ALLEN COUNTY PUBLIC LIBRARY

ACPL ITEM

S 1833 03250 7797

DISCARDED

332
Har
The (almost) per
investment syst

SO-BWM-513

THE (*Almost*) PERFECT INVESTMENT SYSTEM

Robert Harper

Halifax Publishing Co., Inc.

N O T E

While the strategy of stock market investing presented in this book is believed to be effective, there is no guarantee that these methods will result in profits in the future. Thus, neither the publisher nor the author will assume liability for any losses that may be sustained by a reader of this book. Any and all such liability is hereby expressly disclaimed. This book is sold with the understanding that the Publisher or Author is not engaged in rendering legal, accounting or other professional service. If legal advice or other expert assistance is required, the services of a competent professional person should be sought.

Copyright 1996 by Robert L. Harper

All rights reserved. Printed in the United States of America.
No part of this book may be used or reproduced in any
manner whatsoever without written permission except
in the case of brief quotations embodied in
critical articles and reviews.
All clip art from Corel Gallery, Version 1.0
Printed in the United States of America

For information contact
Halifax Publishing Co., Inc.
PO Box 39
Tarboro, NC 27886

ISBN   0-9650682-0-X

Allen County Public Library
900 Webster Street
PO Box 2270
Fort Wayne, IN 46801-2270

DEDICATION

This book is dedicated to my wife, Judy, who
with love and devotion has always supported
every project that I have ever pursued.

ACKNOWLEDGMENTS

Special thanks go to my daughter Lee who edited time
and again every draft of my manuscripts and
offered advice, as well as encouragement.

To so many others who read the various drafts and gave me so much
valuable feed back: My daughter Janis and J.H. Koonce, Denton
Hardee, Charles Flowers, Fred Fountain, Herb Alloy, Gary Sutton,
Joyce Towns, Yale Hirsch, Mike Snell, Dr. Robert Brock, Art
Goodwyn, Vint Fountain, Mac Fountain and to Dan Williams an old
college creative writing buddy who focused his years of publishing
knowledge toward helping me with this project (and Julia Williams
who does all the work). To all of the above and to others too, thank
you so very much.

THE ALMOST PERFECT INVESTMENT SYSTEM
by
Robert Harper

PREFACE

In this book I do not wish to talk down to the reader and risk having the reader say "Who does he think I am, some twelve-year-old kid who doesn't know anything about stock market investing?"

By the same token, many readers may be exploring the world of stock market investing for the first time, and the last thing they need is some super complex, highly sophisticated tome designed to impress, confound, and bore one to death. And most important, I couldn't write a book like that because I'm just not a very complex or sophisticated guy.

As you will see, I'm a great believer in the importance of using historical data to aid us, not so much for predicting the future, but in setting up strong percentage probabilities of what should be our best road map for successful investing.

I also believe that most often the best investment strategies are the simplest ones. I think the best way to read this book, like most others, is from page one to completion to have the total picture. However, if you are a young person with absolutely no investment capital and you have your doubts about your ability to save from your income, you might just skip to the last chapter "Obtaining Your Investing Capital" and after reading and digesting that, then start back with Chapter One.

One problem I've had with this book that I never could completely solve is how to make the large number of tracking years (1929 - 1993) be easy to read.

In looking at other investment books I rarely find one that has tracked their investing system over more than just the past 20 years. In doing this they make their tracking years much shorter and easier to read. However, this leaves the reader not knowing how those proposed strategies would have performed in other, harsher market time-frames.

I elected to track the entire 65 year period and to show how both the Hits-Plus and Super Hits-Plus systems would have performed year-by-year. While knowing this may put a heavier reading burden on some I believe I had the obligation to be thorough in my presentation. Some readers may choose to use the tracking years chapters as reference after they have read to the point of understanding how the Hits-Plus systems really work.

In any event, I believe you will find *The Almost Perfect Investment System* eye-opening, challenging, and hopefully very rewarding in your quest for successful investing.

TABLE OF CONTENTS

PART ONE
A Little Background Music...Please!

**CHAPTER ONE: Why Common Stocks May Be Your
                        Very Best Investment   17**

The S&P 500 Index   18
Picking a Future Wal-Mart   24
Active, Semi-Passive and Passive Investing   25
Liquidity, Liquidity, Liquidity   28

**CHAPTER TWO: Why Mutual Funds Can Be The Best
                        Vehicle To Ride and Drive Your
                        Common Stock Investment   31**

How Many Eggs? How Many Baskets?   32
Choosing A Mutual Fund   33
A Load is an Unneeded Burden   35
Table 2.1, $10,000 With Load vs. No Load   36
Hold My Hand   38
Table 2.2, Load vs. no Load, Trading In and Out   39
A Fund For Everyone and Every Occasion   40

**CHAPTER THREE: History Is Where It's At..
                        Where It Was...Or Where It Will Be   43**

How Common is Common Sense?   44
Advertising   45
Warts and All Advertising   46
Great Complexion, No Warts, No Truth   47
A Different Breed Of Cat   48
And Now, Confession Time   50

CHAPTER FOUR: The Market Searching For
                Its Proper Level   51

    Cast Your Vote, Buy or Sell   52
    The Market Goes Searching   53

PART TWO
Hits (Historical Indicator Timing Strategy)
Comes Comes Alive

CHAPTER FIVE: The Hits System   55

    Table 5.1, S&P 500 Performance 1946-1993   59
    What's Up? What's Down?   60
    Down Two Go; Up Two Whoa   61
    Down Three, In for Four   62
    A Touch of Margin, Perhaps?   64

CHAPTER SIX: The Use Of The January Barometer   67

    January May Set the Trend   68
    Going With the Historical Probabilities   69
    The Mule Barometer   69

CHAPTER SEVEN: The Fail-Safe Trigger   73

    "Grizzly Bear", 1973 and 1974   74
    The Fail-Safe Sell Signal   75
    The Fail-Safe Buy Signal   76
    End-of-the-Month Tracking   77
    Adjust for Dividends for Proper Value   79
    Summary   81
    Figure 7.1, Hits-Plus "What To Do" Flow Chart   83

CHAPTER EIGHT: Forty -Four Years of Hits-Plus Success   85

Playing With Percentages   86
Tables 8.1, 8.2 and 8.3, Buy & Hold, Making the
    Right Call & Missing the Call (2 out of 8)   87-88
Forty-Four Years With Hits-Plus   88
First Use of January Barometer   91
Popping Champagne For 1954   92
First Use of Margin   93
First Ten Years Results   94
$100,000...A Nice Feeling   95
There Will Be Disappointments   97
How will the '73 - '74 Bear Affect Hits-Plus?   98
Unused Fail-Safe Signals Still Directs Us   99
$500,000...A Better Feeling   100
$1,000.000...Felling Better Still   101
$2,357,907...We Could Learn to Like It   102
The Strange Year of 1987   102
1989, A Reason to Smile   103
Over a Million in One Year   104
Mutual Funds for Hits-Plus   105
One-Stop Shopping   106
Hits-Plus vs. Buy-and-Hold   108
Table 8.4, Hits-Plus vs. Buy-and-Hold Comparison   109
A Copywriter's Dream   110

CHAPTER NINE: Hits-Plus, Its Toughest Test
**   1929 Through 1949   113**

How High the Moon?   114
The Year of the Crash   115
Hotel Rooms for Jumping   116
Being Cut by the Whipsaw   117
And Then There was Grief   119
Hawley-Smoot: The Worst Reaction   120
How Some Individual Stocks Faired   122

The Pendulum Swings Back   123
The SEC is Born   124
1937, A Good Year to Be on the Sidelines   125
War Clouds Gather   126
A Bad Looking World   128
A Gutsy Move: Full Margin   129
Victory in Sight   130
21-Year Economic Mine Field   132
Table 9.1, Hits-Plus vs. S&P 500
    Buy and Hold 1929 - 1949   133

CHAPTER TEN: Super Hits-Plus   **135**

Discipline and Patience Truly Tested   137
What is Risk?   139
Using The January Barometer   143
A Pay-off for Discipling   144
A Big Help From the January Barometer   145
Angry After 1965   147
Wow! What a Year   148
Super Hits-Plus and the '73-74' Bear Market   149
Fortune Smiles On Us in 1974   150
A Magician in 1974   150
Table 10.1, Super Hits-Plus vs. Hits-Plus
    1950-1993   154

CHAPTER ELEVEN: Terrible Fall, Great Recovery,
               Super Hits-Plus 1929-1949   **155**

The Mother of All Re-bounds   158
How About That Rainbow   162
Table 11.1, Super Hits-Plus vs. Hits-Plus
    1929-1949   163

CHAPTER TWELVE: What Most Stock Brokers
                Won't Tell You   **165**

The Truth is in The Tables   167

Table 12.1, All Five-Year Periods 1950-1993   168
Table 12.2, All Ten-Year Periods 1950-1993   170
The Worst of Super Hits-Plus is Great   172
Table 12.3, All Fifteen-Year Periods 1950-1993   173
Table 12.4, All Twenty-Year Periods 1950-1993   174
Table 12.5, All Five-Year Periods 1929-1949   176
Table 12.6, All Ten-Year Periods 1929-1993   177
Table 12.7, All Fifteen-Year Periods 1929-1993   178
Table 12.8, All Twenty-Year Periods 1929-1993   178
Sorry, No Crystal Ball   179
Table 12.9, % Return Needed to Increase
     Your Portfoilo   181

PART THREE
Other Stuff, Some Important

**CHAPTER THIRTEEN :   The Power Of Compounded
                         Interest   183**

An Ideal Thirty Day Job   184
Table 13.1, $1,000 A Day vs. One Cent a Day Compounded   185
Table 13.2, $10,000 One Lump Invested at
     Various Compounded Interest Rates   186
Watch Out For "Mr. Slick"   187
Math With Washington's Smoke and Mirrors   188
No One Lump; Go By The Month   189
Various Time Frames...Various Goals   189
Table 13.3, $200 Per Month Invested at
     Various Monthly Compounded Interest Rates   190
Reaching For The Million Dollars   191
The Early Bird Gets The Most Money   192
Table 13.4, $900 Per Month Starting
     Early vs. Starting Late   193

CHAPTER FOURTEEN: The Golden Retirement Years 197
Harvey's Plan   198

The $250 A Month Retiree 198
The Killer Inflation 199
The $300 A Month Retiree 200
The HITS-PLUS Build-Up Time 200
The Hits-Plus 8% Retiree 200
Table 14.1, Hits-Plus Retirement Program 1949-1964 201
Table 14.2, Hits-Plus 8% Retirement Withdrawal 202
The Big Benefits of the IRA 203
Table 14.3, Super Hits-Plus Retirement Program
 1949-1964 204
Table 14.4, Super Hits-Plus 8% Retirement Withdrawal 205
The Saga of Henry and Helen 207
Table 14.5, Henry's Portfolio's 1971-1978 209
Table 14.6, Helen's Portfolio's 1971-1978 210
Table 14.7, Henry's Portfolio's 1979-1993 212
Table 14.8, Helen's Portfolio's 1979-1993 213

CHAPTER FIFTEEN: IRAs, SEP-IRAs, Keoghs,
**   Variable Annuities, 401(k)'s, Etc.   217**

IRAs 218
How Much in an IRA? How Much Outside? 220
Keoghs 221
SEP-IRAs 221
401(k)s 222
Variable Annuities: A Tough Call 222
Pros 223
Cons 224
A Major Breakthrough 226

CHAPTER SIXTEEN: To Margin Or Not To Margin   229

Your Home May Be On Margin 230
The Difference Margin Makes 231
Using Margin With Super Hits-Plus 232

CHAPTER SEVENTEEN: The Psychological Make-up
**   of the Investor   235**

Where's the Investor's Psychiatrist?   236
Forty-four Years of Little Stress   237
1987, The Pressure Was There   238
Gut Wrenching, Mind Twisting Twenty-one Years   238
It's No Action-Packed Horse Race   239
Margin Twice in a Row   240

CHAPTER EIGHTEEN :   Another Look at Dollar
**   Cost Averaging   243**

Table 18.1, XYZ Mutual Fund Quarterly Investing   244
Table 18.2, XYZ Mutual Fund Quarterly Investing
   Continued   246
Dollar Cost Averaging With Hits-Plus   247
Keep Tracking to Keep on Track   251
Progressive Dollar Cost Averaging   253
You Will Get Promotions, Right?   254

CHAPTER NINETEEN: Obtaining Your
**   Investment Capital   257**

Don't Wait For the Ship or the Luck   258
A Road Map For Your Financial Trip   258
Establishing the Budget   259
Automobile Poor or Portfolio Rich   260
No Big Spender, No Miser   261
Pay Yourself First   261
Ongoing Management a Must   263

ALMOST THE FINAL WORD   265

LAST MINUTE UPDATE   269

APPENDIX A: Selected Mutual Funds   273

APPENDIX B: Selected Discount Brokers   275

APPENDIX C: Resources   276

Index   279

PART ONE:

A little background music...please!

CHAPTER ONE

Why Common Stocks May Be Your Very Best Investment.

"...Over the years, the record shows that the average stock has paid a better return and provided a better balance of protection against the evident and unseen risks than any other form of investment."

--- Louis Engel

There are many investment avenues you may take to put your money to work for growth and future monetary reward. First off, I know nothing about rare coins, stamps, and other collectibles. I enjoy and appreciate art, but I'm not a collector.

I have invested in rental property in the past with very good success. For many years, I have owned and operated a business that proved to be both monetarily and emotionally rewarding; I have never owned raw land and I never intend to.

All of these investments have merit and I know of many people who have been highly successful in all of these and many other investment vehicles. But, I firmly believe that for the average person common stocks represent one of the best, if not *the* best, investment source to achieve the kind of net worth, inflation-beating growth one must have to improve their future standard of living and to make their retirement years truly golden.

The S&P 500 Index

Throughout this book I will use the Standard & Poor's 500 as my main reference to the stock market. Indeed, you will later see that the S&P 500 will be our prime source of stock market investing, but not the only one.

The Standard & Poor's 500 tracks the stock of 500 companies made up of mostly large companies. The S&P 500 also includes over-the-counter stocks and some foreign stocks. It represents a broad view of the market itself.

The S&P 500 is by no means the only stock index that is widely followed by the investment community. The best known to most people is the Dow Jones Industrials, which tracks the stock of just thirty large industrial companies. Then there is the Wilshire 5000 Index, a tremendous index, representing small and medium-size companies; the Nasdaq Composite reflecting a huge number of small capital over-the-counter companies; the S&P 400 mid cap; and the Russell 2000. There are a number of other indexes, and some mutual funds and brokerage houses are now introducing their own indexes, some of which are a combination of several of these and other long established standard indexes.

I prefer the S&P 500 Index because I feel that the Dow Jones Industrials with just thirty companies is entirely too narrow of an index to be truly representative of the market and, therefore, too unpredictable. For almost the opposite reason, I don't feel as comfortable with an index as large as the Wilshire 5000. Although the Dow Jones Industrials, The Wilshire 5000, and all the others have strong followers and do indeed serve a very valuable service to many investors, I simply find the S&P 500 to have a long historical data base that over the years has represented quite well the performance of the common stocks of the market place and historically has behaved in a more logical, predictable pattern. Plus the S&P 500 is very easy to buy. You don't have to go out and buy individual shares in the 500 different companies that make up the S&P 500. There are a number of mutual fund companies that feature funds that successfully mirror the S&P 500 Index. I think the Vanguard 500 Index is one the best, but there's also the Dreyfus Index, Portico Equity Index, SEI Index, and others. We will go into this a little more later. In any event, by just investing as little as $1,000 or less in one of these Index mutual funds, in effect you have invested in all 500 companies of the S&P 500.

O.K., so why are common stocks the best investment vehicle? Well, like so many writers about this subject I'm going to throw a few statistics at you and then we'll analyze them.

$1,000 invested in the S&P 500 stocks in January 1932 and left to grow with all dividends re-invested would have grown to $931,406 by the end of 1993 (personal income tax not figured). That's an average annual compounded return of 11.66%. *$1,000 invested in the same stocks in January 1929 before the great crash and depression would have grown to $363,018 through 1993,* an average annual compounded return of 9.49%. And this is going through one of the worst economic periods possible which would have had you with a net value of still less than $1,000 in February 1943, fourteen years later.

Two things should jump out at us right away from these two investment scenarios. First, even a simple buy-and-hold investment position in a broad common stock index can produce excellent long term results. Second, being in the market at the wrong time and staying in during a long bear market period can cost you quite a lot and probably tax your confidence, discipline, and staying power.

The "Hits-Plus" system (Historical Indicator Timing Strategy), which this book is all about, utilizes historical trends from the S&P 500 Index to guide the investor toward being invested in the market on the vast majority of the upside years and to move to cash equivalents and low risk U.S. Government Bonds during most of the downside years. The effect is to greatly reduce downside exposure and to produce overall total return performance that rivals the most successful aggressive mutual funds without the stressful volatility. In later chapters we will examine "Super Hits-Plus" and its truly outstanding performance but I believe it is an essential prerequisite to learn the basic Hits-Plus system first.

Utilizing the basic Hits-Plus system from January 1932 through December 1993, would have turned a $1,000 investment into $10,690,024 (taxes not figured). That's an average compounded return of 16.14%. And yes, that 4.5% in additional annual growth does make that much difference, compared to buy-and-hold over this length of time.

Using Hits-Plus, the return from 1929 through 1993 would have been an average annual compounded growth of 14.81%. *That means an original investment of $1,000 with Hits-Plus would have grown to $7,911,410 instead of just $363,018 with an S&P 500 Buy-and-hold strategy.*

From 1929 through 1942 (14 years) the S&P 500 buy-and-hold investor would have lost over 12.5% of his or her original investment. This surely would have tested the confidence of any investor. But, over this same time frame the Hits-Plus program quadrupled its original investment.

Here are a couple of more S&P 500 investment projections. $1,000 invested in the S&P 500 at the beginning of 1950

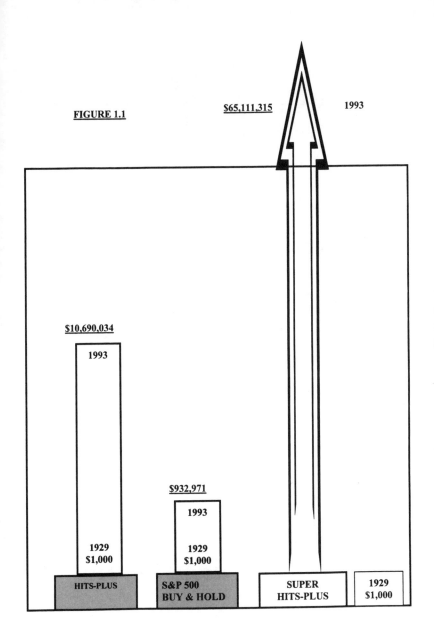

FIGURE 1.1

$65,111,315   1993

$10,690,034
1993

$932,971
1993

1929
$1,000

1929
$1,000

HITS-PLUS

S&P 500
BUY & HOLD

SUPER
HITS-PLUS

1929
$1,000

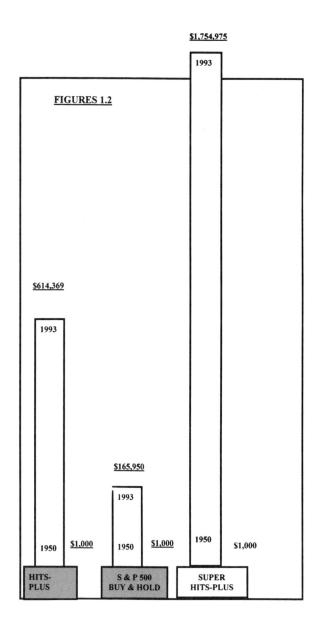

FIGURES 1.2

$1,754,975
1993

$614,369
1993

$165,950
1993

1950 $1,000
1950 $1,000
1950 $1,000

HITS-PLUS
S & P 500 BUY & HOLD
SUPER HITS-PLUS

22

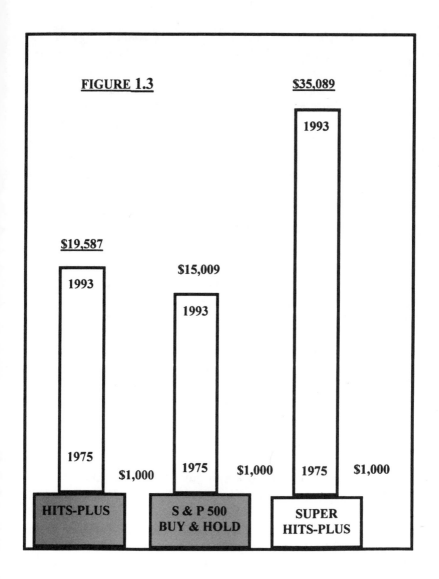

FIGURE 1.3

HITS-PLUS: 1993 — $19,587; 1975 — $1,000

S & P 500 BUY & HOLD: 1993 — $15,009; 1975 — $1,000

SUPER HITS-PLUS: 1993 — $35,089; 1975 — $1,000

and held with all dividends re-invested through 1993 would have grown to $165,950, an average annual compounded return of 12.31% (tax not figured).

$1,000 invested in the S&P 500 at the beginning of 1975 would have grown to $15,009 by the end of 1993, an average compounded return of 15.32% (tax not figured).

Now these are simple buy-and-hold positions in the S&P 500 with no attempt whatsoever at market timing or individual stock selection. Some people say the average investor should not attempt market timing at all. You will see clearly how and why I disagree a little later. *Again, by following the Hits-Plus system an original $1,000 investment at the beginning of 1950 would have grown to $614,369 by the end of 1993.* $1,000 invested with the Hits-Plus program in January 1975 would have delivered 29% more growth than that achieved by the buy-and-hold strategy. And just to whet your appetite a bit, a **$1,000 investment with the Super Hits-Plus strategy would have grown to $65,111,315 from 1929 through 1993.** The graph page won't hold it. But, remember you really must learn the basic Hits-Plus system first and there may be times you will want to use both programs.

Picking A Future Wal-Mart

Other advisors will advise you to not buy a market index such as the S&P 500 or Mutual Funds but to put your money in individual selected stocks and buy and sell at just the right time to achieve fantastic results.

How fantastic? How about buying Teledyne Inc. in 1970 at $2.00 per share and selling in 1984 at $250, turning a $10,000 investment into $1,250,000.

You could have gained over 4,000% with Wal-Mart from January 1980 through December 1989 and over 3,700% with Lin Broadcasting during the same time period. Or by investing $5,000 for 200 shares of McDonalds in 1965 you could be holding McDonalds stock worth around $1,500,000 today.

All right, some readers may be screaming. Stop all the talk about the S&P 500 Index and just tell me what will be the Teledynes, Wal-Marts, and McDonalds of the future.

Sorry, I don't have that ability. And I don't know of anyone else who does either. Oh, there are advisory letters out there that will imply in a very indirect way that they just may be able to advise you on what the tremendous individual growth stocks of the future will be. Usually you will receive an advisory letter listing as many as thirty or more individual stocks that they think just might, maybe, perhaps will turn into another Wal-Mart or McDonalds in the next ten years. But which one or two stocks do you buy? Do you buy all thirty or more and do you sell various ones of these stocks when they fall 20% or fail to perform in a strong upward manner and then purchase other would-be Wal-Marts or McDonalds that replace the old ones on the magic stock list. And all the time keep your broker happy with fat commissions?

Sure there are companies out there that will perform in the future similar to a Teledyne or Lin Broadcasting but they are hidden among thousands of stocks and you just might hit a $10 million lottery before you find the right ones. In other words, just don't count on it. I will take a flyer in an individual stock once in a while, but my prime investment program will continue to be in no-load mutual funds and following a systematic, proven system.

Yes, I do believe that investing in common stocks primarily through no-load mutual funds is the best investment avenue for the average person.

Active, Semi-Passive, & Passive Investing

You may look on various investment vehicles in several ways insofar as how much "active" effort it will take on your part to manage your investment.

For example, if your primary investment is in the private

ownership of your own business, be it a shoe store, a pizza parlor, or automobile dealership, then this is certainly an "active" investment. You must work daily in the overseeing and management of this primary investment. Of course, I believe that once your own business is established well enough and is profitable you should begin to take some of your profits from your business or some of your savings from the management salary you pay yourself and begin a separate investment program in common stocks of other companies through no-load mutual funds.

It only makes good sense to diversify and have separate investments in other baskets, as opposed to letting your entire financial future ride exclusively on the back of one investment horse—a horse that might perform like a thoroughbred race horse for many years only to turn into a broken down old nag later with you left holding the empty feed bag without even stud fees to see you through.

I have owned and operated my own business and still have investment positions in small, closely held companies. Believe me, it can be one of the most lucrative and rewarding investments you could make. By the same token, it can also turn out to be one of the most torturous and devastating ventures you could ever undertake.

It's kind of an American dream to own one's own business, but too often too many people are attracted to wanting to own and operate their own small business in a field where they have little or no expertise. It's the old greener pasture concept and it's always easier to fantasize how great it would be and how successful you would be owning and operating, say, a golf retail outlet because you simply love to play golf. You should take a big second or third look first before you go out and buy or start a golf retail outlet.

Loving to play golf may help a little, but not a great deal, and in fact after you're in the business you'll probably play less golf than ever. You simply won't have the time. To be successful in this area you need business background knowledge and experience in operating such a business. You'll also need to be in the right market place with an excellent location. In this particular case, if you had operated a pro shop at a country club successfully for several years and had acquired the knowledge of inventory control, buying for your clientele, merchandising, record keeping, personnel management, and all the other needed business operations skills, then this could put you in a good starting position.

I was fortunate enough to have been in the business in which I would later purchase a 50% ownership position for 14 years. For 12 of those years I served as General Manager. I knew the business as thoroughly as you could and our market area like the back of my hand. In my case it was Radio Broadcasting with AM and FM radio stations and I truly loved the business, but you will find that once you become an owner, you will put in those 12 and 14 hour days.

In any event, owning your own business can be great or it can be disastrous, but it will be a very "active" investment on your part.

If you own rental property, say an apartment house, this could be what I would call a "semi-passive" investment. Depending on the set-up, it should not take the time that managing a shoe store or radio station should take but it certainly will not be a "put your money in and forget it" situation. You will have to stay on top of things but it should not be close to a full-time management job.

A lot of people say stock market investment is a "passive" investment in that you are not actively managing any one company. No one is going to call you and tell you your lease will not be renewed or that the plumbing and electrical wiring has just gone haywire in all your apartments. In this comparison it definitely is a "passive" investment. But don't make it too "passive."

I can't accept the idea of investing in common stocks and walking away to forget it and maybe taking an end-of-the-year look at how things are at tax time. On the other hand, a lot of people over-manage their common stock investment. They live and die each day according to how their stocks performed the previous day. They constantly call their brokers with endless questions and issue buy and sell orders almost weekly or monthly. They do indeed put in as much time as an apartment house owner and in most cases over-manage their portfolio to its detriment in performance.

My prime investment program is through my "Hits-Plus" and "Super Hits-Plus" systems. It would seem very "passive" compared to an "active" investment and more "passive" than a "semi-passive" apartment house owner-ship, but you are required to keep up with what's going on. Actually, as little as thirty minutes per month and maybe an extra thirty minutes the last of each December and the last of each January could do the job. But I think human nature will cause you to take a peek at the stock market page more often than that.

Liquidity, Liquidity, Liquidity

One of the most favorable aspects of investing in common stocks through no load mutual funds is "liquidity."

There's an old saying that the three most important factors in a retail business are "location, location, and location."

I would almost proclaim that liquidity, liquidity, and liquidity are the most important factors in "passive" and "semi-passive" investments although this could be a bit of an overstatement. However, liquidity is extremely important.

The owner of that raw land who expected a new six-lane highway to go through and then learns it won't happen has really got a liquidity problem.

Owners of real estate, even homeowners, are learning that real estate of all kinds can go down in value under certain economic conditions and that you can't just pick up the phone and call your local Realtor and say sell and get a check in a week.

But, that is exactly what you can do with common stocks. You can pick up the phone and say sell and receive your check in about a week. For almost instant liquidity, if you also have a money fund established with the mutual fund company or discount broker, you could order the sell of your stock or mutual fund shares and have the redeemed cash deposited in the money fund. Then you could write a check on that money fund account the next day, but do double check this with your mutual fund or broker when you phone in your sell instructions. This liquidity means a great deal.

Last but not least is the historical performance of common stocks using any long established index. Over the long term in the United States, common stocks have an excellent performance record and are one of the few investment sources that has handily beaten inflation.

Notice I said "over the long term." This means that if you're looking for a really good investment for just a year or two the stock market may not be a good idea. But for an investment time of at least five years and preferably longer I'll take common stocks every time with the proper systematic proven investment strategy.

CHAPTER TWO

Why Mutual Funds Can Be The Best Vehicle to Ride and Drive Your Common Stock Investment.

"Anyone with a portfolio of, say, under $100,000 is unlikely to do as well investing his own money as he can do in a mutual fund."

Paul Samuelson,
Nobel Prize winning economist

Claude Rosenburg, founder of RCM Capital Management and Publisher of *Investing with the Best* and other good investment books wrote that investors with less than $250,000 should invest in mutual funds. Later in an interview with Kurt Brouner for Brouner's book *Kurt Brouner's Guide to Mutual Funds* (an excellent book), Rosenburg said, "Even people with millions to invest often would be better off with mutual funds."

One of the reasons, I think, and almost any investment advisor should agree with Paul Samuelson and Claude Rosenburg, especially for the small investor, is that it will take a pretty good sum of money to buy enough individual stocks to give you the diversification you really should have. Some people say you should own at least ten different individual stocks to have any real diversification. I think a more realistic number would be twenty to thirty different stocks. This would mean a small investor would have to buy small lots, resulting in higher broker commissions and even more commissions as he/she re-positions his/her portfolio from time to time by selling some issues and buying others.

How Many Eggs...How Many Baskets?

"Don't put all you eggs in one basket."
"Put your eggs in one basket and watch the basket."
I don't know who to credit for the above quotes; they've been around a while and there's a good deal of truth in both.
Buying one good mutual fund with a good solid track record in effect puts your eggs in more than one basket, twenty, thirty, or even five hundred different stocks. But, you only have one basket to watch—that one mutual fund.

You could buy an Index fund, an Aggressive Growth fund, a Sector fund or two, an International Investment fund plus several others and really have broad diversification. But, indeed, this could be entirely too many eggs in too many baskets and diversification alone is not your investment goal.

Mutual funds have been around for many years, but they did not represent a real big player in the stock market until the '70s and even more in recent years. In the early '50s the entire mutual fund industry had assets of less than $4 billion; today the Fidelity family of funds alone would eclipse this figure many times over. In fact, in 1992 alone stock funds received over $75 billion in investor dollars.

In the '50s and '60s many mutual funds demonstrated

performance records that began to attract investors in large numbers. The big bad bear market of 1973 and 1974 chased many small and not so small investors out of the stock market and out of mutual funds, too. But since that time, the overall market performance and the growing appeal of mutual funds as being an ideal investment vehicle for so many has caused the mutual fund industry to become the stock market's major player.

Randall Smith wrote an excellent article under "Heard on the Street" in the May 22, 1992 issue of *The Wall Street Journal* explicitly pointing out just how big and important the mutual fund industry has become to the stock market as an influential driver in both bull and bear markets.

What kind of mutual fund do I look for as my main vehicle of investment? As we will see later the mainstay of the "Hits-Plus" System will go with an S&P 500 Index Fund when we are in the market and with a balance of a T-Bill Mutual Fund and an Intermediate-term Government Bond Fund when we are not in the stock fund. With the "Super Hits-Plus" program we will be going with a small companies stock index fund for our in-market investment.

Choosing A Mutual Fund

Here are some basic rules that are a must for me when I choose a mutual fund:

1. The fund must be large enough and old enough to have a solid track record. And I don't mean two or three years. I look for a record of ten to twenty years and even more.
2. The fund must be a "No-Load" fund. This is essential because "Hits-Plus" calls for some selling and buying, although in the 44-year period since 1950, we were out of the market only 20 times and the rest of the time we were in. This was not a lot of

buying and selling but even with this low amount of buying and selling had we had even a low-load commission it would have cost us quite a bit.

3. The fund must not have 12-b-1 fees. This is just another cost to the mutual fund investor that holds down the potential performance of his or her investment. It's unnecessary and there are too many excellent mutual funds that do not have 12-b-1 fees.

4. Management expenses for the fund should never be over 1.4 percent and preferably no more than 1 percent. And as you will see with the primary investment vehicle of Hits-Plus being an S&P 500 Index fund, the management expense of the fund can be less than .25% (one quarter of one percent).

The primary investment source for "Super Hits-Plus" will be a good small capitalization stock index fund, also available through Vanguard and other good mutual fund families.

Other advantages with mutual fund investing are that with many funds as little as $100 can get you started and you don't have to buy a round number of shares; i.e., $1,000 invested in a fund that's selling for $6.23 per share will purchase you 160.5136 shares. You can make additional purchases as you can afford it or as your investment strategy directs you. With many funds you can switch from the stock fund to one of their money funds or other funds in the family company with just a telephone call. Also, with many funds you can cash-out or sell your position with a telephone call, or at least a quick letter of instructions, and receive your check in a few days. You can also instruct the fund to automatically re-invest all dividends and distributions to work toward a maximum compounded total return. We will always do this unless we are setting up an automatic withdrawal payment for retirement.

A Load Is An Unneeded Burden

Load vs. no-load mutual funds is one of the most debated questions, at least by brokers talking to their clients. The brokers will usually come down on the side of load funds. After all, they receive no commissions on no-load funds. Now, I have many friends who are brokers and I don't want to anger them. They do play a very important role in the investment world and can offer many valuable services. But, in this case let's examine the question of load vs. no-load funds.

One of Webster's definitions of load is "...to weigh down as with a burden." And this is exactly what a mutual fund load is, a burden.

A front load is a sales commission up front, normally from 5% to 8 1/2%. A back load is like we don't charge you to get in, we just charge you to get out. The results of a back load can be the same although some funds may lower this back load if you stay in a certain number of years. But, this will hamper you or cost you if your investment strategy, such as "Hits-Plus," directs you to sell.

There are low-load funds. The Fidelity family and other fund companies have a number of these. These low loads of 1% to 3% do not go to a broker as a commission but stay with the company. Their rationale usually is "we spend so much money advertising to keep investment money coming in and we offer better service to our customers and, after all, we perform better than most funds." Sorry, but this ain't necessarily so.

The bottom line is that for every load mutual fund a broker can show me with an outstanding performance track record I believe I can show him or her a no-load fund with a performance record that can match or beat the load fund. No two mutual funds have identical past records, but it's not difficult to compare their past performance records. There are a number of mutual fund services and other periodical sources you can turn to to compare such past records. *Barron's*

Table 2.1

$10,000 Invested, Buy-and-Hold 5.5% Load Mutual Fund
You start with 5.5% less, i.e. $9450

			Years Held			
Annual % Growth	5	10	15	20	25	30
10	$15,219	$24,511	$39,475	$63,575	$102,388	$164,897
11	$15,924	$26,833	$45,214	$76,189	$128,383	$216,332
12	$16,654	$29,350	$51,725	$91,157	$160,651	$283,131
13	$17,411	$32,079	$59,103	$108,893	$200,629	$369,645
14	$18,195	$35,033	$67,454	$129,876	$250,065	$481,479
15	$19,007	$38,231	$76,895	$154,664	$311,084	$625,701
16	$19,848	$41,688	$87,559	$183,904	$386,262	$811,281
17	$20,719	$45,425	$99,591	$218,348	$478,716	$1,049,561
18	$21,619	$49,460	$113,152	$258,864	$592,219	$1,354,852
			(Taxes Not Figured)			

$10,000 Invested Buy-and-Hold No Load Mutual Fund
Your Entire $10,000 Goes to Work

			Years Held			
Annual % Growth	5	10	15	20	25	30
10	$16,105	$25,937	$41,772	$67,275	$108,347	$174,494
11	$16,851	$28,394	$47,846	$80,623	$135,856	$228,923
12	$17,623	$31,058	$54,736	$96,463	$170,001	$299,599
13	$18,424	$33,946	$62,543	$115,231	$212,305	$391,159
14	$19,254	$37,070	$71,379	$137,435	$265,619	$509,502
15	$20,114	$40,456	$81,371	$163,665	$329,190	$662,118
16	$21,003	$44,114	$92,655	$194,608	$408,742	$858,490
17	$21,924	$48,068	$105,387	$231,056	$506,578	$1,110,650
18	$22,878	$52,338	$119,737	$273,930	$626,686	$1,433,707
			(Taxes Not Figured)			

publishes a track record comparison. So does *Forbes Magazine* and many others. I believe the most definitive and useful service is the one offered by Morningstar; 53 W. Jackson Blvd.; Chicago, IL. 60604; Phone: 800-876-5005. Morningstar isn't cheap, but it is excellent.

How much does a load really cost you in investment performance? Let's look at a comparison table and see (See Table 2.1). Looking at an annual percentage growth of 15% we find that the load fund (5.5%) only cost us $1,107 the first five years. Not too bad, but for what purpose? At the end of twenty-five years it has cost us $18,106. If we want to look at an 18% annual percentage growth and look at a 30-year period the cost jumps to $78,855.

But this is not the real cost that will occur with any investment system that calls for you to sell your mutual fund shares from time to time and move into a money fund position or other investment vehicle.

Remember, the real purpose of any systematic timing investment strategy is to increase up-side performance by a greater annual percentage growth than will be achieved with a simple buy-and-hold approach.

For example, with a buy-and-hold approach with the S&P 500 from 1967 through 1991 (a 25-year period) your average annual growth would have been 10.85%. But, by using "Hits-Plus" you would have achieved an average annual percentage growth of 15.25%. This means with an initial investment of $10,000, "Hits-Plus" would have returned you over $215,000 more than the buy-and-hold approach. That is an increase in end results performance by almost 150%.

But, although "Hits-Plus" does not require a lot of buying and selling, it does require some and, by dealing with load funds*,every time you sell and re-purchase you are setting yourself back by the percentage of the load. Full load funds will usually have an up-front load of from 5% to 8.5%, but there are a number of good load funds with a 5.5% up-front load so this is the comparison load I will use vs. a no-load fund.

In our comparison tables we will hypothetically have you in the market for two years straight and out for one year.

Both comparison funds will return 15% annual growth. During the year you are out of the market, you will be credited with an annual growth of 6%, with no load charged in either case. This is an assumed return you would receive by being in a no-load money fund or other no-load, low risk investment vehicle during the year you are out of the mutual stock fund (See Table 2.2).

In this case, trading in and out of a 5.5% front-end load fund has cost you $32,822 or almost 33% (over a 20-year period) of what you would have gained dealing with a no-load fund. If you had started with a $100,000 investment, the raw dollar cost, or loss, would have been $328,220. In any event, 33% is 33%. In most cases in this book I will be using $10,000 when projecting the performance of a one-lump-sum investment. This way it will be easy for you to calculate your own projected investment results.

If you are planning to invest a one-lump sum of $1,000 then divide the results by ten for your projected return. For a $5,000 investment, divide by two; $50,000 investment multiply by five; $100,000 investment multiply by ten and so on. I will cover Dollar Cost Averaging investing in a later chapter.

Hold My Hand

What do you receive when you invest in a load mutual fund? Mostly you get hand holding, plus, of course, a hand in your pocket for the load commission. Actually, I know a number of people who really feel they want and need the hand holding. They just don't like investing by mail, bank transfer, or dealing with telephone calls with a customer service person whom they don't know personally, no matter how strong and reputable the no-load mutual fund may be. They like the

---

*Some load mutual fund companies do have an "old money" concept that may not charge you a second load if you switch to another fund within their same company. However, the company may not have all the types of funds you want, and if you will be trading basically with an S&P 500 Index fund, a small cap index fund, a bond fund, and a money fund, there's absolutely no reason to consider a load fund.

Table 2.2

No-Load Mutual Fund Investment

Investment	End of Year	Value at End of Period
$10,000	Two (in market for two years)	$13,325
$13,225	Three (out of market for one year)	$14,018
$14,018	Five (in market for two years)	$18,539
$18,539	Six (out of market for one year)	$19,651
$19,651	Eight (in market for two years)	$25,989
$25,989	Nine (out of market for one year)	$27,548
$27,548	Eleven (in market for two years)	$36,433
$36,433	Twelve (out of market for one year)	$38,619
$38,619	Fourteen (in market for two years)	$51,074
$51,074	Fifteen (out of market for one year)	$54,138
$54,138	Seventeen (in market for two years)	$71,598
$71,598	Eighteen (out of market one year)	$75,894
$75, 894	Twenty (in market for two years)	$100,370

5.5% Up-Front Mutual Fund

Investment	End of Year	Value at End of Period
$9,450	Two (in market for two years)	$12,498
$12,498	Three (out of market for one year)	$13,248
$12,519	Five (in market for two years)	$16,557
$16,557	Six (out of market for one year)	$17,550
$16,585	Eight (in market for two years)	$21,933
$21,933	Nine (out of market for one year)	$23,249
$21,970	Eleven (in market for two years)	$29,056
$29,056	Twelve (out of market for one year)	$30,799
$29,105	Fourteen (in market for two years)	$38,491
$38,491	Fifteen (out of market for one year)	$40,800
$38,556	Seventeen (in market for two years)	$50,990
$50,990	Eighteen (out of market for one year)	$54,049
$51,076	Twenty (in market for two years)	$67,548

soothing talk they can have with Joe, Harry, or Mary, and they like meeting them personally, even though Joe, Harry, or Mary have nothing to do with managing their money in the mutual fund. I might add that over the years, all the customer service people with the mutual funds I have dealt with over the telephone have been very friendly, helpful, and highly competent.

As I said before, I have a number of friends who are stock brokers and they do earn their keep and perform valuable services. And I guess selling load mutual funds to some people and holding their hands and listening to various gripes and complaints deserves a commission. But if you don't feel you need hand holding, you don't need load mutual funds. Unless, perhaps, you have a brother-in-law whom you dearly love and he's a broker and you're searching for a way to contribute money to him without outright giving, then buy load mutual funds from him.

A Fund For Everyone and Every Occasion

You'll find over 3,500 mutual funds (over 1,000 general stock funds alone) in the market place. There are many types of mutual funds: Growth, Aggressive Growth, Income, Growth and Income, Equity Income, Balanced, Index Funds, Bond Funds, International Investment Funds, Sector Funds and a number of others. In general you should be able to expect the following:

(a) **Growth funds** seek growth of your assets with little attention toward dividends and with a medium risk factor.

(b) **Aggressive Growth funds** imply a higher risk factor with the potential of greater performance.

(c) **Income funds** should be mostly invested in bonds and income-oriented issues with dividends and distributions of income being their main focus.

(d) **Equity/Income funds** should seek a middle ground of asset growth and dividend income mostly from good dividend-paying stocks.

(e) **Balanced funds** usually mean a balance between stocks, bonds, and other investment issues.

(f) **Index funds,** such as funds set up to mirror the S&P 500 Index or other indexes, should achieve just that, and you should know what you're getting with an Index fund.

(g) **International investment funds** mean just that, with some funds earmarked toward one particular nation or another.

(h) **Sector funds** are funds that invest in just one basic area or general industry, such as health science, technology, energy, utilities, real estate, etc.

Add to this Bond funds, Gold funds, Tax-exempt funds and on and on and you can quickly surmise that there's a fund for almost every investment desire.

I said a little earlier you should be able to expect your mutual fund to invest in the instruments that their category implies. But we are learning now that some funds hedge a bit here and there and may not be investing entirely in the areas that they supposedly should.

There was an excellent article in *The Wall Street Journal* recently under "Your Money Matters" by Barbara Donnelly that explored the idea that there is some deception going on, as some funds that supposedly are low-risk investors are actually investing in higher risk stocks in hopes of beating out other funds in their same category by achieving higher performance.

This deception is being noted and many of these mutual funds are being re-classified in such mutual-fund rating services as those published by Morningstar.

In our particular case with "Hit-Plus" we will be working primarily with Index Funds which you can count on. Also, with "Hits-Plus" and "Super Hits-Plus" our out-of-market investments will be with "T-Bill Mutual Funds," "Intermediate-Term Government Bond Funds," or "Money Funds," all of which you can depend on for being just what they say they are.

Do all mutual funds perform just great? Not at all. Like individual stocks, there are mutual funds that have performed lousy. A lot of the really terribly performing mutual funds have been in the Aggressive Growth category and have followed highly suspect investment philosophies of a very speculative nature. Good mutual-fund advisory and rating services have smoked out these funds and have separated them from the much higher quality aggressive growth mutual funds that still represent more volatility but do have good solid long-term performance records. You will find that "Hits-Plus" is not cast in concrete and will offer you several adjustment options to better suit your own "Comfort Zone" investment goals.

Another reason I think some not-so-sophisticated investors invest in individual stocks as opposed to good mutual funds is what I call the cocktail party/coffee break syndrome.

When they go to a cocktail party or are on a coffee break and the conversation turns to stock investing, it sounds so much more glamorous and savvy to talk about your stock holdings in Wal-Mart, AT&T, IBM, and, of course, that hot new over-the-counter high tech issue that just might be the next Xerox.

Most of these people will tell you about their great success in some individual stocks and never mention their losses unless it might sound a little more glamorous to say, "Well, I did take a small bath on a little issue that went south last week, but I should get that back and more with XYZ Mining!"

Now we might sound like the proverbial nerd when all we have to report is we have our money in an S&P 500 index mutual fund or Small Cap Index fund or at other times a bond fund and money fund. They just might look at us as if to say, "Oh, too dumb to select and buy and sell individual stocks with the big boys, huh?"

Personally, I can take that attitude and laugh all the way to the bank and feel a lot more secure about my investment situation.

CHAPTER THREE

History is Where It's At . . .
or Where It Was . . .
or Maybe Where It Will Be

"I know of no way of judging the future but by the past."

--- Patrick Henry

"A generation which ignores history
has no past...and no future."

---- Robert A. Heinlein

My major in college was social studies, not business. I once believed I would be a history teacher upon receiving my degree and did my high school practice teaching in American history and world history. However, once I received my Bachelors Degree there were no history teachers positions available. I was already working part-time as a radio announcer and was offered a full-time position with the radio station to continue with some air shifts and to also embark on a career as a radio advertising salesman, which in turn evolved into management and ownership. But a history buff I remained.

I do believe that history repeats itself, only differently. That is to say that we will not see history repeat itself lock-step, but that we will see different elements of past events in a different mix coming around again. And, yes, perhaps with a new twist. It may be a little different the second, third, or forth time around, but it will be similar enough that the person who has made a careful study of past events will have a definite advantage in judging the probabilities of just what might be about to take place.

How Common Is Common Sense?

Insofar as recent history is concerned, it might simply be called the wisdom of experience. Barry Lepatner once said "Good judgment comes from experience. And experience comes from bad judgment."

I think most of us will agree that it's just good common sense to learn from our past mistakes and thereby gain a strong element of good judgment that will serve us well in the future. Some call it simply gaining maturity. However, I do recall a conversation I had many years ago with a good friend concerning "what makes a good business manager." After a long discussion we reached the conclusion that the one main strong suit the few really good business managers have is "good common sense." We then quickly agreed that the term "common sense" was a misnomer because what most of us call "common" sense is indeed very "uncommon."

In any event, we can't personally experience everything that has happened to anyone or anything in the past. But, we can read and study and look for distinctive patterns and learn from this history and gain an extremely valuable tool of good judgment to utilize in calculating the strong probabilities of *what* will happen in the *future*.

Advertising

"We can easily represent things as we wish them to be."
Aesop

I had a very difficult time deciding in which chapter to write about the pros and cons of advertising. It could have been in Chapter Two on Mutual Funds or somewhere else concerning advisory letters and services. But, in most cases advertising reflects on something that has happened in the past and offers a promise in the future (but, of course, with the necessary disclaimer that past performance cannot guarantee similar future performance).

Now, most of my private business success has come from the advertising industry, and I offer no apologies for this much needed and valuable service for both the business sector and the John and Jane Does who read, listen to, and view thousands of advertising messages.

I'm crazy about advertisements. I read, listen to, and view a lot of advertisements, perhaps a little more intently and critically than most. And I learn a great deal from advertisements. But, one must know how to dissect and digest advertisements. In other words, to cut through or cut out the crap that so many contain and get to the factual bottom line.

There is good, solid, honest advertising and there is some that I do think gives the industry a bad name by being misleading and sometimes just plain dishonest. We need to develop the senses to detect the good from the bad and why and what makes up the difference.

Any business that advertises has the right, and the advertising agency has the obligation, to show their wares or services in the best light. Very few businesses advertise their warts and all. They spotlight their strong points and leave out the negatives. And this is perfectly O.K. as long as its not blatantly misleading. But, we, as recipients of the advertising, must keep our antennae tuned to what may be left out and how this left out material could effect the true total picture.

Warts and All Advertising

I have seen what I thought was very effective advertising that did, in a most honest and open way, display warts and all, and this, to me, comes off as being so sincere that we have to be favorably impressed. An excellent example of this was the 1984, 34th annual report of the Guardian Mutual Fund, managed by Neuberger and Berman.

Guardian was started June 1, 1950, and has a long and successful history of good solid growth performance. I don't know what their most recent advertising material looks like, but the 1984 Annual Report was a great example of openness and honesty. First, Guardian gave you its total performance history, the good years and the not-so-good. And then they broke these years down into the best periods, the medium periods, and the worst periods.

I don't know of many mutual funds that would lay out their worst performance periods for all to see and contemplate. In other words, 1965 through 1974 was a terrible ten-year period for Guardian. It was also a terrible period for practically every other mutual fund, but how many will own up to it?

During this awful ten-year period Guardian struggled to increase a $10,000 investment to $14,476, an almost 45% total increase, but an average of just 3.77% annual compounded return. But, this was one of the worst ten-year periods, and a buy-and-hold investment in the S&P 500 of $10,000 would have increased to just $11,306.

Of course, *I'm happy to report that Hits-Plus over the same period would have turned $10,000 into $22,101 and Super Hits-Plus turned a $10,000 investment into $34,863.* The point is that Guardian is a good solid mutual fund that has performed very well over the years and is not afraid to point out their not-so-good performance during a time when other mutual funds and individual stocks were also staggering around like an intoxicated bear.

Guardian's report is an exemplary example of "warts and all" open, honest advertising and I think it's good. However in a later chapter I will show how when we learn the investment results in all possible five, ten, fifteen and twenty year periods of various portfolios, a much clearer picture will emerge on what kind of investment performance we must expect to really be satisfied.

Great Complexion, No Warts, No Truth

On the other extreme I received an advertising piece from a broker on a load fund with a 57-year performance history and it was anything but honest.

What's so baffling is that the fund performed very well but they had to try to enhance their performance by deception.

When they compared their performance with the S&P 500 they included all dividends and distributions to be re-invested in their mutual fund for total return performance. But with the S&P 500 they left out the re-investing of dividends and distributions altogether so naturally they beat the S&P 500. In the fine footnote print they noted that their figures included dividend re-investment but they did not note anything about the S&P 500. I caught it because I knew what the total return performance year-by-year of the S&P 500 was. This was very misleading and, in my opinion, dishonest. Their performance figures did not reflect the load sales charge either. And of course Hits-Plus beat the pants off of 'em.

This was probably the most dishonest presentation I have seen from a mutual fund. Most others are very interesting and contain valuable data if you are just aware of certain guidelines you should follow in judging their advertisements and performance claims.

In their advertising material most mutual funds will pick out the time periods where they performed best. The funds that have been around long enough like to start with the beginning of 1975 since 1973 and 1974 were such terrible bear market years. This is O.K. but you should be aware of what's going on. *Most mutual funds that were in existence during the early '70s would show pretty bad performance results in the five-year period from 1971 through 1975.* 1971 and 1972 were good years, but 1973 and 74 were a disaster with 1975 coming back as an excellent year. *However, this five-year period won't be shown much in most mutual fund advertisements.*

Yet and still mutual fund advertisements can be very helpful. With thousands of funds out there, often these ads will point the way toward a number of interesting funds. But, then you need to check them out further to be sure they really do represent what you're looking for, and this is when you need to turn to a good independent rating source such as the Morningstar Publications or other services you can trust.

A Different Breed of Cat

When it comes to advisory newsletters you're looking at another breed of cat altogether. There are some excellent newsletters that offer a great service, and there are others that will drive you nuts and cost you money (more than just the subscription rate).

In most cases its much more difficult for you to judge the value of an advisory newsletter as opposed to that of a mutual fund when you look at their individual advertising. With mutual funds they do have to follow fairly tough S.E.C. (Securities and Exchange Commission) regulations. *With the advisory newsletter advertising it's almost anything goes.*

I have read some advertisements for advisory newsletters that are sent out like sleek little magazines or newspapers that seem to promise to make you rich week-after-next and all the while cure your dandruff problem and enhance your sex life. I would be slightly wary of all this hype.

Fortunately, some years ago a gentleman by the name of Mark Hulbert saw the need and started a newsletter of his own, The Hulbert Financial Digest. This publication rates the "real" performance of the advisory letters themselves. Mr. Hulbert is often quoted in *The Wall Street Journal, Forbes,* and other quality publications. His service is very valuable. It's *The Hulbert Financial Digest*; 316 Commerce St.; Alexandria, Va. 22314; (1-800-334-4679).

Unfortunately, some advisory letters might claim in their advertisements they have had a high rating in The Hulbert Financial Digest "recently," but they don't define "recently." That good rating could be several years old and since that time their poor performance has caused Hulbert to lower that rating quite a bit.

Some advertisements for advisory letters claim they will guide you to profits of 500% or more, but they don't say how long it will take. A 500% growth over a 25-year period is not so great (an average of just 7.43% per year).

With hundreds of investment advisory letters out there you will find all kinds of claims. Some letters feature such large buy lists that few subscribers could take meaningful positions with any logical portfolio. Then they are advised to buy and sell so often that transaction costs would drain most profits. And according to Mark Hulbert, a few advisory letter publishers have no scruples when it comes to misrepresenting their track record and indeed outright lie to the point of claiming to have been rated number one by Mark Hulbert when they never were.

So much of the public is swayed by the most outrageous claims, such as "...If you had followed our advice a $10,000 investment would have grown to $28 million in just twelve years." Apparently this line of advertising is bringing in the highly gullible who turn away from excellent and truthful performances of 15% to 20% average annual compounded returns to grab for the big gold ring without ever double checking with an objective source such as The Hulbert Financial Digest to see if such outrageous claims hold any grain of truth.

I only wish there had been a publication similar to The Hulbert Financial Digest back in the sixties and seventies so we would know how the advisory letters faired during some of the really bad bear years.

To quote Mark Hulbert himself, *"The bottom line? Don't believe everything you read in advertisements for advisory letters... especially the breathless stuff and doubly so when the hype isn't based on a specific portfolio."*

Again, I say looking back at historical data can lead to devising an excellent systematic investment strategy—a kind of road map for the highest future probabilities and percentages that will give you a much stronger return on your investments. But, we do need to be looking at reliable, truthful, historical data.

And Now, Confession Time

O.K., it's true, I too publish a newsletter. It's not so much an advisory letter as it is a guide or service. I started it very small for a few friends who had read earlier drafts of the Hits-Plus System and asked for a simple monthly guide that directed them where their investment dollars should be and at what time in order to be in adherence to the Hits-Plus Program. I pointed out that they could do this on their own with *The Wall Street Journal* and *Barron's* weekly publication and if they didn't subscribe to these publications, their library probably did. Nevertheless, some of them said they wanted this tracking and guidance done for them to save them time and to assure them of accuracy if, of course, the cost would be very modest.

So, from those requests came the *Hits-Plus Mutual Fund Guide*. No one really has to have it in order to follow the Hits-Plus System; this book will tell you exactly how you can do that on your own. But, if, like some of my friends, you would like to devote only five minutes of your time per month for an explicit, concise Hits-Plus Monthly guide instead of spending thirty minutes a month doing it yourself and if this is worth $69.95 per year, then you'll find more information about the service on the last page of this book. End of Pitch.

CHAPTER FOUR

The Market Searching for its Proper Level

"The market is a voting machine, whereon countless individuals register choices which are the product partly of reason and partly of emotions."

Graham & Dodd

"...I've been searching...searching every which of way...."

**Number
one hit, 1957.
The Coasters**

The story is told that back around 1907 the famous, or infamous, John P. Morgan was asked what would be the future movement of the stocks. His legendary answer was "They will fluctuate, young man, they will fluctuate." Now, on the surface that may appear to be a rather silly, flippant statement. But, to me it was also very profound.

Cast Your Vote, Buy or Sell

As Graham & Dodd said the market is a voting machine. It's a voting machine that casts its votes daily—indeed constantly—throughout the day except Saturdays, Sundays, and holidays. The votes are stating, in effect, what they think the value of all these stocks of thousands of individual companies are truly worth and, in turn, what the value of the market as a whole is believed to be. All of this voting is taking place on the New York Stock Exchange, The American Stock Exchange, NASDAQ (over-the-counter), the Foreign Exchange, and other minor exchanges as well as with the buying and selling of various mutual funds, which is just an indirect vote in the stock market as well.

The sellers may be stating they think the individual stock they are now selling has become overvalued and they're going to take a profit and invest elsewhere. They may still think the stock has a little upside potential but not as much as another they have their eyes on. They may be saying this thing has lost me money and I'll be damned if I'll keep riding this loser down further. Or they just might need the money for college tuition, a divorce settlement, or any other of so many reasons.

The buyers may be saying this stock is undervalued and if I buy and hold for six months or longer I can turn a good profit. Indeed, most buyers must feel that the stock is a good investment, at least in the long run. Oh, it might go down a bit more, but they do believe it will eventually rebound and perform well for them.

All this, of course makes J.P. Morgan's statement very true. The individual stock prices will fluctuate and the stock market, as a whole, will fluctuate. An individual stock could jump upward 10%, 20%, or even more in one single day; it could go down this much or more in a single day. In a roaring bull market the Dow Jones Industrials, the S&P 500, and the NASDAQ could post nice gains almost every day, only pausing occasionally for a retreat with profit-taking, catching a second wind and surging ahead again. The reverse could be true in a depressing bear market. And you could have a rather long sideways market with the market going up a few days or weeks, then going down a few days or weeks and in general moving in a fairly narrow box and drifting no where in particular.

The Market Goes Searching

And so we see the market is doing exactly what the Coasters sang about in 1957: Its searching...searching every which of way.

What is it searching for? Well, I submit the individual stocks and the market itself is constantly searching for its proper real value.

When does it find it? It never really does, or if it does its only for a fleeting brief moment and only the omnipotent Deity of the stock world could know that; mere humans can only keep voting.

However, we humans never let the proper real value of the stocks or the market get too much out of kilter for too long before we vote it back toward the other direction. Even we humans can determine when something obviously becomes too overvalued and we'll vote by selling. Thousands of others will do the same and the overvalue situation will begin to correct itself. Now, I readily agree with Graham & Dodd that we humans vote both with sound reason at times and with unreasonable emotions at others.

Often the result is the old swinging pendulum theory of history. *That is, from an overvalued position the market will swing back, not just to the exact point of the proper real value that only the omnipotent Deity knows about, but it keeps over-swinging to the point where its out of kilter in the other direction, where it might pause and start a new swing back again.*

With all these voters, voting with both reason and emotions, and with all this fluctuation and searching every which of way, the pendulum swings are certainly not in the mechanical perfection pattern of the pendulum on a grand old Grandfather clock. The market might go up 30% one year and down 22% the next. It might go down 15% one year, down 28% the next and up 40% the following year. But in all this searching for its proper real value level a pattern does indeed emerge. And it is with the study of these historical patterns and with the belief that history repeats itself, only differently, that I believe that there can be a **Historical Indicator Timing Strategy, i.e., Hits.**

PART TWO:
HITS
(Historical Indicator Timing Strategy)
Comes Alive

CHAPTER FIVE
The Hits System

*"...A time to plant, and a time to pluck up that which is
planted...a time to keep, and a time to cast away...."*
Ecclesiastes 3.2-5

Market timing is controversial. Many argue that the
market simply can't be timed and that it's non-productive, and
maybe even dangerous, to try. They say the best strategy is to
select certain blue chip individual stocks or high quality
mutual funds and stay with a buy-and-hold position for the

long duration.

Other market timing evangelists sing high praises on how well they can time the market getting you in at just the right time and out at just the right time. In other words, you ride on the bull markets straight up and sit on the sideline in a money fund or other less volatile investment vehicle while the raging bear market turns millionaires into paupers.

Over the years some of the most successful investors we have ever known have been market timers, to some degree. However, they have never claimed that they could even rarely buy at the bottom and sell at the top. In fact, most of the best don't even try to time it that close.

"Don't try to buy at the bottom and sell at the top. This can't be done, except by liars." Bernard Baruch.

"I never buy at the bottom and I always sell too soon." Baron Rothchild.

I certainly won't argue with Baruch and Rothchild. In essence, I believe they are saying, don't try to fine tune market timing to such a minute degree; let the market itself tell you what it most probably will do and if you buy above the bottom, be it weeks or months after it touched bottom or even before it reached bottom and is now making its return pendulum swing upward, that's just fine. And don't expect to sell at the top. You may sell before the market reaches the top or after it has reached the top and is on its way back down.

Recently, there has been much written about how a buy-and-hold strategy will beat the best market timing system because the buying and selling required by the market timer triggers more taxes to be paid and thereby reduces the after tax total return.

This is true enough, as far as it goes. It is true, especially with the hyperactive trading that some of your not-so-successful advisory letters require. It's not true at all if your portfolio is within a self-directed IRA, 401(k) type program, or with some variable annuities.

And I think I can show you how a decent timing strategy has beaten the buy-and-hold approach, hands down, in many of the market's time frames that contained prolonged bear markets.

The only study I have seen for the buy-and-hold vs. market timing strategies, utilizing the tax adjustment, is the ten years through the end of 1991. This is, of course, was one of the best bull markets we've had which always greatly favors a buy-and-hold approach. The argument is made that the 1987 crash gave the market timers a chance to show their talents. But, did it really?

Sure, 1987 was a dramatic crash with its tremendous one day drop. But, it's quick recovery again greatly favored the buy-and-hold program. How about a time frame beginning with 1973? And what about the '60s? And if you really want to test the buy-and-hold strategy, especially when you figure the all important psychological factor, let's take the time frame from 1929 through 1938.

In Figure 5.1 you will see how *a buy-and-hold approach with the S&P 500 would have reduced your $10,000 investment to $9,147 after ten years*. Whereas *Hits-Plus would have turned $10,000 into $32,400 over the same time frame* and *Super Hits-Plus would have delivered $52,241 from the original $10,000 investment*, in this, one of the worst possible ten year investment periods.

The bottom line is simple. How good is the market timing strategy? How much trading activity does the timing system call for? (Hits-Plus requires a lot less than almost all other timing and switching programs.) Do we expect future markets to be basically a re-run of the eighties, or should you be prepared for another 1973, 1974, and other less favorable periods of time?

The answer, for me, is that if I will be following a historically proven timing strategy that calls for very limited buying, selling, and switching and if this gives me appreciably better results through all kinds of market conditions and with strong protection against such ulcer causing bear markets as 1973 and 1974, then by all means lead me to it.

Figure 5.1

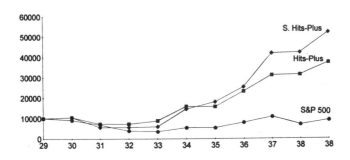

First, as I stated earlier in this book, my favorite market index is the Standard & Poor's 500. The S&P 500, representing the stock of 500 different companies, is broad enough to be an excellent measuring stick. You can trade in and out of the S&P 500 with just one Index mutual fund. And most importantly, the S&P 500 has many years of true historical data that give you the distinct advantage of looking back at past performance patterns leading to not a perfect market timing machine (there is no such animal), but to the development of a systematic strategy that simply projects the strong probabilities of what will happen in the market in the upcoming years. The fact that the S&P 500 Index performance has beaten the performance of 82% of the mutual funds over this past ten years, without any market timing says a lot too.

Let's turn now to a table on the yearly performance of the S&P 500 from 1946 through 1993. Table 5.1 shows total return; total return simply means stock price growth, plus all dividends and capital gains distributions being automatically reinvested. Total return is the only way to really judge the true performance of any investment vehicle. You will note that throughout this book I will always use plus(+) and minus (-) symbols in front of percentage movements. I do this for easy

Table 5.1

*S&P 500 Performance-Total Return
(Dividents & Capital Gains Reinvested)

Year	S&P 500 Perf.	Year	S&P 500 Perf.
1946	- 7.9%	1970	+ 4.9%
1947	+ 5.8	1971	+13.8
1948	+ 5.9	1972	+19.3
1949	+19.0	1973	- 13.9
1950	+32.1	1974	- 27.1
1951	+23.8	1975	+36.9
1952	+17.9	1976	+24.1
1953	- 1.8	1977	- 6.9
1954	+53.1	1978	+ 6.8
1955	+31.4	1979	+18.6
1956	+ 6.4	1980	+32.6
1957	- 10.6	1981	- 5.2
1958	+43.7	1982	+21.7
1959	+11.8	1983	+23.0
1960	+ 1.0	1984	+ 5.9
1961	+26.6	1985	+31.9
1962	- 8.5	1986	+18.8
1963	+23.1	1987	+ 4.9
1964	+15.9	1988	+17.1
1965	+13.2	1989	+31.2
1966	- 9.9	1990	- 2.9
1967	+24.2	1991	+31.1
1968	+10.9	1992	+ 6.8
1969	- 8.3	1993	+10.1

*These are not true performance caculations and are used for illustratiion purposes only

59

clarity for the reader so there is no question of how the market moved.

What's Up? What's Down?

At first look we can see that the S&P 500 was up 37 out of these 48 years, being down only 11 years. But to me the market was down 9 additional years. "What are you saying?" you may ask. "Don't you know up from down?" Yes, but in the case of investing in common stocks you must expect appreciably better returns than when you invest in much more conservative vehicles, such as bank accounts, money funds, CDs, government bonds, high quality corporate bonds, etc.

When you take a higher risk, you also must expect a higher return. If this were not true there would be no stock exchanges, as we know them, with all those voters, all that fluctuating and all that searching. We'd all be investing in mostly fixed income units and leaving the fluctuation alone.

I put the cutoff on whether the S&P 500 has had an up year or down year at 10%. That is, if the S&P 500 is up less than 10% I count it as a down year. You will rarely see a growth mutual fund advertising in bragging tones that their total return was up less than +10% for a particular year unless it was during a really bad year when the market went down and they managed to go against the tide with a plus performance.

With that in mind we will go back and circle 1947, 1948, 1956, 1960, 1970, 1978, 1984, 1987 and 1992 as down years (the actual eleven negative performing years are underlined). As you see, I'm using one-year measuring units. Why? Well, we have to select some time unit of measurement and there are many good reasons for one of those units of time measurement to be the calendar year. So much money is committed for an annual investment by the year. Mutual funds measure their success rating by the year, so do most companies and individuals.

I interpret the observations of Bernard Baruch and Baron Rothchild as advising us not to try to use very narrow time-

60

frames to make snap decisions in market timing. Later, we will use one month and quarter time frames, too, but this will be limited and under special situations.

Now let's go back to the S&P 500 total return yearly performance from 1946 through 1993 (counting the circled years as down years) and take another look. In general, we see that the market is searching for its proper level in a type of swinging pendulum manner. A number of down years are followed by up years. A number of up years are followed by a down year or years. Mostly there are fewer down years in a row because overall the market has always moved in an upward mode.

Down Two Go; Up Two Whoa

In general, if the market has been down (remember down is less than a +10% rise) two years in a row, Hits is going fully invested that third year, even with some margin, because the probabilities are overwhelming that the market will go up that next (third) year. If it doesn't, Hits will stay in fully the next (fourth) year and with full margin, because now the historical probabilities that the S&P 500 will go up this upcoming year are unprecedented in our favor.

By the same token if the market has been up for two years in a row (with exceptions we will cover in a moment) we will sell and invest in more conservative vehicles for the third year.

What we are doing, of course, in trying to increase our chances of being in the market for the up years and out of the market during the down years. We won't hit it just right every year, but we are playing the probabilities or percentages of being right more often with the pendulum swing than we would be with a simple buy-and-hold position.

We have just touched on the simple core of Hits: Two years up, sell and be out the third year. Two years down, buy and be in the third year. But, there are exceptions. Hits becomes slightly more complex, but not very much.

It stands to reason that if the pendulum has swung more

drastically in one direction for more than two years in a row that a corrective swing back in the other direction would also last more than just a year or two.

Down Three, In For Four

So we add the rule that if the market is down three or more years in a row, we will automatically commit to a buy-and-hold position for four years in a row (there will be a Fail-Safe Sell Signal we will add to this shortly). If we are in the market with a four-year buy-and-hold commitment because the previous three years or more were down years, we will definitely sell after this four-year commitment period and move into more conservative investment vehicles.

We do not, however, do exactly the same after a string of up years. If we have a run of three or more up years in the market we will not automatically stay out any more than one year. This is because historically the market does move in an upward mode a much higher percentage of the time. However, there are two more devices we will add to Hits to make it Hits-Plus that might take us out of the market for two or more years in a row.

Let's recap briefly the basic Hits system before we add the "Plus" factors:

1. If the market has been down (remember, down is less than a +10% rise) two years in a row we will go into the market the third year and use one-third margin.
2. If the market goes down that investment year (again, down is less than a +10% rise) we stay in and use full margin.
3. If the market has been up two years in a row we will sell and move into more conservative investment vehicles for the upcoming third year.
4. However, when we look back at the S&P 500 total return performance and see that it has been down (the failure to go up at least +10%) three or more

years in a row we will make a buy-and-hold commitment for the next four-year period.

Where do you find the information on what the S&P 500 Index Total Return is by the month or other time period? At the time of this writing, no publication that I know of, except the *Hits-Plus Mutual Fund Guide,* publishes the S&P 500 Index Total Return on a timely monthly basis and on a projected basis. But, this does not mean that you can't calculate this or learn this very easily.

Almost any good daily newspaper will show you how much the S&P 500 went up or down on the previous day, but since this figure does not include the dividend factor, this alone is of little value to us. So we turn to *The Wall Street Journal* which recently greatly improved their mutual fund listing pages. The Journal now lists Total Return Percentages year-to-date (% Ret Ytd) for each mutual fund (See Figure 5.2)

We see that Vanguard Index 500 ended February 1993 being up +2.2% Total Return for the year (since 12-31-92), with a closing price of $41.86 on the last trading day of the month.

Figure 5.2

	Inv. Obj.	NAV	Offer Price	NAV Chg.	– Total Return – YTD	26 wks	4 yrs	R
Vanguard Group:								
AdmST	BST	10.25	NL	+0.01	NA	0.000	NA	..
AdmIT	BND	10.48	NL	...	NA	0.000	NA	..
AdmLT	BND	10.58	NL	...	NA	0.000	NA	..
AssetA	S&B	14.21	NL	+0.01	+4.2	0.000	0.520	..
BdMkt	BND	10.13	NL	...	+3.6	0.000	0.160	..
Convrt	S&B	11.83	NL	+0.03	+0.3	0.000	0.810	..
EqInc	STK	13.63	NL	+0.03	+5.5	0.000	0.440	..
Explr	SML	42.76	NL	+0.14	−2.5	0.000	0.690	..
Morg	STK	12.55	NL	...	−0.8	0.000	0.460	..
Prmcp	STK	16.71	NL	−0.02	+3.2	0.000	0.680	..
Prefd	BND	9.42	NL	+0.01	+4.0	0.000	0.580	..
Quant	STK	16.81	NL	+0.06	+3.1	0.000	0.430	..
STAR	S&B	13.29	NL	+0.03	+3.1	0.000	NA	..
TC Int	WOR	25.16	NL	+0.01	+3.0	0.000	0.380	..
TCUsa	STK	29.27	NL	+0.03	+3.0	0.000	0.440	..
GNMA	BND	10.53	NL	...	+2.0	0.000	0.290	..
HYCorp	BHI	7.67	NL	+0.01	+4.8	0.000	0.340	..
IGCorp	BND	9.24	NL	+0.01	+5.6	0.000	0.310	..
STCorp	BST	11.01	NL	+0.01	+2.5	0.000	0.260	..
STFed	BST	10.44	NL	+0.01	+2.6	0.000	0.260	..
ST Tsry	BST	10.47	NL	...	+2.5	0.000	NA	..
IT Tsry	BND	11.00	NL	+0.01	+5.1	0.000	NA	..
LT Tsry	BND	10.28	NL	...	(+5.7)	0.000	0.260	..
Idx 500	STK	41.86	NL	+0.10	(+2.2)	0.000	0.200	..
IdxExt	SML	17.46	NL	+0.07	−0.6	0.000	0.190	..
IdxTot	STK	11.00	NL	+0.03	+1.5	0.000	NA	..
IdxGro	STK	10.06	NL	+0.04	−1.9	0.000	NA	..

(Illustration from the Wall Street Journal 3/1/93 issue.)

Next we turn to *The Wall Street Journal*, April 1 issue which has the closing for March (See Figure 5.3).

Figure 5.3

	Inv. Obj.	NAV	Offer Price	NAV Chg.	— Total Return —		
					YTD	26 wks	4 yrs R
STFeq	BST	10.43	NL	...	+3.0	+2.8	+10.2 B
ST Tsry	BST	10.46	NL	−0.01	+2.9	+3.2	NS ..
IT Tsry	BND	10.99	NL	...	+5.5	+5.8	NS ..
LT Tsry	BND	10.24	NL	−0.01	+6.2	+8.1	+13.4 A
Idx 500	STK	42.49	NL	−0.02	+4.4	+9.5	+14.7 B
IdxExt	SML	18.04	NL	+0.13	+3.5	+14.6	+12.9 D
IdxTot	STK	11.20	NL	+0.03	+3.7	+10.7	NS ..
IdxGro	STK	10.15	NL	...	−0.6	NS	NS ..
IdxVal	STK	11.17	NL	−0.01	+9.2	NS	NS ..
IdxEur	WOR	9.89	NL	+0.11	+4.8	+1.3	NS ..
IdxPac	WOR	8.85	NL	+0.01	+16.9	+9.1	NS ..
IdxInst	STK	42.96	NL	−0.02	+4.4	+9.5	NS ..
Idx Bal	S&B	10.63	NL	+0.01	+3.8	NS	NS ..
SmCap	SML	14.77	NL	+0.08	+4.4	+18.8	+11.2 D
MuHY	MUN	10.81	NL	...	+3.8	+6.8	+11.1 A
MuInt	MUN	13.12	NL	...	+3.4	+6.0	+10.3 A
MuLtd	MUN	10.73	NL	...	+1.7	+3.5	+8.1 E
MuLong	MUN	11.01	NL	−0.02	+4.3	+7.1	+11.2 A

(Illustration from the *Wall Street Journal* 4/1/93 issue.)

This issue shows that the Vanguard Index 500 Fund ended March with a Total Return year-to-date of +4.4%. That means that Vanguard Index 500 gained +2.2% during just the month of March. This is the Total Return of the S&P 500 itself except for the Vanguard management expenses which is less than .25% (one quarter of one percent) per year. On a monthly tracking, this is as close as a cat's whiskers.

During the month of March, Vanguard declared and paid a 24¢ dividend, but this was calculated in the Total Return percentage performance by the *Journal*. We will cover more about dividend adjustment in Chapter Seven. If you ever have any doubts about your tracking of the S&P 500 via the Vanguard Index 500 fund with *The Wall Street Journal*, don't hesitate to call Vanguard (see Appendix A).

A Touch of Margin, Perhaps?

I know by now some of you caught me saying we might use either one-third or full margin when we are in the market and if you know what margin is and don't like it you could be a bit upset at this point. Let me say quickly that if you're dead set against the use of margin don't use it, and Hits-Plus will still deliver much greater performance results than buy-and-hold.

We will discuss the pros and cons of margin use in a separate chapter.

To those who are a little mystified about just what margin is I'll touch very simply on it now before we reach the chapter that's devoted to a discussion of margin.

Margin is simply borrowing money from your broker and using your stock as collateral. You would do this if you are comfortable with the use of margin and are fairly confident that the odds are good that the investment year coming up will be a profitable one.

At the time of this writing the maximum margin allowed is 50%. This means that if you own $10,000 in stocks you can borrow an additional $10,000 from your broker to take a total $20,000 stock position. Your margin loan is 50% of your total portfolio's worth.

To use one-third margin and you own $10,000 in stocks you would borrow $5,000 (one half of your totally paid for position) and use this $5,000 to buy additional stock so the $5000 loan position represents one-third of your total holdings. Your total stock position is now $15,000.

You do pay the broker interest on this margin loan, usually around the prime interest rate, but this could vary to a little over prime or a little under depending on your individual investment strength. And if the value of your stock falls over 30% you must come up with more money or the broker will sell enough of your stocks to bring the loan back into legal requirements. This will not bother the Hits-Plus investor who uses margin and I'll tell you why a little later.

What margin does for the margin user is to allow the investor to leverage his or her position and to control more stock than just his available cash will allow him or her. And if the market goes up more than his or her interest cost it can be very profitable indeed. For margin to be successfully used you must be right about the market more times than you're wrong and the shares purchased on margin must go up more than your margin loan interest rate cost. Historically this has not been a problem at all with Hits-Plus. But, again the use of margin is strictly up to the individual and Hits-Plus gives you outstanding results even without margin.

Two other points. You can use margin with the buying of no-load mutual funds by going through a discount broker such as Charles Schwab or others. And for comfortable margin users, it's worth the reasonable discount commissions and interest to do so. Of course, if your stock holdings are in a self directed IRA, 401 (k) type plan, or variable annuity you cannot use margin, but you can use Hits-Plus without margin in many of these cases.

Also by now some of you readers may have noticed that Hits calls for an investment decision after two down years or more or after two up years. What do you do if just the previous year was up or down, i.e. no two years in a row of the same type movement to give you a strong definite indication for the upcoming years.

This is when we turn to the January Barometer.

CHAPTER SIX
The Use Of The January Barometer

JANUARY

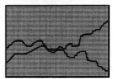

*"I was gratified to be able to answer promptly.
I said I don't know."*

- Mark Twain

*"I don't know why or how the thing works, but it
does and I use it."*

*---- Millions of us people who use everything
from automobiles to computers without
knowing the why or how it works.*

The January Barometer works. Not all the time, but
over 75% of the time. I do like to know the reasoning behind
why something works and there is reasoning to support why
the January Barometer works so often.

In Yale Hirsch's *1994 Stock Traders Almanac* (as well
as in earlier issues), an excellent publication that I will buy
every year, he traces his reasoning for the January Barometer's
success back to the Twentieth Amendment to the Constitution,

which became effective in 1934. Before that time the January Barometer did not work so well. Basically, the Twentieth Amendment put Congress in session on January Third instead of the first Monday of December, which had previously been the case, and the congressmen who had been defeated were gone and the new winners were in. So we have the full month of January for Congress to begin to set the tone for the upcoming year. Hirsch's analysis does make good sense.

January May Set the Trend

I would add to this the same basic argument I made for using one calendar year as our main unit of time measurement. In January many investment commitments are made for the upcoming calendar year. Thousands of individuals make their IRA investment for the year as well as other investment decisions. We are so acclimated to calendar year decisions and commitments. Even though many companies operate on various fiscal year calendars, they still tend to plan on a calendar-year basis. Many bank trust departments, portfolio managers of insurance companies, and other money managers and investment advisors will make at least some of their investment decisions and commitments for the year during the month of January, thereby setting a possible trend for the year.

Some analysts argue that many investors sell their losers before the end of the year to take a tax loss position and then reinvest in January (if they feel there are enough good bargains out there), thereby influencing the January market. Also, those who have had big gains that qualify for more favorable capital gains treatment (and if they believe that there's little or no gains left to come from these stocks) will sell them in early January and then reinvest or sit on the sidelines during the month of January, again helping to create a January Barometer. Others say many of the mutual fund managers like to start the new year with a freshened-up portfolio and to do so either with a more conservative or more optimistic approach.

Going with the Historical Probabilities

After saying all of this, there is still not an overwhelming amount of evidence to tell us exactly why the January Barometer correctly calls the Market's performance for the year so often. There is, however, a number of good reasons to support it and it does have an excellent track record since 1934.

Simply put, if the S&P 500 is up at all during the month of January the historical probabilities are very strong that the market will be up for the year as a whole. And if the month of January is down at all, the historical probabilities are very strong that the market will be down as a whole for the year.

Some followers of the January Barometer just look at the January performance of the S&P 500 without including the automatic reinvestment of dividends, etc. for total return results. Hits-Plus will always go with total return for the true picture.

Hits-Plus does not use the January Barometer every year. We _only_ use the January Barometer when we do _not_ have two down years or more in a row in the market or when we do _not_ have two up years in a row with which to make our Hits decision. If the market has been down (always remember with Hits down is less than a 10% rise) two years in a row, we will invest the upcoming third year regardless of what the January Barometer says. The same goes with multiple up years in a row. Hits will always override the January Barometer when we have multiple-year indicators.

But, when just the previous year was up or down then we will turn to the January Barometer to make our investment commitment for the year.

The Mule Barometer

I understand that in the March 12, 1984, issue of Barron's there was an article implying that the success of the January Barometer is based on erroneous reasoning. I missed this article, but have read the gist of it in Mark Hulbert's *The Hulbert Guide to Financial Newsletters.*

It's my understanding that the Barron's article concludes that often the month of January itself may be up more than the entire year or nearly as much as the entire year. Therefore, by including January in with the other eleven months the followers of the January Barometer may buy into the market on the first trading day of February only to find he or she will have a very lackluster performance or even lose money for the remainder of the year.

I have a very high regard for *Barron's*, but I don't believe they have ever heard of the mule Barometer.

I was born and raised on a farm in eastern North Carolina, and I'll always remember a story that was told to be true. It seems a farmer in our area, whom I'll call Willard, had just spent what he considered a good bit of money having a much needed mule stable built. After the carpenters had left, Willard tried to herd his mules from the pasture into the new stable, but there was a problem. The roof of the stable slanted from a low point over the entrance gate to a point several feet higher at the back of the stable. When Willard tried to herd his mules into the new stable the roof above the gate proved to be too low. The mules hit their heads on the too low roof over the entrance gate resulting in lacerated ears and head bumps. This further resulted in unhappy mules and a very unhappy Willard who could ill afford to pay to have the roof reconstructed at a higher level.

But, then Willard's neighbor Reuben arrived on the scene. Willard pointed out his awful problem with the too low roof level just over the entrance gate. Reuben, in turn, studied the situation for a few minutes and then called for a shovel. Reuben took the shovel and within a few minutes he dug out a little valley in the dirt floor under the entrance gate so when the mules walked in or out of the stable, they would walk at a lower level under the entrance gate roof-line. No more cut ears or head bumps.

The point is Willard saw the problem only from the perspective of the stable having a too low roof-line over the gate. Reuben saw things form a broader perspective, including the idea that the dirt floor could be lowered with good results for the not-so-hard-headed mules.

Maybe it was from my farm raising, but at the very beginning, I did not look at the January Barometer as a tool you would use only while waiting on the sidelines outside of the market.

We will go ahead and make our market buy on the first trading day in January and wait, in the market, to see what January does. We will not wait outside the market to see what January will do. The reasons are simple. The market still goes up more than it goes down, and, historically, we would be worse off waiting for the January results on the outside rather than on the inside. January, 1975 alone was up +12.6%, and January of 1976 was up +12%. Plus, from 1934 there were fourteen other Januarys that were up over 5% whereas there were only five years that January was down over 5%. Thus, it would be better for us to be in the market the first of January on the years we will be acting on the January Barometer than to be out of the market to await the January decision. Remember January only has to be up or down just a fraction for us to make the call.

During the 44-year time frame from 1950 through 1993 the January Barometer was correct over 79% of the time. However, since we use the January Barometer to supplement "Hits," it is not a yearly tool for us.

From 1950 through 1993, when Hits-Plus did use the January Barometer, it paid off 90% of the time. I am not selecting 1950 through 1993 as a time frame just to prove a point. Actually this book will cover historical investments since the beginning of 1929 through 1993. I have, however, separated the years from the beginning of 1929 through 1949 and from the beginning of 1950 through 1993.

My purpose in this is that I want to devote one chapter to the great stock market crash and depression of the thirties and the tumultuous World War II years and immediate post-World War II years. The reader will be able to see explicitly the performance record of Hits-Plus from the outset of 1929 through 1993 and to select any five, ten, fifteen, etc. year period of time and then to judge the performance of Hits-Plus for that particular time frame.

The January Barometer is an excellent investment tool and is added to Hits as one of the pluses, to make up Hits-Plus.

CHAPTER SEVEN
The Fail-Safe Signals

"There are old traders around and bold traders around but there are no old, bold traders around."
----Bob Dinda, Dean Whitter

"A loss never bothers me after I take it. I forget it overnight. But being wrong...not taking the loss...that is what does damage to the pocketbook and to the soul."
----Jesse Livermore

With Hits-Plus we would like to avoid all bear markets from the little "Teddy Bears," "The Cub Bears," on through, and especially, the ferocious "Grizzly Bear." But, we just can't do this.

No investment strategy that I know of can avoid or escape all bear markets. Hits-Plus is more conservative than many investment systems, although its long term performance results rival the most aggressive, chance-taking strategies without the heart-stopping roller coaster rides featuring five-year time frames that leave you with holes in your pocket.

Back in 1973 and 1974 I was out of the market altogether, but not because of any great investment insight on my part. It just so happened that in 1973 I was selling all of my rental property and raising all the cash I could to invest in the broadcasting business I had been managing for over thirteen years. I had first invested in the stock market in the early sixties and had been in and out of the market from time to time. But in 1973 and 1974 my focus was elsewhere.

"Grizzly Bear"—1973 and 1974

Although I would not again become very active as a stock market investor until the late seventies, because all of my capital was tied up in the broadcasting company, I did continue to keep track of the market and study various investment strategies.

The devastating results of the free-fall "Grizzly Bear" market of 1973 and 1974 really got my attention. And as a history buff I had always had a fascination with the stock market crash of October 1929 and the terrible depression that followed.

The 1973-1974 bear market clawed and ripped a -37% loss in the S&P 500, but this was minor compared to a -58% loss in the famous Fidelity Magellan Fund, a -69% loss in the now highly regarded Nicholas fund, a -46% loss in 20th Century Growth, and a disastrous -70% loss in the crash and burn performance of the 44 Wall Street Fund. Many other individual stocks fell further and on into near oblivion.

It's true that many of these funds staged a dramatic comeback in 1975, 1976, and on. But, it's also true that many investors rode the grizzly bear all the way down and then sold out swearing never again to buy another share of common stock or shares in a mutual fund as long as they lived.

If you think 1973 and 1974 were bad wait until we cover the Great Depression of the 1930s. But that horror story warrants its own chapter. I also think you'll find it interesting how Hits-Plus and Super Hits-Plus performed during these chaotic times.

In any event, the 1973-1974 bear market impressed upon me that regardless of what investment strategy or system you follow, *you need some kind of fail-safe signal that would get you out of the market before you have pretty much lost it all.* After all a little nip from a mild "Teddy Bear" is one thing, a little slapping around by a frisky "Cub Bear" hurts a bit, but a mean, hungry "Grizzly Bear" with fangs and claws flashing and slashing can leave you bleeding from every financial vein in your basket-case investment body.

By the same token you need some kind of signal to let you know when the mayhem is over and when to get back in.

The Fail-Safe Sell Signal

I worked and researched to fashion a fail-safe signal for a number of years. I never sought to develop an early warning, fine-tuned method of when to sell and when to buy. All I wanted was to avoid the very worst of "Grizzly Bear" markets.

The fail-safe signal I adopted is simple and will be unappealing to many investors. It appears to sell you out too late when the market heads south and gives up too much of the early rise of the returning bull market. So be it. Just remember the fail-safe signal is rarely used; the rest of Hits-Plus will have you out of the market for most bear periods and back in early for the bull markets, but we do need a fail-safe signal for that added protection.

The fail-safe signal directs you to sell out when your S&P 500 index mutual fund falls -31% from its highest high price at the end of a trading month. "Take a -31% loss," you scream. No, not necessarily, and, even if you do, it would be better than the -70% hold-til-you-die fall that the 44 Wall Street Fund experienced. I said "not necessarily" because remember I also said a -31% drop from its <u>highest high</u>. Suppose you bought the fund on the first trading day of January at $10 per share and watched it climb to $12.60 a share by the end of June. Then the bear comes clawing in and the fund ends November at $8.65. This is a drop of a little over -31% from the highest high end-of-the-month price of $12.60. But, it is only a 13.5% loss from your $10 purchase price. I say <u>only</u> 13.5% reluctantly because a 13.5% loss is pretty bad, but if its the only last ditch fail-safe signal that will save me from a financial blood bath, I'll take it. ***Remember to always reset your Fail-Safe Sell Signal as a new end-of-the-month <u>high</u> is reached.***

The Fail-Safe Buy Signal

"Don't gamble! Take all savings and buy some good stock and hold it till it goes up, then sell it. If it don't go up, don't buy it.
Will Rogers

This is an example of the great humor of Will Rogers. It's too bad we can't make retroactive stock buying decisions where we see that a stock is now selling for $10 per share, but ten months ago it was selling for $7 per share, so we just call our broker and direct him to buy it at $7 and immediately sell it at $10.

The humor of the Will Rogers quote is obvious, but I think there's good investment advice there too. When we have been sold out by the Fail-Safe Sell Signal, when do we buy back in? I submit we wait until the market makes a significant enough move upward to be making a statement that "The Bear" is over and the bull is coming on the scene.

The Fail-Safe Buy Signal directs you to buy back in the S&P 500 Index Mutual Fund when it climbs +21% from its lowest low end-of-the-month trading price.

So if the same fund that we sold at $8.65 continued to fall until the following year when its end-of-the-month trading price had reached $4.79 and then begins to rise again, and if $4.79 turns out to be the lowest end-of-the-month trading price we will track the price until its end-of-the-month trading price is over $5.80 per share (a gain of +21%) and then we'll buy back in. ***Remember (when you have sold out) to always reset*** *your Fail-Safe Buy Signal every time a new end-of-the-month trading low is reached.*

Yes, there may be times when we are whipsawed, in that we buy back in at a higher price than we sold. If the lowest low had been around $7.94, we would have bought back in at $9.61, a price higher than we sold. I do not fret about this possibility because the Fail-Safe Buy Signal is so rarely used, and, although it can cost you a bit at certain rare times, its like taking out catastrophic insurance. Under certain conditions it can literally save your financial back-side.

A little reasoning please? Why sell -31% from the highest high and buy at +21% from the lowest low. Well, the total is 52%, a swing of two points over 50%, and, historically, this percentage swing more than indicated that a real true "Grizzly Bear" is already in effect with a -31% drop from the highest high and that a true bull market is already in effect with the +21% rise from the lowest low. This strategy is no more "Totally Fool Proof" than any other strategy, but it lets the market itself tell you what its doing. When the market moves this drastically, it's telling you in no uncertain terms that, *in the case of the "Sell Signal" even worse may yet be coming. And in the "Buy" signal case its saying, "The worst is over and a much better market is ahead."*

End-of-the-Month Tracking

So why is the Fail-Safe Sell Signal price set at the end-of-the-month price rather than selling as soon as a 31% drop occurs regardless of when it occurs? Why not track the price daily or weekly? Again, we are being asked to select the best unit of time. Our main Hits program uses a one-year commitment unless the January Barometer is in effect and then naturally it's the month of January.

Frankly, I feel that what happens in the market in any time frame of less than one month is simply too narrow a period of time to make a judgment.

Historically, using the end-of-the-month time for us to measure the Fail-Safe Sell Signal and the Fail-Safe Buy Signal will cost us a bit on some occasions. At other times it will keep us from making false premature moves as the market takes a stab in one direction or the other and then right back in the opposite direction without a true trend being cast. Overall, the end-of-the-month share price will serve us well in the very rare occasions we might have the Fail-Safe Signals flash their signals.

When and if the Fail-Safe Sell Signal does flash, we sell out and move into 50% U.S. Treasury Bills and 50% Intermediate Term Government Bonds right away regardless of any other indicators. The Fail-Safe Sell Signal takes precedent over all other indicators when it flashes. Once we sell, we stay out until the end-of-the-month share price moves up +21% from its lowest low regardless of any other indicators. In other words if we're out of the market because of a   -31% Fail-Safe Sell and the market stays down for two years and then moves up +10% to +15%, we still stay out until that +21% from the lowest low price is realized. I have been asked, "Wouldn't a narrower range Fail Safe Sell and Buy Signal work?" The answer is yes, in many market time frames. A sell at -21% and a buy at +11% would do very well in many historical market periods but not during the terrible thirties. During this time, a -21% Sell Signal and +11% Buy Signal would have whipsawed you to death. The Hits-Plus System itself keeps you out of the vast majority of bear markets; i.e., we never actually had to use the Fail-Safe Signals from 1950 through 1993, but it is good insurance to have it in place as part of your program.

We must remember that when we have tracked the S&P 500 performance in this book we have used a trading price that reflected the re-investment of all dividends so we did not have to worry about tabulating and converting dividends into additional stock for total return value. Fortunately, Ibbotson Associates SBBI Year Book did all this for us.

Adjust for Dividends for Proper Value

When we actually own shares in an individual mutual fund, we will always direct the fund to automatically reinvest all dividends to buy more shares in the fund. So if a mutual fund that is selling for $10 a share declares a $1.00 dividend, the NAV (Net Asset Value) or share price of the fund will go down to $9 per share. However, if we had a $1,000 position (100 share) in the fund our $100 dividend would have purchased 11.111 additional shares for a total of 111.111 shares, and out total value position is still $1,000. Now if the share price fell to an end-of-the-month trading price of $6.90 per share, at first glance one might surmise that the mutual fund had lost -31% in value (a -31% drop from $10). Of course, our 111.111 shares at $6.90 per share are now worth $766.67 which is a -23.33% drop in total value. The point is we don't sell because the per share price of a mutual fund drops -31% from its highest high end-of-the-month trading price. We must be sure that the fund had not paid a dividend during this period of time that would have artificially lowered the share price more than the real total return value of the fund. If you actually own the mutual fund you will receive this dividend information from the fund itself.

Hits-Plus Mutual Fund Guide publishes this information each month. Or, if you have any doubt simply call the mutual fund and ask, "How much (in percentage) has the mutual fund declined, total return, since the end of last month?" Never hesitate to call and ask. It's not a dumb question. The only dumb qusestion is the one you don't ask.

If I am tracking a mutual fund, be it the Vanguard Index 500 fund or a small companies stock index fund, I use both *The Wall Street Journal* (published daily Monday through Friday) and *Barron's*, a weekly financial newspaper published by Dow Jones and Company.

For example, if at the end of January the NAV (share price) of the mutual fund is $10.00 and this is the highest end-of-the-month high I will set my Fail-Safe Sell Signal at $6.90 (-31% from $10.00). If at the end of February the NAV is

$10.85, a new highest end-of-the-month high, the new Fail-Safe Sell Signal goes to $7.49 (-31% from $10.85).

If at the end of March the NAV drops to $10.30 the Fail-Safe Sell price of $7.49 stays the same as we are still working with $10.85 as being the highest end-of-the-month high.

Now let's say that on April 15 we see the little x sign right after the IDX 500 x listing under the Vanguard family of funds. This tells us that the Vanguard Index 500 Fund has declared a dividend that is reflected in the NAV price of the Shares. (We also note that on April 14 the fund traded at $10.32 per share). However, *The Wall Street Journal* does not tell us how much the dividend was. For this information we must wait for the next issue of *Barron's* where we find that the dividend was 62¢ (6% of $10.32) and, therefore, lowered the NAV to $9.70. But since the dividend would be used to buy additional shares the true value of the fund remains the same. We must also re-set the NAV price that would signal when a new highest end-of-the-month high has been reached. Again, we just lower the last highest high price of $10.85 by -6% which says that the NAV share price must rise to over $10.20 a share to achieve a new end-of-the-month high in true value. A -31% fall from $10.20 would drop the share price to $7.04 therefore this will be where we will set our new Fail-Safe Sell Signal. Always remember when a new highest end-of-the-month trading price is reached, we must re-establish our Fail-Safe Sell Signal at -31% below this price.

Make it a point to familiarize yourself with the quotations footnotes in *The Wall Street Journal* and *Barron's:* e-Ex-Distribution, s-Stocksplit or Dividend, x-EX-Dividend. Watch for these little signs right after the listed name of the individual mutual fund in the Journal and then check the next Barron's to see what happened and when. *If you're ever in doubt, telephone the mutual fund in question. Most have 800 numbers.*

The proper use of the Fail-Safe signals will become explicitly clear as we track the performance of Hits-Plus over the years. For example, in 1974 we will see how we went into the market the first of January to await the January Barometer. When January was down we sold and were out of the market for the rest of the year. But, because we tracked the end-of-the-month prices we saw that had we stayed in, the Fail-Safe Sell Signal would have taken us out. Therefore, we do not buy back in and begin to utilize Hits-Plus again until the Fail Safe Buy Signal is flashed; then we buy back in the market in accordance with what Hits-Plus tells us to do. This may be beginning to sound a little complex, but I assure you that when we track the use of Hits-Plus year by year, clearly defining each year what we're doing and why, it will be very clear as we learn by observing and doing under actual market conditions.

Summary

1. If the market has been down (down is less than a+10% rise) two years in a row, we will buy into the S&P 500 for the third, up coming year, and use one-third margin.

2. If the S&P 500 goes down that third year (Down, as always, is the failure to rise +10% or more), we stay in the market and now with full 50% margin. This would continue to be true if the market went down a fourth year.

3. If the S&P 500 is down three years or more in a row we will automatically invest fully with one-third mar gin the first investment year. And thereafter, we invest without margin for three additional years. This is a four-year commitment to be in the market. Exception: If we have been sold out of the market because of the Fail-Safe Sell Signal, then we stay out until the Fail-Safe Buy Signal is flashed and then proceed as planned.

4. If the S&P 500 has been up two years in a row (and it is not a four-year commitment to be in the market, as presented in rule #3) then we will sell out of the S&P

500 and use 50% of our funds to buy U.S. Treasury Bills and 50% of our funds to buy Intermediate-Term Government Bonds.

5. If the S&P 500 has been up just the previous year or down (down being a rise of less then +10%) and if rule #3 is not in effect (the commitment to be in the market for four years in a row) and if the Fail-Safe Sell Signal is not in effect, then we will go fully in the S&P 500 (without margin) on the first trading day in January and stay through the month of January to read the January Barometer. If the S&P 500 is up (total return) for the month of January we will stay in the market for the full year. If the S&P 500 (total return) is down for the month of January, we will sell out and use 50% of our funds to buy U.S. Treasury Bills and 50% of our funds to buy Intermediate Term Government Bonds.

6. The Fail-Safe Sell Signal and the Fail-Safe Buy Signal, when flashed, take precedence over everything. This is your catastrophe insurance. When and if the S&P 500 falls -31% from its highest high at the end-of-the-month trading price, we sell out. Now let's be clear we are talking about a total return -31% loss from any previous end-of-the-month highest high to the current end-of-the-month trading price. In other words, if the highest end-of-the-month trading price of our S&P 500 Index Mutual Fund several months ago was $14.50 and even if it fell to $9.86 (a -32% drop) some time during the month, we would not sell. We would wait until the end of the month. At that time, if the price had gone back up to $10.15 (a -30% drop from $14.50), we would not sell. However, if the end-of-the-month trading price was $10.00 or less, we would sell. It doesn't make any difference to us what happens on a daily or weekly basis, our decision time frame is at the end of each month. Once we have sold

Figure 7.1

What to Do

Hits-Plus First-of-the-Year Flowchart

Has the S&P 500 Index (Total Return) been down Three years or more in a row? **1**

NO

YES → **A** — We will buy into the S&P 500 Index with 1/3 margin the first year and make a four-year commitment to stay in the market. If the market is up this upcoming year, we will not use margin the next three years. If the market goes down this first upcoming year, we will use full margin the following year.* **2**

Has the S&P 500 Index been down two years in a row? **1**

NO

YES → **B** — We buy into the S&P 500 Index for one calender year and use 1/3 margin. **2**

Was the S&P 500 Index down last year? **1**

NO

YES → **C** — We buy into the S&P 500 Index on the earliest trading day in Jan. If at the end of Jan. the index is up, at all, we stay in. If it is down at all, we sell and move into T-Bills and Bonds. *

Was the S&P 500 Index up for the last three years in a row? **3**

NO

YES → Unless this comes during a four-year commitment (see A), we will invest for the upcoming year in T-Bills and Bonds.

Was the S&P 500 Index up for the last two years in a row? **3**

NO

YES → Unless this comes during a four-year commitment (see A), we will invest for the upcoming year in T-Bills and Bonds.

Was the S&P 500 Index up last year? **3**

YES → We buy into the S&P 500 Index on the earliest trading day in Jan. If at the end of Jan. the index is up, at all, we stay in. If it is down at all, we sell and move into T-Bills and Bonds.

1 Down means the S&P 500 Index failed to gain +10% Total Return.

2 The use of margin is optional. You do not have to use margin to receive excellent performance from Hits-Plus.

3 Up means the S&P 500 Index, gained +10% Total Return, or more.

* The Fail-Safe Sell Trigger will interrupt and take precedence over all investment plans that may be in effect.

out, we put 50% of our funds in U.S. Treasury Bills and 50% in Intermediate-Term Government Bonds, and we keep tracking the market on an end-of-the-month basis. But do not buy back in until a Fail-Safe Buy Signal is flashed.

7. The Fail-Safe Buy Signal comes when the S&P 500 Index rises +21% from its lowest low end-of-the-month trading price. Once this +21% rise takes place, we buy back into the market fully and in accordance with whatever Hits-Plus directive may be in effect at the time.

In addition to this seven step summary explaining the Hits-Plus Program here is a "Yes"/"No" Flow Chart that some may find more helpful (See Figure 7.1). I would urge you to go over both the seven step summary and the Flow Chart several times until you feel comfortable you understand what you are supposed to do and when. I promise when we actually put the total Hits-Plus program into a 44-year trading experience in the next chapter, all of this will become very clear and will be a lot of fun and eye-opening.

CHAPTER EIGHT
Forty-Four Years of Hits-Plus Success

"...Steady, moderate gains will get you where you want to go."
-- John Train

"In investing, the return you want should depend on whether you want to eat well or sleep well."
-- J. Kenfield Morley

I'm in total agreement with John Train. Steady, moderate gains will get us where we want to go. This, of course, begs the questions of "What is moderate?" and "How long will it take us to get where we want to go?" To me moderate would be an average annual compounding return of at least 15% or better over a long term. To many this is not moderate at all but rather optimistic. To the hot-hand high rollers who usually only talk about what happens in a five-year bull market time period this would seem too conservative.

Most analysts, however, usually feel an average 15% annual compounded return is excellent. A 15% annual compounded return will double your money every 5 years. This is a standard many would love to duplicate. We are talking about averages. There will be five-year and ten-year time frames where the average will be less and other five- and ten- year time frames when the 15% goal will be greatly exceeded.

As for the J. Kenfield Morley quote, I think most of us would like to eat well and sleep well. I believe Hits-Plus will enable you to do both.

However, I think both Train and Morley may be advising us not to overreach. There are times when we should pick up our marbles and stand on the sidelines.

Taking a substantial loss in the market can set us back for years even if from time to time we are out of the market and in a more conservative vehicle when with hindsight we should have been in. It is those years when we were out of the market and correctly so that will do so much to catapult us ahead of the rest of the gang that stayed in and took a beating.

Playing with Percentages

Let's play a percentage game. Let's say we invested $10,000 in a volatile aggressive growth mutual fund with a buy-and-hold strategy and the results for the next eight years went like this:

Year #1	-25%
Year #2	+35%
Year #3	-15%
Year #4	+25%
Year #5	-20%
Year #6	-14%
Year #7	+60%
Year #8	+12%

So, how well did we do? Many of you readers will know right away how we did. Others will fail badly in their estimation.

We quickly see that we had four up years and four down years. The four up years were +35%, +25%, +60%, and +12%, a total of 132%. The down years were -25%, -15%, -20%, and -14%, a total of -74%. Some people will say "Hey, we didn't do too badly; just look at that plus 60% year and plus 35% year."

But, in actuality, our $10,000 investment performed as shown in Table 8.1.

Table 8.1

$10,000 Buy-and-Hold Investment Performance (8 years)

Year	Investment	Performance	End-of-Year Value
#1	$10,000	- 25%	$ 7,500
#2	$ 7,500	+35%	$10,125
#3	$10,125	-15%	$ 8,606
#4	$ 8,606	+25%	$10,757
#5	$10,757	- 20%	$ 8,606
#6	$ 8,606	- 14%	$ 7,401
#7	$ 7,401	+60%	$11,842
#8	$11,842	+12%	$13,263

In eight years we added only $3,263 in growth to our $10,000 original investment; that's an average annual compounded growth of only 3.6%.

You see if we lose -25% one year, it will take a 33 1/3% gain the next year just to draw back even. And if we lose -50%, we will need a 100% gain to get back even.

Now, just suppose we were sharp enough to stay out of the market those down years and just earned 6% in conservative investment vehicles. Table 8.2 shows how the picture would look. Quickly we see that we doubled our money in five years, and with a total of $38,179 at the end of eight years this represents an average annual compounded growth of 18.23%.

Table 8.2

Investment Performance, Down Years Replaced with +6% Vehicle (8 Years)

Year	Investment	Performance	End-of-Year Value
#1	$10,000	+ 6%	$10,600
#2	$10,600	+35%	$14,310
#3	$14,310	+ 6%	$15,169
#4	$15,169	+25%	$18,961
#5	$18,961	+ 6%	$20,099
#6	$20,099	+ 6%	$21,305
#7	$21,305	+60%	$34,088
#8	$34,088	+12%	$38,179

On a yearly basis this would be perfect timing—a little too much to expect. Lets do another hypothetical eight years where we miss the call two out of the eight years, one year being when we should have been out (year #3) and one year being when we should have been in (year #8). See Table 8.3.

Table 8.3

Investment Performance, Missing the Call Two Years

Year	Investment	Performance	End-of-Year Value
#1	$10.000	+ 6%	$10,600
#2	$10,600	+35%	$14,310
#3	$14,310	- 15%	$12,163
#4	$12,163	+25%	$15,204
#5	$15,204	+ 6%	$16,116
#6	$16,116	+ 6%	$17,083
#7	$17,083	+60%	$27,333
#8	$27,333	+ 6%	$28,973

With this hypothetical eight-year $10,000 investment where we miscall when we should be in or out 25% of the time (a larger percentage error than the historical performance of Hits-Plus), we have achieved an average annual compounded growth of 14.22% at the end of the eight years.

What we should really see here is the extreme importance of being out of the market on down years and the willingness to make this move when it seems the probabilities, the percentages, the odds (you name it) indicate that we indeed should be out of the market and in more conservative investment vehicles.

Forty-Four Years with Hits-Plus

O.K., let's set the stage for our 44-year experience with Hits-Plus.

The starting year is 1950, a year when inflation was almost 6%, but the prime interest rate was just over 2%. At the outset of 1950 we have $10,000. You can imagine you have saved it, inherited it, or whatever. And remember, if you want to use $1,000 as a starting sum you just divide the results by ten, or five for $5,000. Of course, you could multiply by five for a hypothetical $50,000 initial investment.

88

In any event, here we go. First, we will look back at the S&P 500 performance for the past four years which shows 1946 at -8.1%, 1947 at +5.7%, 1948 at +5.5%, and 1949 at +18.8%. Since the performance for 1947 and 1948 were less than a 10% gain each year, we circle these years and call them down years. This gives us three down years in a row, and Hits-Plus directs us to commit to a full investment position in the market for four years in a row when this happens. Therefore, if we had obtained our $10,000 at the beginning of 1949, we would have invested totally in the S&P 500 and with one-third margin. But, since we didn't have the $10,000 until the beginning of 1950, we still play by the Hits-Plus rules; we will invest the $10,000 in the S&P 500 (without margin since this is the second year) and stay in for three continuous years. For this 44-year study I have used the S&P 500 pricing and performance from *Stock, Bonds, Bills, and Inflation Yearbook*, published by Ibbotson Associates, Chicago (annually updates work by Roger G. Ibbotson and Rex A. Sinquefield). Used with permission. All rights reserved. (See Appendix C). *SBBI* from Ibbotson is, in my opinion, the absolute best source book for professional research of this type. The share price itself reflects the automatic reinvesting of all dividends for the "Total Return" picture so don't expect to find S&P 500 data in past issues of *The Wall Street Journal* that are the same as these figures. I have rounded off Ibbotson's share prices to the nearest penny and other statistics to the nearest fraction. 1950 results look like this:

Year 1950

Investment	$10,000
Share Price	$4.83
Total Shares	2070.4
End-of-Year Share Price	$6.36
End-of-Year Total Value	$13,167

1950 was a very good year with a gain of 31.7 % . Now we have two more commitment years to go in the market, starting with 1951:

Year 1951

Investment	$13,167
Share Price	$6.36
Total Shares	2070.4
End-of-Year Share Price	$7.89
End-of-Year Total Value	$16,335

Even though the Korean War was in full swing and inflation was still close to 6%, it was a very good year in the investment world of the stock market. Our S&P 500 Index investment gained 24%. And so we enter the last of our total commitment years of investment with 1952:

Year 1952

Investment	$16,335
Share Price	$7.89
Total Shares	2070.4
End-of-Year Share Price	$9.34
End-of-Year Total Value	$19,338

1952 gives us a very nice 18.4% gain, and, so with our commitment years over, we gladly sell out and move 50% of our funds into U.S. Treasury Bills and 50% of our funds into Intermediate-Term Government Bonds. Today, this could be done by putting 50% of our money in a good Mutual Fund Money Fund and 50% in a good Mutual Fund Intermediate-Term Government Bond Fund. You will find that in the early fifties, U.S. Treasury Bills did not give the return they do in later years, and, although an investment in Intermediate-Term Government Bonds is a conservative investment, it will fluctuate. In any event, by 1953 inflation had dropped to less than 1% and the prime interest rate was just a little over 3%. Here's how the 1953 investment looks:

Year 1953

Investment	$19,338
U.S. T-Bills	$9,669
Ind. Bonds	$9,669
End-of Year T-Bills Value	$9,845
End-of-Year Bonds Value	$9,981
End-of-Year Total Value	$19,826

First Use of January Barometer

We end 1953 with $19,821, just a +2.5% gain, but still a little better than the market which was down -1%. Remember on January Barometer years January only has to be up or down by just the smallest fraction to direct us. Now, the market has had just one down year after the up years, so Hits-Plus tells us to use the January Barometer. We will sell our T-Bills and Bond Fund and put all of our money into the S&P 500 on the earliest trading day of January 1954 and wait to see if January goes up or down. The January market looks as follows:

Year 1954 Through January

Investment	$19,826
Share Price	$9.24
Total Shares	2145.67
End-of-January Price	$9.74
End-of-January Total Value	$20,899

January is up so we will stay in the market for the year. The rest of 1954 looks like this:

Year 1954 February Through December

Investment	$20,899
Share Price	$9.74
Total Shares	2145.67
End-of-Year Share Price	$14.11
End-of-Year Total Value	$30,275

Popping Champagne for 1954

If you were so inclined, you would have popped a bottle of champagne after the tremendous +52.6% gain in 1954. This leaves the market with one up year after the down year for 1953, so we stay fully invested in the S&P 500 and await the January Barometer for 1955. January was up almost +2%, therefore we stay in for the rest of the year:

Year 1955

Investment	$30,275
Share Price	$14.11
Total Shares	2145.67
End-of-Year Share Price	$18.56
End-of-Year Total Value	$39,824

Another fantastic performance year for the S&P 500, being up +31.6% for 1955. Now that we have had two up years in a row Hits-Plus directs us to sell and go 50% into U.S. Treasury Bills and 50% into Intermediate-Term Government Bonds for 1956. The 1956 results are as follows:

Year 1956

Investment	$39,824
U.S. T-Bills	$19,912
Ind. Bonds	$19,912
End-of-Year T-Bills Value	$20,402
End-of-Year Bonds Value	$19,828
End-of-Year Total Value	$40,230

You would have been a little disappointed with "Hit-Plus" in 1956 because the S&P 500 did go up +6.6%, and we gained only a little over +1% as our bond fund actually lost a bit. But not to worry, we'll stick with our Hits-Plus program. Since the S&P 500 was only up +6.6% (less than a +10% rise) we count it as a down year. Therefore, with 1956 being a down year, after 1955 was up, we buy back into the S&P 500 on the first trading day of January, 1957 and await the January

Barometer. January was down -4%, which leaves us with a total of $38,579 to invest between U.S. T-Bills and Intermediate-Term Bonds. On the first trading day of February, we split this $38,579 between U.S. T-Bills and Intermediate-Term Bonds. The remainder of 1957 results are as follows:

Year 1957 (from Feb.)

Investment	$38,579
U.S. T-Bills	$19,289
Ind. Bonds	$19,290
End-of-Year T-Bills Value	$19,841
End-of-Year Bonds Value	$20,321
End-o-Year Total Value	$40,162

First Use of Margin

After January's loss of -4%, the S&P 500 went on to lose almost -7% more to end 1957 being down -10.8%. Since we counted 1956 as a down year (with less than a +10% gain) and 1957 lost -10.8%, we now have had two down years in a row. We go back into the S&P 500 totally for 1958, and, for the first time, Hits-Plus calls for the use of one-third margin. Our total cash is now $40,162; therefore, we borrow $20,081 on a margin loan at 3.83% (the average prime rate in 1957). Our 1958 results are:

Year 1958

Investment	$40,162
Margin Loan @ 3.83%	$20,081
Total Investment including Margin	$60,243
Share Price	$17.65
Total Shares	3413.20
End-of-Year Share Price	$25.30
End-of-Year Total Value (Gross)	$86,354
End-of-Year Value after Loan Paid	$65,504

After we pay back our margin loan, including interest, we have a net value of $65,504 at the end of 1958. Had you chosen not to use margin you would have had $57,569. The S&P 500 was actually up a tremendous +43.4% in 1958, but the margin user would have gained +63.1%. With one up year after the two down years, we stay in the market (without margin) for 1959 to await the January Barometer. January was up +.05%, so we stay in the market. The 1959 results are:

Year 1959

Investment	$65,504
Share Price	$24.30
Total Shares	2589.209
End-of-Year Share Price	$28.32
End-of-Year Total Value	$73,323

First Ten Year's Results

With a gain of 12% for 1959 we have now completed ten years with Hits-Plus. At the end of the first five years we had tripled our money with an average annual compounded growth of +24.78%. At the end of ten years we had a total gain of +663% for an average annual compounded growth rate of +22.54%. Now, the fifties were indeed fabulous years for the stock market, but Hits-Plus made it much better.

We will continue to track Hits-Plus but now with a shorter format to depict each year's performance except when I feel an expanded explanation is necessary. With two up years for the S&P 500 Index we switch to 50% T-Bills and 50% Intermediate Government Bonds.

Year	Investment	Total Return	End-of-Year Total Value
1960	$73,323	+7.2%	$78,609

Hits-Plus directed us correctly in 1960 as the market was up only a half of a percent (+.05). We ended the year with total funds of $78,609, a gain of over 7%, thanks primarily to a good performance from our Intermediate-Term Government Bond Fund. With less than a 10% gain in the S&P 500 for 1960, it is counted as a down year. Therefore, we buy back in the market for 1961 and await the January Barometer. January, 1961 is up +6.45%, a good justification for awaiting January's results in the market instead of on the sidelines.

Year	Investment	Total Return	End-of-Year Total Value
1961	$78,609	+26.9%	$99,774

1961 was up +26.9%. With one up year, we stay in the market to await the January Barometer. January 1962 is down -3.66% so we sell and go to our T-Bills and Bonds with $96,122.

Year	Investment	Total Return	End-of-Year Total Value
1962	$99,774	+.05%	$100,237

$100,000 . . . A Nice Feeling

For us, 1962 ended up with a slight increase for the year as a whole and we topped $100,000. The S&P 500 itself was down -8.7% for the year. With one down year following one up year we sell our T-Bills and Bonds and invest back into the S&P 500 to await the January Barometer for 1963. January is up by +5.1%, so we stay in. 1963 results are:

Year	Investment	Total Return	End-of-Year Total Value
1963	$100,237	+22.8%	$123,113

The total gain for 1963 was +22.8%. With one up year following one down year, we stay in the market for 1964 to await the January Barometer. January is up +2.8%.

Year	Investment	Total Return	End-of-Year Total Value
1964	123,113	16.5%	43,404

As I feel the reader now understands how and why we are switching into the S&P 500 according to the directives of the Hits-Plus system and when and why we switch to a 50% bond and 50% T-Bill position as directed by the Hits-Plus system I will now convert to an even shorter format in the interest of time and space. 1964 picked up +16.5%. Now with two up years in a row, Hits-Plus tells us to sell and go back into U.S. T-Bills and Intermediate-Term Government Bonds.

Year	Investment	Total Return	End-of-Year Total Value
1965	$143,404	+2.5%	$146.953

The S&P 500 has now had three up years in a row. Hits-Plus says the odds are much heavier now that the market should go down for 1966 and for us to stay in T-Bills and Bonds:

Year	Investment	Total Return	End-of-Year Total Value
1966	$146,953	+4.7%	$153.896

(still in T-Bills & bonds as was up 3 years in a row through 1965)

We end 1966 with $153,896. The S&P 500 lost -10.1%. This, I think, reaffirms Hits-Plus over the buy-and-hold strategy. If you had bought and held for the years 1965 and 1966 you would have been worse off than staying with T-Bills and Bonds as Hits-Plus directed for both years.

Now, with one down year Hits-Plus instructs us to buy back into the S&P 500 on the first trading day in January to await the January Barometer. January was up a big +8%.

Year	Investment	Total Return	End-of-Year Total Value
1967	$153,896	+24%	$190,796

Year	Investment	Total Return	End-of-Year Total Value
1968	$190,796	-.05%	$189,852

(out of market, Jan. Barometer)

There Will Be Disappointments

1968 proved to be a pretty tough year for us. We ended the year being down a fraction of one percent. But, we saw the S&P 500 go up +11.1%. This is one year the January Barometer didn't work. But, the vast majority of the time it does, so we shrug our shoulders and stick with Hits-Plus. The S&P 500 has now had two up years in a row so we stay where we are with T-Bills and Bonds.

Year	Investment	Total Return	End-of-Year Total Value
1969	$189,852	+2.9%	$195,454

With a gain of just $5,602 for 1969 *we finish our second 10-year period and the overall 20-year period with $195,454.* The S&P 500 for 1969 was down -8.5%, so we were correct to be out of the market.

The sixties were not kind years for the stock market investors. The S&P 500 buy-and-hold grew by an average annual compounded rate of +7.81%. Many mutual funds during this time frame did a lot worse. Hits-Plus did manage an average annual compounded growth of +10.3%, and our 20-year average annual compounded growth rate was +16%, not too shabby. The good news about the sixties was that inflation only averaged 2.54% per year, and the prime interest rate averaged 5.29%. These numbers, however, would change quite a bit in the seventies and early eighties.

With 1969 being a down year, Hits-Plus calls for us to buy back into the S&P 500 on the first trading day in January and await the January Barometer. January, 1970 is down a big -7.4%, therefore we sell and move into T-Bills and Bonds on the first trading day in February.

Year	Investment	Total Return	End-of-Year Total Value
1970	$195,454	+2.9%	$201,240

Year	Investment	Total Return	End-of-Year Total Value
1971	$201,240	+18.6%	$238,738

(in market, with margin, because market had been down previous two years)

After we pay back the margin loan with interest, we have net funds of $238,738. The market was up +14.3% for the year but the use of margin gave us a return of +18.6% for the year. Now with one up year we stay in the market to await the January Barometer for 1972. January is up +2%; we stay in for the year:

Year	Investment	Total Return	End-of-Year Total Value
1972	$238,738	+19%	$284,038

We achieved a nice +19% gain in 1972, and with two up years in a row, Hits-Plus says move into U.S. T-Bills and Intermediate Term Government Bonds for 1973:

How Will the '73-'74 Bear Affect Hits-Plus?

Year	Investment	Total Return	End-of-Year Total Value
1973	$284,038	+5.8%	$300,427

In 1973 our T-Bills returned +6.9% and our bonds grew in value by +4.6%. The total portfolio was up +5.8%. But, oh what happened in the market. *The S&P 500 lost -14.7%, and many mutual funds and individual stocks took dives double this amount.* Many brokers were saying that 1973 was a needed correction that left many bargains for the bold buyers.

We'll just stick with Hits-Plus, which instructs us to buy back in on the first trading day of January 1974 and let the January Barometer direct us from there. Our total funds at the beginning of 1974 are $300,427. January was down a little less than -1%, leaving us with $297,873 to split between U.S. T-Bills and Bonds on the first trading day of February.

Year	Investment	Total Return	End-of-YearTotalValue
1974	$300,427	+5.6%	$317,110

Hooray for the January Barometer! From February to December, *our T-Bills gained over +7% and the Bonds +5.6% whereas the S&P 500 tumbled -26.5% for the year. Many mutual funds fell -50% or more and some individual stocks dropped -70%* or more. Pity the poor, first-time investor who bought on a buy-and-hold strategy the first of 1973 only to find over half of his or her money (or more) gone by the end of 1974. *Hits-Plus gained +11.6% for 1973-1974.*

Unused Fail-Safe Still Directs Us

Remember, we track the market on a month-to-month basis, and we look back and see that on the last trading day in December 1972, the S&P 500 reached a highest high of $84.96 per share. Even though we were out of the market all of 1973 and eleven months of 1974, we saw the market drop to $55.20 per share the last of August 1974 (a drop of more than -31% from the $84.96 highest high). If we had been in the market, the Fail-Safe Sell Signal would have sold us out at this time. We kept tracking the market (while we held our T-Bills and Bonds) and saw that the lowest end-of-the-month low was reached the last of September 1974 at $48.74. This means that we will not re-enter the market until it rises +21% above this $48.74 level at the end of a month. At the end of December 1974, we have had two down years, therefore Hits-Plus directs us to go back in the market fully invested plus one-third margin for 1975, but we won't do this until the Fail-Safe Buy Signal flashes. This signal does flash the last of January 1975 when the end-of-the-month trading price rises to $58.98, more than a +21% increase from the lowest low. After picking up an additional $1,760 from our T-Bills and Bonds in January, we move totally into the S&P 500 Index Fund on the first trading day of February 1975 and with one-third margin: that's $318,870 plus $159,435 margin borrowed at 7.85%.

Year	Investment	Total Return	End-of-Year Total Value
1975	$317,110	+30%	$412,340

The S&P 500 was up a total of +37.2% for 1975, but we were not in on a tremendous +12.5% of this rise that came in January alone. We don't have a working crystal ball, we just have Hits-Plus which has served us so well. We end 1975 with net funds (after paying off the margin loans plus interest) of $412,340. With 1975 being an up year, we stay in the market through January 1976 for the January Barometer's instructions. This was another record fantastic January, being up by +12%.

Year	Investment	Total Return	End-of-Year Total Value
1976	$412,340	+23.8%	$510.661

$500,000 . . . A Better Feeling

With a good solid +23.8% performance for 1976, the two up years in a row point us toward T-Bills and Bonds for 1977.

Year	Investment	Total Return	End-of-Year Total Value
1977	$510,661	+3.3%	$527,334

The S&P 500 dropped -7.2% in 1977 as we watched from our T-Bill and Bond position that left us with $527,334 to invest for 1978.

Year	Investment	Total Return	End-of-YearTotalValue
1978	$527,334	-1.2%	$520,762

(out of market , Jan. Barometer)

Year	Investment	Total Return	End-of-YearTotalValue
1979	$520,762	+21.3%	$631,838

(in market, with margin, after two previous down years)

Year	Investment	Total Return	End-of-YearTotalValue
1980	$631,838	+32.4%	$836,675

(in market, Jan. Barometer)

Year	Investment	Total Return	End-of-YearTotalValue
1981	$836,675	+12.1%	$937,746

(out of market, two previous years up)

Year	Investment	Total Return	End-of-YearTotalValue
1982	$937,746	+17.1%	$1,098,161

(out of market, Jan. Barometer)

$1,000,000 . . . Feeling Better Still

The January Barometer was wrong in 1982, but it didn't hurt us very much. The S&P 500 ended with a total gain for the year of +21.6%, and we gained a total of +17.1% for the year thanks to the Intermediate-Term Government Bonds growing by +28.6% from February through December and a +10.5% performance by the T-Bills.

With over a million bucks and with one up year for the S&P 500, we go back into the market to see what January will tell us to do in 1983. January is up by +3.5%.

Year	Investment	Total Return	End-of-YearTotalValue
1983	$1,098,161	+22.5%	$1,345,386

(in market, Jan. Barometer)

Year	Investment	Total Return	End-of-Year Total Value
1984	$1,345,386	+11.9%	$1,505,958

(out of market, after two up years)

Year	Investment	Total Return	End-of-Year Total Value
1985	$1,505,958	+32.2%	$1,990,256

(in market, Jan. Barometer)

$2,357,907 ... We Could Learn to Like It

Year	Investment	Total Return	End-of-Year Total Value
1986	$1,990,256	+18.5%	$2,357,907

An +18.5% growth in the S&P 500 pushes our portfolio value to $2,357,907. With the S&P 500 having two up years in a row, we once again move into our 50/50 T-Bill/Bond position for 1987.

The Strange Year of 1987

Year 1987

Investment	$2,357,907
U.S. T-Bills	$1,178,953
Ind. Bonds	$1,178,954
End-of-Year T-Bills Value	$1,243,442
End-of-Year Bonds Value	$1,213,144
End-of-Year Total Value	$2,456,586

1987 was a very strange year. I'm sure if you had been on the Hits-Plus program, and, therefore, in T-Bills and Bonds instead of the market, you would have been screaming by the end of August as the market had soared upward by +39% and here *we were holding mediocre T-Bills and Government Bonds. But on October 19, 1987, the Dow Jones Industrial averages fell 508 points in that one day. In just ten trading days*

from the morning of the October 19, the market fell -34%.
From the end-of-the month highest high of $459.86 on the last trading day in August, the S&P 500 closed at its lowest end-of-the-month low on the last trading day of November at $324.05, a drop of -29.5%. So, although the market had fallen more than -31% in mid-month trading it did not reach our Fail-Safe Sell Signal of -31% with end-of-the-month tracking. Of course, we were already out of the market anyway, and *we could stop fussing about missing out on the great bull market of 1987.*

Although 1987 saw one of the worst short term market crashes of all time, the market had been up so much the first eight months of the year and it began to stage a recovery in December, so the S&P 500 actually ended the year being up +5.2%.

Since an end-of-the-month -31% from the highest high was not reached we do not have to wait for a +21% gain from the lowest low to go back in. All told, with a +5.2% being less than -10%, we simply count 1987 as a down year and buy back into our S&P 500 Index Fund on the first trading day of January 1988 and await the results of the January Barometer. January was up +4.3%.

Year	Investment	Total Return	End-of-YearTotalValue
1988	$2,456,586	+16.8%	$2,869,510

1989, A Reason to

Year	Investment	Total Return	End-of-YearTotalValue
1989	$2,869,510	+31.5%	$3,773,159
		(in market, Jan. Barometer)	

1989 put smiles back on the faces of the common stock investors as the S&P 500 rose +31.5%. Now we have had two up years in a row, so it's time once again to step out of the market and into our U.S. Treasury Bills and Intermediate-Term Government Bond Fund for 1990.

Year	Investment	Total Return	End-of-Year Total Value
1990	$3,773,159	+8.8%	$4,104,065

Over a Million in One Year

Year	Investment	Total Return	End-of-Year Total Value
1991	$4,104,605	+30.6%	$5,358,510

(in market, Jan. Barometer)

It sure is nice to make $1,253,905 in one year in the market. That's what the +30.6% gain in the S&P 500 gave us for 1991.

Year	Investment	Total Return	End-of-Year Total Value
1992	$5,358,510	+4.2%	$5,547,247

(out of market, Jan. Barometer)

Year	Investment	Total Return	End-of-Year Total Value
1993	$5,547,247	+10.0%	$6,101,434

(in market, Jan. Barometer)

1993 made a +10% gain right on-the-button which leads me to say that if the gain had been +9.5% or more I feel it still should have been counted as an up year but a +9.4% gain should have been listed as a down year. This ends our 44-year old test of Hits-Plus. Too bad my Dad didn't invest $10,000 in a Hits-Plus program in 1950.

We need now to analyze this 44-year experience. First of all, as I stated earlier you will not find share prices of the S&P 500 in *The Wall Street Journal* that match those which I used.

The reason is I used "Common Stocks: Total Return Index" from *Stocks, Bonds, Bills, and Inflation Yearbook* published by Ibbotson Associates; PO Box # 528456, Chicago, Ill. 60652-8456; Phone (800) 758-3557. This source is the best of all research tools in my opinion. *SBBI* started with a $1.00 value of the S&P 500 Index January 1, 1926 and, thereafter, adjusted the share price to automatically include the re-investment of all dividends for a clear picture of the total return. If we had invested in a S&P 500 Index Fund, as they are available today, we could receive the automatic re-investment of dividends without a problem.

Mutual Funds For Hits-Plus

In reality, the average S&P 500 Index Mutual Fund will deliver approximately .5% (one half of one percent) per year less in performance than that quoted from Ibbotson's publication in this chapter. However, at the time of this writing Vanguard's Index 500 Mutual Fund expense is less than one quarter of one percent per year (actually .19%).

For our U.S. Treasury Bills Investment, today we could use a good money fund from one of the large mutual fund families. If we use this source, we should be careful not to go just with the highest return around but be sure their money instrument portfolio is solid and short term. To most closely duplicate the return and safety of U.S. Treasury Bills, I suggest Capital Preservation; 755 Page Mill Rd.; Palo Alto, Calif. 94303; Phone: (800) 472-3389. Capital Preservation invests solely in U.S. Treasury Bills and may average about .05 percent less than other money funds but the safety of T-Bills is certainly there. However most money funds in the best known mutual fund families do offer good safety and return that will closely mirror U.S. Treasury Bill performance.

There is no exact reflection of Intermediate-Term Government Bonds in a Mutual Fund. I suggest the Vanguard Fixed-Income Short-Term Govt. Bond Fund, (800) 662-7447. This particular Vanguard Fund has only been around since the beginning of 1988, but the Vanguard Family has a long and strong history. Value Line U.S. Government Securities Mutual Fund does not invest totally in Intermediate-Term Government Bonds, but its performance has closely mirrored the Government bond performance since its inception. Other mutual funds for your bond investment you might consider are California U.S. Government Securities, Dreyfus U.S. Government Intermediate, and Fidelity Intermediate Bonds.

Remember, our 50% U.S. T-Bills and 50% Intermediate-Term Government Bond portfolio serves as a parking place for our money for those years when Hits-Plus tells us the probabilities are strong that the S&P 500 Index will not perform well. A parking place, yes, one that is conservative and safe. But, we still want a reasonable return during this parking time period.

One-Stop Shopping

What is it worth to have a one-stop shopping center and full service for your Hits-Plus program? I'm talking about using a discount broker who deals in many mutual funds of all types and also offers margin on no-load funds for those who wish to use it. Some of the discount brokers who offer such turnkey services are Freeman-Welwood & Co., Charles Schwab & Co., Waterhouse Securities, Jack White and Co., and others.

I'm more familiar with Charles Schwab and Co. because I have had an account with them for several years, and I'm very pleased with the full service they perform. Of course, this service comes with a price tag, but you may feel, as I do, that since the cost is very nominal compared to full charge brokers it makes trading and record keeping so much easier.

At the time of this writing, Charles Schwab offers over 900 Mutual funds including Vanguard 500 Index Fund, Dreyfus Index, and SEI S&P 500 Index Fund. Schwab has its own money fund in case you decide to use a money fund for your U.S. T-Bill account instead of dealing direct with Capital Preservation or other money funds. Schwab also offers its own

U.S. Government Bond Fund (with an average portfolio maturity of 5 years or less) and the Vanguard Fixed Income Short-Term Federal Fund, either of which could suffice for your Intermediate-Term Government Bond investments.

Charles Schwab charges a minimum of $39 per trade. The transaction fees depend on the size of the transaction. For $0 to $14,999, you pay 0.7% (seven tenths of one percent) unless the trade is so small that the percentage fee would be less than $39 then you would pay the $39 minimum. For $15,000 to $99,999, you pay 0.7% on the first $14,999 and 0.2% (two tenths of one percent) on the $15,000 to $99,999. For $100,000 plus, you pay 0.7% on the first $14,999, 0.2% on the amount between $15,000 and $99,999, and 0.08 (eight one hundreds of one percent) over $99,999. Plus, when the time comes for you to sell one mutual fund and move into another, you will be charged the percentage fee or minimum fee (whichever is applicable) and only $25 when you buy into another mutual fund.

Example: If you buy $15,000 in mutual funds, the fee will be $105. If you buy $50,000 in mutual funds, the fee would be $105 on the first $14,999 (.07%) and $70 (0.2%) on the $35,001 amount for a total of $175. If you buy $150,000 in mutual funds, the fee would be $105 on the first $14,999, $170 on the next $85,000, and $40 on the last $50,000 amount for a total of $315.

I have no monetary interest in Charles Schwab & Co. or any other broker firm, and you might choose to deal entirely with a large family of funds such as Vanguard or others. It will cost you less, but, in many cases, you will find you will face some restrictions such as no margin and, perhaps, not being able to switch from one fund to another as easily as your program calls for. It would pay you to check this out for yourself as mutual fund families do change their policies from time to time.

I have not tried to figure, at all, any personal income taxes on the 44-year performance of Hits-Plus. Of course, you would have had to have paid taxes on your gains, on the federal level and perhaps on the state level too (depending on your state of residence), but tax laws do change and you or your accountant will best know your own taxable situation.

You will note that at no time in this 44-year tracking of Hits-Plus did we actually use the Fail-Safe Sell Signal. We would have used it after the last trading day of August, 1974, but we were already out of the market due to the January Barometer for 1974. At the end of 1974, the S&P 500 had experienced two down years in a row, thereby directing us to go back into the market for 1975. But our Fail-Safe program insists that once a Fail-Safe Sell Signal is flashed we don't buy back in until the S&P 500 rises +21% from its lowest low end-of-the-month trading price. So we waited until the Fail-Safe Buy Signal was flashed as it was on the last day of January 1974.

The Fail-Safe Sell Signal was almost flashed in 1987. Again we were already out of the market so we had no S&P 500 position to sell. Although the Fail-Safe Sell Signal was almost flashed, it didn't actually occur, thereby not becoming a factor at all.

As I have said earlier the Fail-Safe program is rarely used, but it is important to keep it as part of Hits-Plus as a kind of catastrophe insurance. I think the value of having the Fail-Safe plan as part of Hits-Plus will be very clear in the next chapter that will cover the chaotic time from 1929 through 1949.

Hits-Plus Vs. Buy-and-Hold

Let's look back now and see how the performance of Hits-Plus compared with an S&P 500 buy-and-hold strategy (See Table 8.4).

In all of the percentages, I have rounded the percentage off to the nearest tenth of a percent. I have also rounded off to the nearest fraction on stock prices and shares of stock purchased; therefore, some tabulations might not agree by a very small fraction.

Table 8.4

"Hits-Plus" Compared to S&P 500 Buy-and-Hold Strategy. 1950-1993

Year	S&P 500 %End-of-Year Value	Hits-Plus %End-of-Year Value
1950	$13,167	$13,167
1951	$16,335	$16,335
1952	$19,338	$19,338
1953	$19,143	$19,826
1954	$29,212	$30,275
1955	$38,443	$39,824
1956	$40,980	$40,230
1957	$36,554	$40,162
1958	$52,418	$65,504*
1959	$58,708	$73,323
1960	$59,002	$78,609
1961	$74,873	$99,774
1962	$68,359	$100,237
1963	$83,945	$123,113
1964	$97,796	$143,404
1965	$110,020	$146,953
1966	$98,908	$153,896
1967	$122,646	$190,796
1968	$136,260	$189,852
1969	$124,678	$195,454
1970	$129,665	$201,240
1971	$148,207	$238,738*
1972	$176,366	$284,038
1973	$150,440	$300,427
1974	$110,573	$317,110
1975	$151,706	$412,340*
1976	$187,812	$510,661
1977	$174,290	$527,334
1978	$185,793	$520,762
1979	$219,979	$631,838*
1980	$291,252	$836,675
1981	$276,981	$937,746
1982	$336,225	$1,098,161
1983	$411,912	$1,345,386
1984	$437,862	$1,505,958
1985	$578,854	$1,990,256
1986	$685,942	$2,357,907
1987	$721,611	$2,456,586
1988	$842,842	$2,869,510
1989	$1,108,337	$3,773,159
1990	$1,072,870	$4,104,065
1991	$1,401,168	$5,358,510
1992	$1,508,637	$5,585,175
1993	$1,659,501	$6,143,692

*Years we used 1/3 margin.

A Copywriter's Dream

As an old advertising man, the performance of Hits-Plus is a copywriter's dream. You don't have to build around fluff, hype, and put on some sort of dog and pony show complete with smoke and mirrors.

You simply state that whereas *a buy-and-hold S&P 500 strategy would have given you a 16,495% return over forty-four years, Hits-Plus delivered a whopping 61,337% growth.*

This translates into a very respectful +12.31% average annual compounded return (that many mutual fund managers would dearly love) for the buy-and-hold S&P 500 program vs. *a +15.71% average annual compounded return for Hits-Plus.* This 3.65 percentage point difference means that Hits-Plus gave you a 29% better average annual compounded return than the S&P 500 buy-and-hold.

The copywriter points out that Hits-Plus had only three years out of forty-four that actually lost money: 1957 was down -.02% (2/100s of one percent), 1968 lost -.05% (5/100s or one percent), and 1978 was down -1.2%. So Hits-Plus is not perfect.

But, even looking at one of the worst ten-year periods for the stock market (from 1965 through 1974), Hits-Plus returned an average annual compounded return of +8.26%. That's nothing to brag about you might say. Well, if you compare it to the S&P 500 buy-and-hold position that returned only +1.24% as an average annual compounded yield and most of the best mutual funds showed less than a 5% average annual compounded return, it's not bad. And when there are very few places elsewhere you could have received anything close to an average +8.26% return, it doesn't look too bad at all. In fact, in the chapter on retirement and withdrawal plans, a return of over 8% is seen in a more important light.

Again, I picked the 44-year period from 1950 through 1993 in order to separate it from 1929 through 1949, a time frame that I think deserves particular attention as it takes us through one of the world's worst economic depressions, through the upheaval of World War II, and into the first few post-war years. You can easily add the 1929-1949 period to 1950-1993 for a total 65-year analysis of Hits-Plus. So now let's head back to the beginning of 1929.

CHAPTER NINE

"Hits Plus,"
Its Toughest Test: 1929 Through 1949

*"It is wise to remember that too much success (in the market)
is in itself an excellent warning."*
Gerald M. Loeb

The roaring twenties in the United States was really something. Many of our nation's service men had gone through as devastating a war experience as history had seen with our participation in World War I. They witnessed death and destruction beyond imagination, complete with chemical warfare. But, our numbers of participating soldiers and our numbers of casualties were small in comparison to the European nations that had waged the war longer and on their own home turf.

The general feeling in America in the twenties was that we were the world leader that had proven our industrial might and agricultural production ability as being second to none. After all, the war "to make the world safe for democracy" had been won, and we had earned the right to have endless prosperity.

But, the twenties were not great for everyone. The agricultural rural areas in many parts of our nation already had their own brand of depression long before the early thirties. And there were many pockets of poverty and wage disparities across the country. Yet and still the overall mood of vast numbers of our citizens was that of "let the good times roll" with illegal bath tub gin, fun loving flapper girls, romancing the American automobile and getting rich the easy way by speculating in the legal gambling world of the stock market.

How High The Moon?

1928 marked the year when stock market speculation by individuals really went into high gear. ***During 1928, the stock of Montgomery Ward almost quadrupled, Wright Aeronautics did likewise and the glamorous symbol of the world of radio, RCA, went up almost 500% percent.***

This is the scene we survey at the beginning of 1929 when we come into our hypothetical $10,000 all set to try Hits-Plus as our investment program. Here again you can make this $10,000 figure $1,000 by dividing the results by ten, or you could make it $100,000 by multiplying by ten, etc.

As we look back over the past three years at the performance of the S&P 500, we find that 1926 was up +11.6%, 1927 grew by +37.5% and 1928 jumped a big +43.6%. With three up years in a row, Hits-Plus tells us that this market for 1929 is overvalued, and although we can only expect a 4% to 6% return in U.S. Treasury Bills and Intermediate-Term Government Bonds, that is the place where we should invest for the year of 1929.

The Year of the Crash

Year 1929

Investment	$10,000
U.S. T-Bills	$5,000
Government Bonds	$5,000
T-Bills End-Of-Year Value	$5,237
Int. Bonds End-Of-Year Value	$5,300
Total End-Of-Year Value	$10,538

1929 ended with a +5.4% performance for Hits-Plus and the total year results of the S&P 500 was down -8.4%. But, these statistics tell very little of the real story of what happened in the stock market in 1929 and what began to happen in this country that would effect all of the citizens in the United States.

There had been quite a bit of selling on the New York Stock Exchange the few days that preceded ***Thursday, October 24, 1929, the day that history would record as "Black Thursday" as sell orders poured in and stock prices plunged downward.*** It was decided that even the visitors' gallery at the exchange should be closed.

The next day confidence-building statements from business leaders, stock brokers, and even President Hoover helped support the market for the rest of the week, but over the weekend margin calls (that required as little as 10¢ cash on the $1.00) were made by the brokers who had to have the money. Monday saw another free fall, except it wasn't free. It was very costly as many investors and brokers were virtually wiped out. The very non financial headline of the show business newspaper *Variety* said it all: "Wall St. lays an Egg."

Of course, there were still many statements made by prominent people hoping to instill confidence back into the American people. On November 4, Henry Ford said, "Things look better today than they were yesterday." And the President of the National Association of Manufacturers commented, "I can observe little on the horizon today to give us undue or great concern."

Hotel Rooms for Jumping

There were also suicides. As the November 25, 1929 issue of *Time Magazine* reported, James J. Riordan, President of New York's County Trust Co., Stock brokers Frank S. Palfrey and W. Paul Brown, as well as Chicago grain broker, Herman L. Felgenhauer, all took their lives. There were even jokes about suicides, like hotel room clerks asking each new arrival if they wanted a room for sleeping or jumping. And the one about two men jumping from a skyscraper window holding hands; you see they had joint accounts.

Actually the stories about suicides after the stock market crash in 1929 were overblown. There were just not as many as the stories, jokes, and rumors implied there were. ***The sad thing is that 1929 was just a downside blip compared to what was coming up (or going down) in the next several years***.

But, now let's get back to our Hits-Plus account that survived 1929 with what now looks like a terrific gain of +5.4%. As we tracked the performance of the S&P 500 from our sideline position in U.S. Treasury Bills and Intermediate-Term Government Bonds, we saw that the S&P 500 had reached its highest high end-of-the-month trading price of $2.93 on the last trading day of August. From that point, it fell more than -31% at the End-Of-the-Month trading price of $1.96 on the last trading day of November. As throughout this book, these S&P 500 trading prices are from Ibbotson Associates, *Stocks, Bonds, Bills, and Inflation: 1992 Book.* I have rounded off stock prices to the nearest penny and other statistics to the nearest fraction.

This decline of -31% flashed our Fail-Safe Sell Signal, and although we were already out of the market and in T-Bills and Bonds, this meant that we would not buy back into the S&P 500 until it gained +21% from its lowest low end-of-the-month trading price. Therefore, 1930 would see us continue to be on the sidelines with 50% in U.S. Treasury Bills and 50% in Intermediate-Term Government Bonds. We will find that during the Great Depression years U.S. Treasury Bills would return little or nothing and at times Intermediate-Term Government Bonds would return less than nothing, but this is the Hits-Plus program. And the T-Bills and Bonds were safer than the mattress, a tin can buried in the backyard, or, for that matter, many banks.

The January Barometer for 1930 was up as the market gained +6.4% that month. This meant that although we were out of the market because of the Fail-Safe Sell Signal, when the Fail-Safe Buy Signal is flashed with a +21% gain from $1.96 (which proved to be the lowest low end-of-the-month trading price) at the end of any upcoming trading month we will buy back in. This happens at the end of March 1930 when the S&P 500 closed at $2.38. This would turn out to cost us dearly, but then Hits-Plus is not perfect.

Being Cut By the Whipsaw

<u>1930 January through March</u>

Investment	$10,538
U.S. T-Bills	$5,237
Int. Government Bonds	$5,300
T-Bills End-of-March Value	$5,278
Int. Bonds End-of-March Value	$5,414
End-of-March Value	$10,692

1930 April Through November

Investment	$10,692
Share Price	$2.38
Total Shares	4,492.43
End-of-Oct. Share Price	$1.63
End-of-Oct. Total Value	$7,322

Well, we sure got whipsawed on that one as $2.38 proved to be the highest high end-of-the-month trading price only to tumble by over -31%. Again selling us out at the end of November at just $1.63 per share. Remember, "whipsawing" is what happens when any less-than-perfect timing program sells you out of the market and then puts you back in before the bear has run his full course. There is no perfect timing program and many buy-sell strategies try to operate in such a narrow range that they can literally buy and sell you back and forth, in and out of the market, almost daily and the whipsawing effect could bankrupt you in no time flat. The Hits-Plus Fail-Safe Signals give the market a much wider range in which to move but the wild up and down trading of the thirties beat us too. However, 1930 was the only year in the thirties or forties when we really got whipsawed.

Sure, we cried real tears and moved back into U.S. Treasury Bills and Intermediate-Term Government Bonds on the first trading day of December.

1930 Dec. 1 through Dec. 31 (one month)

Investment	$7,322
U.S. T-Bills	$3,661
Int. Government Bonds	$3,661
End-of-Year T-Bills Value	$3,665
End-of-Year Bonds Value	$3,670
End-of-Year Total Value	$7,335

And Then There Was Grief

1930 was a terrible year for Hits-Plus and the U.S.A. I think it is very important to look back at what was actually going on in our nation and the world during the early thirties.

Here are some statistics that may be just figures to some, but believe me they translated into real human suffering during the Great Depression of the thirties. Over 600 banks failed in 1929. This number more than doubled in 1930, and in 1931 more than 2,200 banks went under.

Over one and a half million people were unemployed in 1929, but by 1932 estimations of unemployment ranged from twelve million to over fifteen million.

To put this into perspective in comparison to recent years, *1932's unemployment rate was 23.6% and in 1933 it reached 24.9% and would remain in double digits until World War II, and this was with no unemployment insurance, food stamps and few of the welfare programs as we know them today.*

Across the country you would find families who had once embraced a comfortable feeling of security and financial success now facing unemployment, debt, and despair. In our larger cities, soup kitchens and bread lines were not an unusual sight. By the end of 1932, the wages paid by U.S. Steel had dropped over 60% from their 1929 levels. *Pay scales of six cents an hour and $2.50 per week were to be found in some areas of our nation when there was any work at all.*

But, this was not just an American Depression, it was worldwide. The depressed economy hit Great Britain shortly after World War I and continued to deepen until "on the dole" was a common response from a British would-be-worker when asked what his job was.

Hawley-Smoot: The Worst Reaction

So what did the U.S. Congress do? What turns out to be one of the worse things possible. They passed the Hawley-Smoot Bill (also known as the Smoot-Hawley Bill), imposing a strong upward revision of tariff rates to protect American business from foreign competition. Ignoring the fact that even in the twenties and thirties the United States had to play on a world wide economic playing field, Congress decided we could simply withdraw within the confines of our own borders and somehow become prosperous again. Fair trade practices are one thing; protectionism is quite another. Most economic historians are now very much in agreement that the Hawley-Smoot Tariff Bill prolonged and agonized the Great Depression at the expense of human suffering.

As bad as the Great Depression was, and it was bad, there were still people who had money. More people still had jobs than didn't. Many people still built homes and bought new cars, although a lot fewer than in the twenties. Even new luxury automobiles such as Cadillacs, Lincolns, Pierce Arrows, and Packards were bought (at big discounts) and enjoyed by those who could afford them. However, some millionaires sensing public animosity refused to buy the Lincolns or Cadillacs and drove Fords, Chevrolets, or Plymouths and meanwhile held on to their money in very conservative instruments (U.S. Treasury Bills and Intermediate-Term Government Bonds perhaps) and waited for bargains in real estate, raw land, and in the stock market. Many of those who did have money during the thirties and who were wise and prudent made immense fortunes during these times that were so harsh on so many others.

1931 finds us outside the market again as a result of that horrendous whipsawing of 1930. We stay in a position of 50% U.S. Treasury Bills and 50% Intermediate-Term Government Bonds, continue to track the end-of-the-month performance of the S&P 500, and wait for the Fail-Safe Buy Signal to flash again.

Year 1931

Investment	$7,335
U.S. T-Bills	$3,667
Int. Government Bonds	$3,668
End-of-Year T-Bills Value	$3,706
End-of-Year Int. Bonds Value	$3,620
End-of-Year Total Value	$7,326

Even in U.S. Treasury Bills and Intermediate-Term Government Bonds, we lost nine bucks in 1931. The S&P 500, however, was down a whopping -43.3%. Now the S&P 500 has had three down years in a row, but there's still no sign of the market rising +21% from its lowest low end-of-the-month trading price as it keeps drifting down more and more with each passing month. For 1932 we will stay in our T-Bill and Bond position and keep tracking the S&P 500 to see if indeed the Fail-Safe Buy Signal will flash.

Year 1932 January through July

Investment	$7,326
U.S. T-Bills	$3,706
Int. Government Bonds	$3,620
End-of-Aug. T-Bill Value	$3,738
End-of-Aug. Bond Value	$3,804
End-of-Aug. Total Value	$7,542

An end-of-the-month lowest low of 49¢ was reached on the last trading of June, 1932. From this point it would leap almost +38% in just the month of July. We buy back into the S&P 500 on the first trading day of August, 1932 at a price of 67¢ per share. With this Fail-Safe Buy Signal, we find ourselves going back into the market after it had been down three years in a row and 1932 would also turn out to be down as an overall year. Hits-Plus calls for a 100% commitment to the S&P 500 plus one-third margin only on a calendar year basis, although I doubt it would make much difference either way.

Realistically I must wonder if we would have had the intestinal fortitude to have used margin in 1932. In any event we will stick to Hits-Plus and utilize one-third margin at the beginning of 1933 unless another Fail-Safe Sell Signal is flashed.

Year 1932 Aug. through December

Investment	7,542
Share Price	67¢
Total Shares	11,256.71
End-of-Year Share Price	79¢
End-of-Year Total Value	$8,892

The market jump in the last six months of 1932 gave the Hits-Plus investor a +21.4% gain for the year overall. However, because the S&P 500 had fallen so drastically during the first six months of the year, the Index for the entire year was down -8.2%.

How Some Individual Stocks Faired

At the end of 1932 we have -11.1% less money than we started with at the beginning of 1929. A buy-and-hold S&P 500 position would be down -64.2%. Taking a quick look at what some consider really good individual stocks in 1932, we discover that a $10,000 investment in U.S. Steel in 1929 had been reduced in value to $812 in 1932. Ten thousand dollars in General Motors in 1929 was worth around $340 in 1932; likewise $10,000 in Anaconda Coppers was worth about $175, DuPont just $440, and so on.

The Pendulum Swings Back

Even with the Great Depression very much in effect the United States was still in business, and companies that were in business had a real value. The pendulum had been swinging lower and lower each year now for four years in a row and investors who had money analyzed the stock market and surmised that even with economic conditions as bad as they were many stocks were selling at fire sale bargain prices and now was the time to buy.

With three or more down years in a row (actually four) and with us back in the market following a Fail-Safe Buy Signal, Hits-Plus directs us to commit to being in the market for four years in a row (not withstanding a Fail-Safe Sell Signal) and to begin 1933 with one-third margin. Again margin doesn't have to be used to make Hits-Plus a success, and we will analyze the use and non-use of margin in a later chapter.

Year 1933

Investment	$8,892
Margin Loan at 1.5%	$4,446
Total Investment including margin	$3,338
Share Price	79¢
Total Shares	16,883.54
End-of-Year Share Price	$1.21
End-of-Year Total Gross Value	$20,429
End-of-Year Total Value	$15,916
(after loan pay back)	

Well, the world is still alive and wonderful things can happen in the stock market. 1933 saw the S&P 500 soar +54% and our account, with margin, went up +79%. After five years, *Hits-Plus has increased its $10,000 by +59.2%; that's an average annual compounded return of 9.74%. Not bad for 1929 through 1933,* if we could only forget the whipsawed adventure in 1930 and all the other gut crunching things we witnessed from the sidelines. *The S&P 500 buy-and-hold investor would still have lost nearly half his money at the end of 1933,* and, in fact, it would be October 1936 before he would draw even once again.

With our four year commitment (three more to go) of being in the market we stay with our S&P 500 stock position for 1934.

Year 1934

Investment	$15,916
Share Price	$1.21
Total Shares	13,153.71
End-of-Year Share Price	$1.20
End-of-Year Total Value	$15,784

The SEC is Born

In 1934 we lost $132 or -.08%. A very slight down year. Other important things did occur in 1934. President Roosevelt called for Congress to enact legislation to regulate the stock exchanges. This action would establish the Securities and Exchange Commission (SEC) that curtailed many of the manipulations and false and misleading information that was heretofore fed to investors. Margin transaction, while allowed, was controlled. Overall, the SEC was established to give the stock investor more information and, therefore, more protection. The regulations the SEC would write and enforce would change over the years. It would not, could not, and should not serve as a total security blanket for investors. Investing, by its very nature is taking a chance, but the SEC brought a stability to the market place that would serve it well to this day.

We will continue to track Hits-Plus but again with a shorter format to depict each year's performance except when I feel an expanded explanation is necessary.

1935 marks our third year of the four year commitment Hits-Plus had directed us to take. So, although 1934 was slightly down we still stay in the market.

Year	Investment	Total Return	End-of-Year Total Value
1935	$15,784	+47.5%	$23,282

With a big +47.5% rise in 1935 our Hits-Plus program has now more than doubled our money as we prepare to sit tight with our fourth and final year of our four-year commitment to be in the S&P 500 market.

Year	Investment	Total Return	End-of-Year Total Value
1936	$23,282	+33.9%	$31,174

With the end of 1936 we sell out our S&P 500 position and move back into 50% U.S. Treasury Bills and 50% Inter-mediate Term Government Bonds for 1937. 1936 had a very strong +33.9% performance, so with the exception of the pause the market took in 1934 for profit taking after that tremendous +54% in 1933, the pendulum has swung all the way back to close higher than it had been in 1928. But the nation is still in a depression. Could the pendulum have gone somewhat too far to an overpriced level? 1937 will be viewed from our T-Bill and Bond position.

1937: A Good Year To Be On The Sidelines

Year	Investment	Total Return	End-of-Year Total Value
1937	$31,174	+.09%	$31,465

1937 was a tough year for the S&P 500 as it tumbled -35%. Had we been in the market instead of in T-Bills and Bonds, the Fail-Safe Sell Signal would have taken us out as the market dropped more than -31% from its end-of-the-month highest high of $2.51 on the last trading day of February to an end-of-the month price of $1.61 on the last trading day of

November. Therefore, we now must track the market and not change our T-Bill and Bond position until a Fail Safe Buy Signal is flashed when the S&P 500 climbs +21% from its end-of-the-month lowest low.

For most practical purposes the new deal of FDR ended with a combination of the 1937-38 recession and the President's failed attempt to "pack" the Supreme Court. President Roosevelt had accomplished a lot since 1933, but the economy was still on the ropes and many economists believed that 1937 represented more than a recession; it was evidence that the Depression itself was not over.

1938 would prove to be a better year for the market but it would not come early in the year. With the one down year of 1937 we would have gone back into the market based on the January Barometer, which was up, but until the Fail-Safe Buy Signal flashes we sit tight with the T-Bills and Bonds.

The Fail-Safe Buy Signal flashed with the June closing price of $1.73. This was over +21% higher than the lowest low end-of-the-month trading price of $1.25 which occurred at the end of March. So on the first trading day of July, 1938 we once again buy back into the S&P 500.

Year	Investment	Total Return	End-of-Year Total Value
1938	$31,465	+18.9%	$37,401

War Clouds Gather

1938, after a roller coaster start, turned out to be a good year for the S&P 500 as it gained +31.1%. The Hits-Plus Program only gained +18.9% for the entire year because we had to wait for the +21% Fail-Safe Buy Signal to flash to re-enter the market. However, *for the two-year period of 1937 and 1938 the buy-and-hold investor would have been down -14.4% while the Hits-Plus strategist would have enjoyed a +20% performance.*

On the world scene, things didn't look too well at all. War clouds had been gathering in Europe and in the Far East. In January of 1938 FDR had asked Congress for more military preparedness. The United States and Britain requested naval information from Japan and were refused. Hitler drafted an additional one million troops in August of 1938 and six days later Japan did likewise. In October German troops moved into the Sudetenland and in November FDR called home his envoys in Berlin.

1939 arrived as a year of great uncertainty. The U.S.A. would host the World's Fair in New York and Adolf Hitler would start World War II.

The S&P 500 had experienced one up year so Hits-Plus tells us to stay in the market through January and follow the January Barometer.

Year	Investment	Total Return	End-of-YearTotalValue
1939	$37,401	-4.6%	$35,681

January dropped -6.7%, and we quickly backed out of the S&P 500 and went back into U.S. Treasury Bills and Interme-diate-Government Bonds. Our T-Bill and bond position helped us a bit for the remainder of the year but we ended up with a -4.6% loss.

Britain and France were now at war with Germany, and the world is very nervous about global events. The S&P 500 closed the year down -.04%, so with one down year back again we go into the market to await the January Barometer. The S&P 500 was down -3.2% in January, 1940, and again we sell out of the market and go back into our T-Bills and Bonds.

Year	Investment	Total Return	End-of-YearTotalValue
1940	$35,681	-2.0%	$34,973

A Bad Looking World

Neither Hits-Plus nor the S&P 500 had faired too well since 1938; neither had the world. 1940 saw Paris fall to the Nazis and French and British troops narrowly escaped total disaster on the beaches of Dunkirk. Over the skies of England the Battle of Britain would rage. On October 29, the U.S. draft of young men for military service would begin. "America First" groups would demand that the United States should stay out of other nations' wars. But we would learn that this country cannot ignore world dictators on a rampage any more than we could divorce ourselves from the world economy. The S&P 500 has now had two down years in a row; therefore, Hits-Plus calls for us to go fully invested in the S&P 500 and with one-third margin (for those who choose to use margin).

Year	Investment	Total Return	End-of-Year Total Value
1941	$34,973	-18.1%	$28,626

It had to happen sooner or later. After the S&P 500 was down two years in a row (1939 & 1940), Hits-Plus invested 100% with one-third margin and the market goes down for the third year in a row and this time its a -11.6% loss for the year, and we lost -18.1% because of the use of margin. In retrospect, there's little wonder that the psychology of the market had to have been the big factor.

In Europe, Hitler's armies won battle after battle and invaded deep into Russia to finally encircle Leningrad in September. Meanwhile, in the Far East, Japan rejected all peace proposals from Washington and then on December 7th the sneak attack on Pearl Harbor killed over 2,000 people and destroyed many of our naval warships. The U.S.A. was now totally involved in World War II.

Yet and still, Hits-Plus directs us to continue to be fully invested in the S&P 500 for 1942 and to execute the use of full margin. I admit it would take a little courage to do this and we will discuss later more fully the use or non-use of margin and our personal psychological make-up in facing such market conditions. But, for 1942 we will be totally invested in the S&P 500 with full 50% margin.

A Gutsy Move: Full Margin

Year	Investment	Total Return	End-of-Year Total Value
1942	$28,626	+39.7%	$40,002

We breath a really big sigh of relief after the S&P 500 closed up +20.3% at the end of 1942. This time our gain was +39.7% because of our use of margin. For the two years, 1941 and 1942, the margin investor gained 7.26% more than the non-margin user. But, yes, it would have taken a courageous investor to have used margin during this particular time in our history.

The war news in the early months of 1942 was not good, nor was the performance of the market. However, everyone in America who wanted jobs, and could work, had jobs. Our industries were going twenty-four hours a day churning out planes, ships, tanks, jeeps, guns, etc. Our farms were busy producing food and fiber for our own soldiers, and citizens, as well as our allies around the world. What we really needed now were war victories to boost morale. General Doolittle's bombing of Tokyo, although of little military strategic value, gave the United States something to cheer about. Our naval victory at Midway, followed by the marines landing on Guadalcanal, did much to re-instill optimism and confidence in the American people.

Hits-Plus says that anytime the S&P 500 is down three or more years in a row we are committed to be in the market for four years (Remember, we were in the market in 1942, which was an up year.). So, unless the Fail-Safe Sell Signal takes us out, we will be fully invested in the market for 1943, 1944, and 1945.

Year	Investment	Total Return	End-of-Year Total Value
1943	$40,002	+25.9%	$50,364

Year	Investment	Total Return	End-of-Year Total Value
1944	$50,364	+19.7%	$60,105

Victory Is in Sight

By the end of 1944 most everyone knew that the Allies would be victorious. Of course, they knew too the cost would be high in human lives and destruction, but now at last people were talking about and planning what they would do after the last surrender flag was waved and our troops came marching home.

1945 would be the fourth and last year in a row of our committed investment in the S&P 500 under the Hits-Plus program.

Year	Investment	Total Return	End-of-Year Total Value
1945	$60,105	+36.4%	$82,075

Hitler was dead and Germany surrendered unconditionally. Hiroshima and Nagasaki were destroyed by atomic bombs and Japan signed unconditional surrender papers aboard the *U.S.S. Missouri*. The United States and the free world celebrated the allies' victory in World War II. But in the United States the S&P 500 had now had a four year run of plus years averaging a gain of +25.6 each year with 1945 being up over +36%. Investors are also concerned that a typical end-of-war recession could be waiting in the wings.

After four up years in a row, Hits-Plus goes back into a 50/50 position in U.S. Treasury Bills and Intermediate-Term Government Bonds for 1946.

Year	Investment	Total Return	End-of-YearTotalValue
1946	$82,075	+.07%	$82,628

Hits-Plus didn't deliver a big gain in 1946, but it was better than the -8.1% loss with the S&P 500. With one down year Hits-Plus instructs us to buy back into the market on the first trading day of January and await the January Barometer. We do and January is up so we stay in the market for 1947.

Year	Investment	Total Return	End-of-YearTotalValue
1947	$82,628	+5.7%	$87,395

In 1947, the S&P 500 gained +5.7%, but since this gain is less than +10%, we count it as a down year; therefore, with two down years in a row, we stay fully invested in the S&P 500 and use one-third margin for 1948.

Year	Investment	Total Return	End-of-YearTotalValue
1948	$87,395	+7.3%	$93,780

The S&P 500 gained only +5.5% for 1948. This didn't hurt us, even with the use of margin since the prime rate in 1948 was so low. In fact, Hits-Plus gained +7.39% with the use of margin because of the low 1.75% loan rate. However, again the S&P 500 gain for 1948 was less than 10%. Therefore, 1948 is counted as a down year by Hits-Plus, calling for full investment for 1949 and with full margin.

Year	Investment	Total Return	End-of-YearTotalValue
1949	$93,780	+35.9%	$127,475

In 1949, the S&P 500 went up +18.8%, but with the use of full margin the Hits-Plus investor gained +35.9%

21-Year Economic Mine Field

Thus ends a 21-year experience with Hits-Plus that walked us through an investment and economic mine field period in our history that has been unparalleled. And yet, ***Hits-Plus managed to deliver an average annual compounded return of +12.9%. A buy-and-hold strategy with the S&P 500 would have given you an average annual compounded return of just +3.8%.***

What makes the yearly average return of +12.9% even more impressive is the fact that during this time prime interest rates averaged less than 2% and inflation was practically non-existent. There was a lot of deflation from 1930 through 1932 and some deflation again in 1938, 1939, and 1949. The only inflation years of concern were 1941, 1942, 1946, and 1947. Overall, when you consider the cost-of-living factor, this +12.9% average annual compounded return equals a much higher return by today's standards.

This becomes very evident as we look at Table 9.1 that compares the Hits-Plus return annual performance with that of the S&P 500.

Table 9.1 shows that although in 1930 we lost -30%, Hits-Plus managed to increase our original $10,000 investment to $15,916 by the end of 1933 while the S&P 500 buy-and-hold program lost down to only $5,508.

The depression years and the early World War II years were very frantic times and no investment strategy could withstand it all, but I sincerely believe that any other investment program would have been hard put to beat or even come close to duplicating the performance of Hits-Plus.

Could there be a historical repeat of the Great Depression

Table 9.1

"Hits-Plus" Compared to S&P 500 Buy-and-Hold Strategy, 1929-1949

Year	S&P 500 %End-of-Year Value	Hits-Plus %End-of-Year Value
1929	$ 9,156	$ 10,538
1930	$ 6,878	$ 7,335
1931	$ 3,897	$ 7,326
1932	$ 3,580	$ 8,892
* 1933	$ 5,508	$ 15,916
1934	$ 5,431	$ 15,784
1935	$ 8,017	$ 23,282
1936	$10,740	$ 31,174
1937	$ 6,978	$ 31,465
1938	$ 9,147	$ 37,401
1939	$ 9,111	$ 35.681
1940	$ 8,221	$ 34,973
* 1941	$ 7,269	$ 28,626
**1942	$ 8,743	$ 40,002
1943	$11.012	$ 50,364
1944	$13,185	$ 60,105
1945	$17,990	$ 82,075
1946	$16.538	$ 82,628
1947	$17,482	$ 87,395
* 1948	$18,444	$ 93,780
**1949	$21,910	$127,475

*Years we used 1/3 margin.
**Years we used full margin.

133

years and the World War II years? Many will argue that it absolutely won't happen, that now with the Securities and Exchange Commission, unemployment insurance, social security, and so many other Government programs, it just can't happen. I certainly hope they're right. If awful bad investment years do re-occur in the market they will not be a lock-step duplication of the thirties, but I think it would be good to know that you are employing an investment strategy that held up so well during the worst investment times the nation has ever experienced. All disclaimers must say, "We can't guarantee that future performance will equal past performance, etc." There is absolutely no working crystal ball available anywhere, and if you believe that there is, there is still a lot of swamp land just waiting for your investment dollars.

CHAPTER TEN
Super Hits-Plus

"If passion drives, let reason hold the reins."
-- Benjamin Franklin

"You can't steal second base and keep one foot on first."
-- Unknown

After reading the first nine chapters of this book, I expect there will be a number of readers who will say "OK, Hits-Plus looks and has performed really good over a long historical period of time. But, I like the higher returns I read about that some of the more aggressive mutual funds advertise."

Some people answer this by looking for the recent hot mutual funds that have turned in fabulous performances over the past few years. Too often they buy into the hot funds the same way someone in a gambling casino would bet on a crap shooter with a hot hand. To me too much hot means you might just get burned and research bears me out on this.

There is a better way. We have seen how by investing in the S&P 500, which is made up of about 75% of the value of the New York Stock Exchange, and using the Hits-Plus timing system we have turned this index into a performer that rivals or beats the performance of virtually all mutual funds from 1950 through today and everything in sight in the thirties and forties.

If you have read very much at all about the performance of the stock market you will know that small company stocks have out performed the larger company stocks of the S&P 500 Index quite a bit over long time frames. *In fact $1,000 invested in the S&P 500 (with a buy & hold strategy) at the beginning of 1929 would have grown to $363,012 by the end of 1993. But, $1,000 invested in Small Company Stocks* at the beginning of 1929 (and held throughout this time) would have grown to $1,612,367 by the end of 1993.*

Although this shows that the small company stocks gave over four times the amount of end-of-period return *we know too that by using the Hits-Plus timing system $1,000 invested in-and-out of the S&P 500 Index would have grown to $7,911,410 from 1929 through 1993.* It's only natural that one would wonder could we put the Hits-Plus program into effect with a small company stock index and really get super results. The answer to this is yes ... but not in the manner that you might expect.

A small company index will not behave in as predictable a pattern as the S&P 500 Index. It is not unusual for a small company index to have three or four down years in a row and likewise on up years, except even more so. From January 1975 through December 1983 the Small Company Index had a nine year run of gaining more than +13% every year. In fact the average compounded gain per year during this time frame was +35.99%. That means a $10,000 investment would have jumped to $152,095 but I know of _no one_ who could have

(*selected and published in Ibbotson's SBBI*)*

predicted this performance.

So we can't predict a pattern of performance for a small company index except mostly it will leap, creep, sleep or fall steep. The answer to me is to *follow the basic Hits-Plus trading system using the more predictable S&P 500 Index as our indicator or barometer but to do our investing (when in the market) in a good small company index mutual fund* and of course our out-of-the-market investment will still be 50% in an intermediate term bond fund and 50% in a good money fund. *The results is super in every sense of the word.* But, there are mental or emotional by-products that we must be aware of.

If we follow the Super Hits-Plus system we must realize that it will be tougher to maintain the discipline of sticking with your chosen investment strategy with a strong sense of discipline and patience. This is the secret in successful long term investing no matter what strategy you may chose to employ. I have seen investors switch strategies on a yearly or every other year basis, usually going with the ideas presented in some hot advisory letter and then switching to the suggestions of another letter after not receiving instant success.

Discipline and Patience Truly Tested

In any event if you invest with the Super Hits-Plus program your discipline and patience will be truly tested. For example you would have been out of the market and in bonds and T-Bills in 1977 while the Small Company Stock Index (SCSI) gained +25.38%. This would have been followed by you still remaining out of the market in 1978 while watching the SCSI return +23.46%. After two years in a row of being out of the market and observing great returns being delivered would you still have stuck with the Super Hits-Plus system? Again in 1982 you would have been out of the market and missed out on a +28.01% gain by the SCSI.

But, recall how important it is to be out of the market and not taking the losses. We must remember that a -25% loss will require a +33.3% gain just to draw back even. Super Hits-Plus would have correctly keep us out of the market in 1953, 1957, 1960, 1962, 1966, 1969, 1970, 1973, 1974, 1984, 1987 and 1990. We would have been especially happy to have been on the sidelines in 1969 (a -25% loss), 1970 (a -17.4% loss), 1973 (a -30.9% loss) and 1974 (a -19.9% loss).

In this chapter when I refer to *The Small Company Stock Index* I will be using the *Small Company Stocks* data from *Ibbotson's SBBI* publication. This index is a little complex to explain. From the beginning of 1926 through 1981 it was made up of stocks representing the fifth quintile of the New York Stock Exchange and was value-weighted and re-balanced on a regular basis. The important thing to know is that it was a consistent index representing small company stocks.

From 1982 to date SBBI has simply tracked the total return of the DFA (Dimensional Fund Advisors) U.S. Small Company 9/10 Mutual Fund. This mutual fund is a market-value-weighted index of the ninth and tenth deciles of the New York Stock Exchange plus stocks from Nasdak and the American Stock Exchange. Again, the important thing is it represents a real consistent small company index and does not trade in and out of stocks at a manager's whims or by using any individual stock selecting strategy to try to "beat the market." However most readers of this book will not be able to invest in the DFA U.S. Small Company 9/10 Mutual Fund because the fund is intended primarily for institutional investing and calls for a minimum investment of $100,000.

So how do you invest in a SCSI fund that should give you similar results as the DFA Mutual Fund. Again my current recommendation would be to turn to the Vanguard mutual fund family. We find that Vanguard does not offer a mutual fund that tracks the same small company stock selections that the DFA fund does but in my opinion it is comparable enough. The Vanguard Index Small Capitalization Stock Fund invests in approximately 400 stocks that seeks to mirror the performance of the Russell 2000 Stock Index. Compiled by the Frank Russell Company the Russell 2000 represents about 10% of the value of all publicly traded companies in the United

States. These small companies have a market value of under $750 million each, with an average market value of $250 million. They represent twelve industrial and service sectors.

We can track the Russell 2000 only back to the beginning of 1979. The Vanguard Index Small Capitalization Stock Fund began to mirror the Russell 2000 in 1989. The Russell 2000 does not perform identically to the DFA Fund but since 1979 the overall performance has been very close and utilized with the Super Hits-Plus strategy it has out outperformed the standard Hits-Plus program, without the use of margin. The minimum investment in the Vanguard fund is just $3,000 and the fee and expense rate is typically the lowest in the industry (currently 0.18%).

I found that since the beginning of 1979 through 1993 Super Hits-Plus, using the DFA fund would have grown $10,000 into $171,988, whereas using a mutual fund that correctly mirrored the Russell 2000 would have turned $10,000 into $165,149. Of course another future time frame could bring different results. In any event because of the long term data availability with the Small Company Stock Index published by Ibbotson's SBBI (from 1926 to date) throughout this chapter I will use this index (while believing that most other consistent small stock index's should have performed in a similar manner).

So what did Super Hits-Plus deliver from 1950 through 1993? Well, fasten your seat belt, $10,000 invested at the beginning of 1950 would have grown to $17,307,301 and that's an average annual compounded return of +18.5%.

What is Risk?

Before we get started with our 1950 through 1993 adventure with Super Hits-Plus let's examine the Small Company Stock Index vs. the S&P 500 Index a little more. In recent years you will find that Small Company Stock Index related mutual funds will have very poor performance records and carry high risk ratings.

Here's why. Since 1982 through 1993 the S&P 500 (with a buy-and-hold strategy) has out performed the SCSI in every possible 5-year time period (total of 8). And most rating services judge risk as meaning volatility and how well the mutual fund has performed over a relatively short period of time.

However from 1950 through 1981 the Small Company Index out performed the S&P 500 in 24 of the 32 possible 5-year time periods. As for as volatility is concerned I do not believe this necessarily means risk. You could put your money in bank CD's or money funds and experience very little volatility but inflation could erode your savings and you'd have little chance of real wealth building. *To me the real definition of risk in mutual fund investing is how long can the investor reasonably expect to go without needing to withdraw any of his or her investment money.*

If the investor has a very secure job or business and has good hospitalization benefits, proper disability insurance and no other big expenses expected for at least a five to ten year period (the longer the better) then this in itself lowers the true risk factor.

Also there can be a big difference in the performance of a buy-and-hold approach to that of a limited timing strategy such as Hits-Plus. The whole purpose of Hits-Plus is to be in the market (the majority of the time) when it goes up. And when the Small Company Stock Index has had up years it can really jump. By the same token Hits-Plus strives to have us out-of-the market during down years and here again the Small Company Index tends to drop further during bear markets.

When we look at longer time frames the risk factor deceases drastically with the Super Hits-Plus system investing in the SCSI. For example in the last six 10-year time frames (1980 through 1993) Super Hits-Plus (without margin) was the winner 3 times and regular Hits-Plus (with the use of margin) was the winner 3 times and they were dead even on total return with an average annual compounded return of +18.08%. But, once we go all the way back to 1950 *Super Hits-Plus performed best 29 out of 35 10-year time frames (from 1950 through 1993) and even in its lowest performing 10-year period it produced an average annual compounded return of +12.72%.*

So let's get started. Again we will begin our experience with $10,000 at the beginning of 1950 and at first I will use the same format to depict each investment year. However since I believe that by now the reader should be very familiar with how we invest with the Hits-Plus system later I will shorten the depiction of the yearly investment format in the interest of time and space.

For this tracking of the use of Super Hits-Plus we will not use margin as we did with the regular Hits-Plus strategy. Not because it wouldn't boost returns ... it would. But, since this is a more aggressive investment approach many may choose to be a little conservative when it comes to the use of margin. In any event later I will point out what the difference would have been.

Remember had we had our $10,000 at the beginning of 1949 this would have been after the S&P 500 Index had been down for three years in a row and would have called for us to be invested in the market for four years in a row. But, since we just came into our $10,000 at the beginning of 1950 we'll automatically be in the market for three years in a row (unless the fail-safe sell signal should take us out).

The S&P 500 Index is directing us what to do, but when we invest in the market the investment goes into the SCSI.

Year 1950

Investment	$10,000
Share Price	$6.25
Total Shares	1,598.97
End-of-Year Share Price	$8.68
End-of-Year Total Value	$13,874

141

With a gain of +38.74% the Small Company Stock Index beat the S&P 500 Index by 7 percentage points but the next two years will test one's commitment to the Super Hits-Plus strategy.

Year 1951

Investment	$13,874
Share Price	$8.68
Total Shares	1,598.97
End-of-Year Share Price	$9.35
End-of-Year Total Value	$14,958

A +7.8% gain doesn't exactly call for a celebration when we see that the S&P 500 went up +24%. This is our first little test of our discipline to stick with the Super Hits-Plus system and stay invested in the Small Company Stock Index. Greater test of our patience will come later.

Year 1952

Investment	$14,958
Share Price	$9.35
Total Shares	1,598.97
End-of-Year Share Price	$9.64
End-of-Year Total Value	$15,411

Our next test of discipline came real soon with just a +3.02% performance in 1952 vs. a +18.4% increase in the S&P 500 Index. In reality many investors would now abandon the Super Hits-Plus program and go searching for a better plan to reach their investment goals. But, let's stick with Super Hits-Plus and see what happens. Since 1952 was our last year of commitment to being invested in the market we are directed to switch our investment to 50% U.S. T-Bills and 50% Interme-diate Term Government Bonds. Since the reader can easily refer back to Chapter Eight for a clear break down of just how this investment performed I will present the performance in a shorter format.

Year	Investment	Total Return	End-of-Year Total Value
1953	$15,411	+2.5%	$15,796

Of course Super Hits-Plus and regular Hits-Plus performed the same in 1953 as they both were in the same 50% T-Bills and 50% Intermediate Term Government Bonds investment. The S&P 500 was down -1% but the already struggling Small Company Stock Index dropped -6.06%. Could it be that the small companies are over due to turn in a good positive performing year?

Using The January Barometer

With one down year for the S&P 500 Index Hits-Plus calls for us to switch back into the market on the earliest trading day in January of 1954. With Super Hits-Plus we still are directed by the performance of the S&P 500 Index although we'll be investing in the Small Company Stock Index. This is true in using the January Barometer too, i.e., if in January the S&P 500 is up but the Small Company Stock Index is down (and vice versa) we go by the S&P 500 directive. Same thing if and when a Fail-Safe Sell or Buy Signals comes into play. The Small Company Stock Index could drop -35% from its highest end-of-month high and we would not sell out if the S&P 500 Index only fell -29%.

Year 1954 Through January

Investment	$15,796
Share Price	$9.01
Total Shares	1753.17
End-of-January Share Price	$9.69
End-of-January Total Value	$16,988

Both the S&P 500 and the Small Company Stock Index were up in January but as a directive we're only concerned about the fact that the S&P 500 was up. We stay invested in the SCSI.

Year 1954 February Through December

Investment	$16,988
Share Price	$9.69
Total Shares	1753.17
End-of-Year Share Price	$14.47
End-of-Year Total Value	$25,368

A Pay-off for Discipline

With a big +60.57% gain in 1954 we feel a lot better about Super Hits-Plus although because of our poor performance in 1951 and 1952 we are still behind the performance of the regular Hits-Plus program. With one up year after the down year of 1953 we stay in the market for January of 1955 and await the S&P 500 January Barometer. January is up so we remain invested in the Small Company Stock Index for the rest of 1955.

Year 1955

Investment	$25,368
Share Price	$14.47
Total Shares	1,753.17
End-of-Year Share Price	$17.43
End-of-Year Total Value	$30,558

A nice +20.43% gain for Super Hits-Plus but again not as good as the regular Hits-Plus program which was up +31.6%. *So we see that small company stocks do not always beat large company stocks, during certain time frames, as some stock brokers and mutual fund managers often seem to imply. To me the real key to investing in small company stocks is discipline, patience and the ability to follow your strategy for longer periods of time.*

We will continue to track Super Hits-Plus but now with a shorter format to depict each year's performance except when I feel an expanded explanation is necessary. With two up years for the S&P 500 Index we switch to 50% T-Bills and 50% Intermediate Government Bonds.

Year	Investment	Total Return	End-of-Year Total Value
1956	$30,558	+1.02%	$30,870

1956 was another bit of a disappointment as, while we were out of the market and gaining only +1.2%, the S&P 500 Index rose +6.6% and the Small Company Stock Index was up + 4.28%. With the S&P 500 gaining less than +10% it's counted as a down year and so we go back into the Small Company Stock Index for January.

A Big Help From the January Barometer

The S&P 500 was down a big -4% in January but the Small Company Stock Index was up +2.36%. Although our investment was up the S&P 500 January Barometer says get out of the market and back into T-Bills and Bonds. So we take our $31,599 (which includes the +2.36% gain) and invest in T-Bills and Bonds for the remainder of the year.

In 1957 the S&P 500 loss almost -7% but after the +2.36% gain for the Small Company Stock Index in January it turned very erratic and ended up being down -14.57% for the year. We may not celebrate because of a big gain in 1957 but we can smile because of our avoiding a big loss. And with our additional pick-up of +4.1% in T-Bills and Bonds from February through December our end-of-the year total investment stands at $32,895, representing a total return of a +6.56% gain for the year.

Year	Investment	Total Return	End-of-Year Total Value
1957	$30,870	+6.56%	$32,895

With 1958 coming up we know that the S&P 500 has failed to gain +10% for two years in a row thus with the regular Hits-Plus system we would be investing fully in the S&P 500

Index and with one-third *margin*, however as I stated earlier in this chapter with Super Hits-Plus I will not use margin although I will point out what the results would be with the use of margin.

Year	Investment	Total Return	End-of-YearTotalValue
1958	$32,895	+64.88%	$54,237

1958 really shows how small company stocks can leap. The S&P 500 was up +43.4% which was no less than terrific in itself. If the Super Hits-Plus investor had used one-third margin the end-of-year total value would have been $64,276 (a 95.4% gain) and if the regular Hits-Plus investor had not used margin the total end-of-year value for that approach would have $57,592. In Chapter Twelve we will cover the pros and cons of using margin again as well as analyze various other combined strategies we could employ. With one S&P 500 up year after two down years we stay invested in the SCSI (remember this is not an Index you will find published on a daily basis unless you track the DFA U.S. Small Company 9/10 Mutual Fund) to see how January will direct us. The S&P 500 gained +.05% in January and our position in the SCSI jumped +5.75%. Still another reinforcement of why it's best to be in the market, instead of out, to see how January will move.

Year	Investment	Total Return	End-of-YearTotalValue
1959	$54,237	+16.39%	$63,126

This ends the first ten years of Super Hits-Plus and we find that Super Hits-Plus (without the use of margin) would fall short of performing as well as regular Hits-Plus with margin, but had we used margin in 1958 with Super Hits-Plus it would have beaten regular Hits-Plus by $1,488. In any event I ask you to stay for the entire 44-year trip with Super Hits-Plus. You will discover some very interesting years ahead. With two up years in a row for the S&P 500, 1960 will find our money in T-Bills and Bonds.

Year	Investment	Total Return	End-of-YearTotalValue
1960	$63,126	+7.2%	$67,671

We were right on the button in 1960 as the S&P 500 only gained a half of a percent (+.05%) and the SCSI loss -3.29%. It's January Barometer time for 1961 resulting in the S&P 500 moving up +6.45% and the SCSI gaining +9.15% in just the one month.

Year	Investment	Total Return	End-of-YearTotalValue
1961	$67,671	+32.08%	$89,340

Year	Investment	Total Return	End-of-YearTotalValue
1962	$89,340	+5.7%	$94,432

(out of market, Jan. Barometer)

Year	Investment	Total Return	End-of-YearTotalValue
1963	$94,432	+23.56%	$116,680

(in market, Jan. Barometer)

Year	Investment	Total Return	End-of-YearTotalValue
1964	$116,680	+23.52%	$144,123

(in market, Jan. Barometer)

Year	Investment	Total Return	End-of-YearTotalValue
1965	$144,123	+2.47%	$147,683

(out of market, two previous years up)

☹   Angry After 1965   ☹

Boy, would we have been angry after 1965. While we stayed in mediocre T-Bills and Bonds the S&P 500 went up +12.5% while the SCSI leaped +41.75%. But, before you proclaim that a buy-and-hold strategy would have been better ... double check. With an S&P 500 Index buy-and-hold program you would now have $110,032 and with an SCSI buy-and-hold your portfolio would total $116,032 instead of

$147,683 with Super Hits-Plus. This is where real discipline comes in ... the willingness to be patience and follow your selected investment strategy. Now with three up years in a row we are directed to continue to stay in our T-Bills and Bonds position.

Year	Investment	Total Return	End-of-YearTotalValue
1966	$147,683	+4.7%	$154,624

Well, we have some vindication as 1966 saw the S&P 500 fall -10.1% and the SCSI went down -7.01%. With one down year back in the market we go to let January point the way ... and boy did it ever point the way. The S&P 500 jumped +8% and the SCSI leaped +18.38% in that one thirty day period.

Wow! What a Year

Year	Investment	Total Return	End-of-YearTotalValue
1967	$154,624	+83.56%	$283,828

The S&P 500 investor was happy with a +24% gain but the SCSI investor was ecstatic after racking up a +83.56% increase in the value of his/her portfolio. After one up year (and what an up year) it's January Barometer time again. The S&P 500 dropped -4.3% in January of 1968 whereas the SCSI gained +1.54% and we back out of the market and into our T-Bills and Bonds position.

Year	Investment	Total Return	End-of-YearTotalValue
1968	$283,828	+5.52%	$299,495

Yes, there would have been a frown on our face after 1968 because we would have witnessed the S&P 500 do a U-turn and end the year with a +11.1% gain while the SCSI returned +35.97%. One must wonder who at this point would stick to the Super Hits-Plus strategy and who would say "I'm going to stay in the market for 1969 and reap the rewards." The disciplined Super Hits-Plus followers will simply shrug their shoulders and say "O.K.the S&P 500 Index has registered gains of over +10% for two years in a row so we're going to stick with our T-Bills and Bonds.

Year	Investment	Total Return	End-of-YearTotalValue
1969	$299,495	+2.95%	$308,330

How did we, the Super Hits-Plus disciplinarians, make out in comparison to the buy, hold and hope investors? 1969 saw the S&P 500 drop -8.5% but the SCSI fell -25.05%. So even though the buy and holder would have beaten us +35.97% vs. +5.52% in 1968 by the end of 1969 we would have made $19,078 more in just this two year span.

Year	Investment	Total Return	End-of-YearTotalValue
1970	$308,330	+4.42%	$321,958

(in T-Bill & Bonds, Jan. Barometer down)

Year	Investment	Total Return	End-of-YearTotalValue
1971	$321,958	+16.49%	$375,048

(in market, S&P 500 down two previous years)

Year	Investment	Total Return	End-of-YearTotalValue
1972	$375,048	+4.43%	$391,663

(in market, Jan. Barometer up)

Super Hits-Plus and the '73-'74 Bear Market

With two up years in a row for the S&P 500 Index the Hits-Plus and Super Hits-Plus investors will be in T-Bills and Bonds for 1973 thereby avoiding the big 1973 market decline.

Year	Investment	Total Return	End-of-YearTotalValue
1973	$391,663	+5.76%	$414,223

1973 saw the S&P 500 drop by -14.7% while the SCSI

tumbled -30.9%. Wasn't it great to be out of the market?

☺ Fortune Smiles On Us In 1974 ☺

1974 was a January Barometer year so we invest in the SCSI on the earliest trading day of 1974 and let the S&P 500's January performance direct us from there. The S&P 500 Index dropped a little less than -1% but our investment in the SCSI jumped +13.26%. This could again prove to be a dilemma for the undisciplined investor as he/she would be reading in various publications that after the 1973 bear market it was bargain time to buy into the market. Not for the disciplined Super Hits-Plus investor. He/she feels the S&P 500 index is still the best barometer and so while happy with the +13.26% January gain back into T-Bills and Bonds we go on the earliest trading day in February.

Year	Investment	Total Return	End-of-Year Total Value
1974	$414,223	+20.57%	$499,429

A Magician in 1974

We really would have appeared to be a real stock market wizard in 1974, being in the SCSI in January and then jumping right back out and into our trusted T-Bills and Bonds. We were right on target. With the performance of our T-Bills and Bonds added to the +13.26% SCSI performance we swam against the tide with truly great results as the S&P 500 fell -26.5% and the SCSI did a reverse U-turn to fall -19.95% for the year.

You may remember from Chapter Eight that although we were out of the market and didn't use the Fail-Safe signal it was flashed the last of August 1974 when the S&P 500 registered a drop of -31% from its highest end of the month high. Therefore we will not re-enter the market until the S&P 500 rises +21% from its lowest end of the month low. This will take place at the end of January 1975. We stayed in T-Bills and Bonds throughout the month of January.

Year	Investment	Total Return	End-of-Year Total Value
1975	$499,429	+20.36%	$601,111

Year	Investment	Total Return	End-of-Year Total Value
1976	$601,111	+57.37%	$945,968

(in market, Jan. Barometer up)

Year	Investment	Total Return	End-of-Year Total Value
1977	$945,968	+3.26%	$976,807

(in T-Bill & Bonds, S&P 500 up two previous years)

We were out of the market when we had rather have been in during 1977 and it will happen again in 1978 ... two years in a row. But, patience and discipline is still the answer. We know now by looking back that we were in the midst of a nine-year roaring bull market for the SCSI but hindsight is always 20/20. Keep on keeping on with Super Hits-Plus is the order.

Year	Investment	Total Return	End-of-Year Total Value
1978	$976,807	+3.02%	$1,006,307

(out of market, Jan. Barometer down)

Year	Investment	Total Return	End-of-Year Total Value
1979	$1,006,307	+43.46%	$1,443,648

(in market, S&P 500 down two previous years)

Year	Investment	Total Return	End-of-Year Total Value
1980	$1,443,648	+39.87%	$2,019,230

(in market, Jan. Barometer is up)

Year	Investment	Total Return	End-of-Year Total Value
1981	$2,019,230	+12.08%	$2,263,153

(in T-Bills & Bonds, S&P 500 up two previous years)

Year	Investment	Total Return	End-of-Year Total Value
1982	$2,263,153	+16.72%	$2,641,552

(in T-Bills & Bonds, Jan. Barometer is down)

Year	Investment	Total Return	End-of-Year Total Value
1983	$2,641,552	+39.66%	$3,689,192

(in market, Jan. Barometer is up)

Year	Investment	Total Return	End-of-YearTotalValue
1984	$3,689,192	+11.94%	$4,129,682

(in T-Bills & Bonds, S&P 500 up two previous years)

After nine years of a small company stock bull market it trips up in 1984 but we had moved to T-Bills and Bonds because the S&P 500 had been up two years in a row (1982 & 1983). The SCSI fell -6.67% in 1984 but would come back in 1985 and on but not so dramatic until 1991. However Super Hits-Plus would continue to be a steady performer.

Year	Investment	Total Return	End-of-YearTotalValue
1985	$4,129,682	+24.66%	$5,148,062

(in market, Jan. Barometer is up)

Year	Investment	Total Return	End-of-YearTotalValue
1986	$5,148,062	+6.85%	$5,500,704

(in market, Jan. Barometer up)

Year	Investment	Total Return	End-of-YearTotalValue
1987	$5,500,704	+4.18%	$5,730,633

(in T-Bills & Bonds, S&P 500 up two previous years)

Year	Investment	Total Return	End-of-YearTotalValue
1988	$5,730,633	+22.87%	$7,041,229

(in market, Jan. Barometer up)

Year	Investment	Total Return	End-of-YearTotalValue
1989	$7,041,229	+10.17%	$7,757,322

(in market, Jan. Barometer up)

Year	Investment	Total Return	End-of-YearTotalValue
1990	$7,757,322	+8.77%	$8,437,639

(in T-Bills & Bonds, S&P 500 up previous two years)

Year	Investment	Total Return	End-of-YearTotalValue
1991	$8,437,639	+44.63%	$12,203,357

(in market, Jan. Barometer up)

Year	Investment	Total Return	End-of-YearTotalValue
1992	$12,203,357	+17.21%	$14,303,554

(in T-Bills & Bonds, Jan. Barometer down)

Year	Investment	Total Return	End-of-YearTotalValue
1993	$14,303,554	+21%	$17,307,301

(in market, Jan. Barometer up)

There we have the 44-year experience with Super Hits-Plus with an average annual compounded return of +18.47% without the use of margin. With the use of margin when called for by Hits-Plus, in the years 1958, 1971, 1975 and 1979, the Super Hits-Plus portfolio would have had a value of $23,902,444 at the end of 1993 and that's an average annual compounded return of +19.34%. Always remember personal taxes are not figured and margin could not have been used within an IRA or Variable Annuity program.

See the comparison Table 10.1 at the end of this chapter for a clear picture of how Hits-Plus and Super Hits-Plus performed over this 44-year time frame.

Another phenomenal thing, when we look back, is the fact that Super Hits-Plus did not have a single down year in all 44 years since 1950 but I doubt we could always count on this. As always no one can guarantee that future years will perform as they have in the past.

Again we used SCSI as published in *Ibbotson's SBBI* for all of the total return stock market price data used in this book. However, in the newsletter *Hits-Plus Mutual Fund Guide* we have switched to the Vanguard Index Small Capitalization Stock Fund as of the beginning of 1990. This was done as a practical matter and in my opinion would not make much difference in the overall performance for the Super Hits-Plus investor.

In Chapter Eleven I will quickly take us through the economic mine field years of 1929 through 1949 using the Super Hits-Plus system and then in Chapter Twelve we will analyze various combined strategies of Hits-Plus and Super Hits-Plus that we could employ.

Table 10.1

"Super Hits-Plus Compared to "Hits-Plus". 1950-1993

Year	Super Hits-Plus%	End-of-Year Value	Hits-Plus%	End-of-Year Value
1950	+38.7%	$13,874	+31.7%	$13,167
1951	+ 7.8	$14,958	+24.0	$16,335
1952	+ 3.0	$15,411	+18.4	$19,338
1953	+ 2.5	$15,796	+ 2.5	$19,826
1954	+60.6	$25,368	+52.6	$30,275
1955	+20.4	$30,558	+31.6	$39,824
1956	+ 1.0	$30,870	+ 1.0	$40,162
1957	+ 6.6	$32,895	- .02	$40,162
1958	+64.9	$54,237	+63.1	$65,504*
1959	+16.4	$63,126	+12.0	$73,323
1960	+ 7.2	$67,671	+ 7.2	$78,609
1961	+32.1	$89,340	+26.9	$99,774
1962	+ 5.7	$94,432	+ .05	$100,237
1963	+23.6	$116,680	+22.8	$123,113
1964	+23.5	$144,123	+16.5	$143,404
1965	+ 2.5	$147,683	+ 2.5	$146,953
1966	+ 4.7	$154,624	+ 4.7	$153,896
1967	+83.6	$283,828	+24.0	$190,796
1968	+ 5.5	$299,495	- .05	$189,852
1969	+ 2.9	$308,330	+ 2.9	$195,454
1970	+ 4.4	$321,958	+ 2.9	$201240
1971	+16.5	$375,048	+18.6	$238,738*
1972	+ 4.4	$395,663	+19.0	$284,038
1973	+ 5.8	$414,223	+ 5.8	$300,427
1974	+20.6	$499,223	+ 5.6	$317,110
1975	+20.4	$601,111	+30.0	$412,340*
1976	+57.4	$945,968	+23.8	$510,661
1977	+ 3.3	$976,807	+ 3.3	$527,334
1978	+ 3.0	$1,006,307	- 1.2	$520,762
1979	+43.5	$1,443,648	+21.3	$631,838*
1980	+39.9	$2,019,230	+32.4	$836,675
1981	+12.1	$2,263,153	+12.1	$937,746
1982	+16.7	$2,641,552	+17.1	$1,098,161
1983	+39.7	$3,689,192	+22.5	$1,345,386
1984	+11.9	$4,129,682	+11.9	$1,505,958
1985	+24.7	$5,148,062	+32.2	$1,990,256
1986	+ 6.8	$5,500,704	+18.5	$2,357,907
1987	+ 4.2	$5,730,633	+ 4.2	$2,456,586
1988	+22.9	$7,041,229	+16.8	$2,869,510
1989	+10.2	$7,757,322	+31.5	$3,773,159
1990	+ 8.8	$8,437,639	+ 8.8	$4,104,065
1991	+44.6	$12,203,357	+30.6	$5,358,510
1992	+17.2	$14,303,554	+ 4.3	$5,585,175
1993	+21.0	$17,307,301	+10.0	$6,143,692

*Years Hits-Plus used margin.
  Super Hit-Plus did not use margin.

CHAPTER ELEVEN

Terrible Fall, Great Recovery, Super Hits-Plus 1929-1949

*"The way I see it, if you want the rainbow,
you gotta put up with the rain."*

-- *Dolly Parton*

We will quickly track the 21-year period from 1929 through 1949 with The Super Hits-Plus system. Remember we always use the S&P 500 Index as our more dependable barometer and this includes the Fail-Safe Sell and Buy Signals. In most cases this will keep us from selling and buying too often and keep the whipsawing effect from costing us so dearly. However we will find that in 1930 the more volatile small companies stock fell so much faster than the S&P 500 companies that it really did cost us dearly with a terrible slashing whipsaw effect. We will also see how dramatic a turn-around can be accomplished with the Small Company Stock Index as in 1933 and other sky rocket years.

Again with our $10,000 investment money we will spend 1929 in T-Bills and Intermediate Term Government Bonds since the S&P 500 had up years in 1926, 1927 and 1928. The crash for the Small Company Stock Index was much more devastating than with the S&P 500 in 1929. The S&P 500 only fell -8.42% for the year whereas the SCSI tumbled -51.36%. What a relief it was to be in T-Bills and Bonds while that tragedy struck but of course no investment system could survive completely the years of the great stock market crash and the great depression.

Year	Investment	Total Return	End-of-YearTotalValue
1929	$10,000	+5.38%	$10,538

Our T-Bills and Bonds proved to be a safe haven for 1929. Meanwhile after reaching an end-of-the-month high of $2.93 per share in August of 1929 the S&P 500 fell more than -31% to $1.96 on the last trading day of November, therefore the Fail-Safe Sell Signals was flashed although we were already out of the market. This means we stay out until the S&P 500 climbs +21% from an end-of-the-month low. This would occur at the end of March 1930. From January through March of 1930 our T-Bills and Bond position would push our portfolio value to $10,692. With the Fail-Safe Buy Signal flashing we go back into the SCSI at the beginning of April (much to our later sorrow).

Year	*Months*	Investment	Total Return	End-of-*Period*Value
1930	*April-Nov.*	$10,692	-47%	$5,662

What a disaster ... a -47% crash in just eight months. Finally the Fail-Safe Sell Signals was flashed when the S&P 500 fell below -31% from its previous end-of-the-month high. This was registered at the end of November so we sold out of the still tumbling SCSI to seek refuge in T-Bills and Bonds. The month of December added one dollar to our portfolio to end the year of 1930 with $5,663. Now that we're out of the market we'll stick with the T-Bills and Bonds until the S&P 500 rises +21% from a lowest end-of-the-month low to direct us back into the market. Frankly I would doubt many would want to see that happen too soon as the memory of that April through November whipsaw will haunt us like a nightmare.

Year	Investment	Total Return	End-of-Year Total Value
1931	$5,663	-.005%	$5,660

The way things were in 1931 we couldn't make any headway even in T-Bills and Bonds as we lost three dollars. Still we would see the SCSI drop another -49.75%, which means that the buy-and-holder who held SCSI stock valued at $1.71 per share at the beginning of 1929 would now be looking at shares valued at only 26¢ per share.

The S&P 500 was also still falling with no real sign of turning around. We will be staying in U.S. T-Bills and Intermediate Term Government Bonds for the first seven months of 1932.

Year	Months	Investment	Total Return	End-of-Period Value
1932	Jan-July.	$5,660	+2.95%	$5,827

At the end of July we have $5,827 as compared to the $7,542 value of the regular Hits-Plus investor's portfolio, but if its any consolation both portfolios beat the heck out of the buy-and-hold investor. With the S&P 500 rising over +21% from its lowest end-of-the-month low we re-invest back into the SCSI on the earliest trading date of August. The SCSI jumped +35.23% in July alone. Would this indicate a real recovery trend, or would it set the stage for another whipsaw blood letting?

Year	Months	Investment	Total Return	End-of-Period Value
1932	Aug.-Dec.	$5,827	+3.38%	$6,024

So we gained +3.38% from August through December (total performance of +6.43% for the year) but that doesn't tell the story at all. It would have been a real emotional experience. The SCSI streaked upward by a whopping +73.46% in August alone only to fall -13.2% in September, -17.75% October, -12.27% in November and -4.9% in December. The S&P 500 fell back also from September through December, after an excellent August performance, but not enough to spring the Fail-Safe Sell Signal.

With three or more S&P 500 down years in a row (actually four) the Hits-Plus system directs us to be in the market for a four year commitment (not withstanding a Fail-Safe Sell Signals).

The Mother of All Re-bounds

Year	Investment	Total Return	End-of-YearTotalValue
1933	$6,024	+142.87%	$14,604

The buy-and-hold investor would have seen his stock selling for less than 18¢ per share during 1932 and even with a per share price of 59.4¢ at the end of 1933 he would still be in a world of hurt. The regular Hits-Plus investor would have used one-third margin in 1933 which turned a +54% gain of the S&P 500 into a +79% jump. After the emotional roller coaster ride the Super Hits-Plus investor had experienced I doubt even the strongest of heart would have used margin for 1933. But, if he had (after paying off the margin loan) the SCSI portfolio would have been worth $18,850 or a +213% slam dunk.

With three years to go on our four year commitment to be

in the market we stay put in the SCSI and let it run.

Year	Investment	Total Return	End-of-Year Total Value
1934	$14,604	+24.22%	$18,144

In 1934 the S&P 500 lost a fraction enabling the Super Hits-Plus investor (without the use of margin) to surpass the regular Hits-Plus investor (using margin). At this point the Super Hits-Plus portfolio is worth +14.95% more than the regular Hits-Plus portfolio.

Year	Investment	Total Return	End-of-Year Total Value
1935	$18,144	+40.19%	$25,447

Now we have one more year to go with our four year commitment to be in the market.

Year	Investment	Total Return	End-of-Year Total Value
1936	$25,447	+64.8%	$41,920

Some brave souls might be tempted to stay in the market hoping the good times would continue to roll but not the disciplined Super Hits-Plus strategist. It will be T-Bills and Bonds for us in 1937.

Year	Investment	Total Return	End-of-Year Total Value
1937	$41,920	+.093%	$42,311

1937 really shook investors up after three good solid performing years the SCSI dropped like a stone by -58%, while the S&P 500 fell -35%. Had we been in the market the Fail-Safe Sell Signal would have taken us out the last of November. In any event with one down year we would have gone back in the market to check the January Barometer but we can't go back in now until the Fail-Safe Buy Signal flashes.

Year	Months	Investment	Total Return	End-of-Period Value
1938	*Jan.-June*	$42,311	+2.3%	$43,287

The Fail-Safe Buy Signal put us back into the market on the first of July 1938.

Year	*Months*	Investment	Total Return	End-of-*Period* Value
1938	*July-Dec.*	$43,287	+20.68%	$52,241

It was an excellent turn around for us in 1938 with a +23.46% gain for the entire year. But, as war clouds gather the next three years will test our discipline again. With one up year it's January Barometer time. January was down both for the S&P 500 and for the SCSI. Our SCSI portfolio fell -8.48% to $47,790 and then was placed in T-Bills and Bonds on the earliest trading day in February where it goes back up to $48,745 at the end of the year, but still leaving a minus performance for the year.

Year	Investment	Total Return	End-of-Year Total Value
1939	$52,241	-6.69%	$48,745

Year	Investment	Total Return	End-of-Year Total Value
1940	$48,745	+1.65%	$49,554

(in T-Bills & Bonds, Jan. Barometer)

Year	Investment	Total Return	End-of-Year Total Value
1941	$49,554	-9.06%	$45,064

(in market, S&P 500 down two previous years)

1941 was a one-third margin year for the regular Hits-Plus investor and he lost -18.1%. If the Super Hits-Plus strategist had used margin he would have been down -14.34%. With three very lackluster years in a row for both the Hits-Plus and Super Hits-Plus investors we would enter 1942 with a great deal of apprehension, but because the S&P 500 has been down three years in a row we now have a commitment to be in the market for the next four years (not withstanding a Fail-Safe Sell Signal). As was pointed out in Chapter Nine, with the bombing of Pearl Harbor and the United States fully entering into World War II it certainly would not have been a comfort-able scene. However, by the end of the year the stock market would have staged another dramatic rebound.

Year	Investment	Total Return	End-of-Year Total Value
1942	$45,064	+44.59%	$65,158

The (non-margin) Super Hits-Plus investor beat the (full 50% margin) regular Hits-Plus investor's +39.7%. Had the Super Hits-Plus follower been gutsy enough to have used full 50% margin the results would have been a +87.68% leap.

Now after 1942 we have three more commitment years to go. And what a great three years it will prove to be.

Year	Investment	Total Return	End-of-Year Total Value
1943	$65,158	+88.4%	$122,757

Year	Investment	Total Return	End-of-Year Total Value
1944	$122,757	+53.7%	$188,677

Year	Investment	Total Return	End-of-Year Total Value
1945	$188,677	+73.62%	$327,581

After three terrific leaping years in a row we will now observe three sleeping years.

Year	Investment	Total Return	End-of-Year Total Value
1946	$327,581	+.067%	$329,775

(out of market, after four year commitment)

Year	Investment	Total Return	End-of-Year Total Value
1947	$329,775	+.095%	$332,927

(in market, Jan. Barometer)

Year	Investment	Total Return	End-of-Year Total Value
1948	$332,927	-2.14%	$316,016

(in market, S&P 500 down previous two years)

The regular Hits-Plus investor would have used one-third margin in 1948 and it really didn't hurt as the S&P 500 did go up +5.5% and the margin loan rate was just 1.75%. However if the Super Hits-Plus investor had used margin he would have been hurt a bit more resulting in a -4.02% drop. For the margin user 1949 would have called for the full 50% use of margin but as stated at the beginning of this chapter we are going with no margin use for the Super Hits-Plus investor but will report how the results would have been had margin been used.

Year	Investment	Total Return	End-of-Year Total Value
1949	$316,016	+19.73%	$378,365

(in market, S&P 500 down three previous years)

How About That Rainbow

There we have the 21-year adventure with Super Hits-Plus turning in an average annual compounded return of +18.88%. Quite a performance for this very chaotic time in our history. (See Table 11.1 for a comparison in performance between Hits-Plus and Super Hits-Plus). In 1949 if the Super Hits-Plus investor had used full 50% margin it would have been a +37.47% year. If the Super Hits-Plus strategist had been able to have mustered unheard of courage and used margin, as called for, by the Hits-Plus system in 1933, 1941, 1942, 1948 and 1949 his/her portfolio would have been valued at $692,982 at the end of 1949. And that's a fabulous +22.36% average annual compounded return. As Dolly Parton (who well demostrates peeks and valleys) said *"... if you want the rainbow, you gotta put up with the rain."* **We waded through a flash-flood down pour at times, but wow! what a beautiful Rainbow.**

Table 11.1

"Super Hits-Plus" Compared to "Hits-Plus. 1929-1949

Year	Super Hits-Plus%	End-of-Year Value	Hits-Plus%	End-of-Year Value
1929	+ 5.4%	$10,538	+ 5.4%	$10,538
1930	- 47.0	$5,663	- 30.0	$7,335
1931	- .005	$5,660	- .001	$7,326
1932	+ 6.4	$6,024	+21.4	$8,892
1933	+142.9	$14,604	+79.0	$15,916*
1934	+ 24.2	$18,144	- .08	$15,784
1935	+ 40.2	$25,447	+47.5	$23,282
1936	+ 64.8	$41,920	+33.9	$31,174
1937	+ .09	$42,311	+ .09	$31,465
1938	+ 23.5	$52,241	+18.9	$37,401
1939	- 6.7	$48,745	- 4.6	$35,681
1940	+ 1.6	$49,554	- 2.0	$34,973
1941	- 9.1	$45,064	- 18.9	$28,625*
1942	+ 44.6	$65,158	+39.7	$40,002**
1943	+ 88.4	$122,757	+25.9	$50,364
1944	+ 53.7	$188,677	+19.7	$60,105
1945	+ 73.6	$327,581	+36.4	$82,075
1946	+ .07	$329,927	+ .07	$82,628
1947	+ .09	$332,927	+ 5.7	$87,395
1948	- 2.1	$316,016	+ 7.3	$93,780*
1949	+ 19.7	$378,365	+35.9	$127,475**

*Years Hits-Plus used 1/3 margin.
**Years Hits-Plus used full margin.
Super Hits-Plus did not use margin.

CHAPTER TWELVE

What Most Stock Brokers Won't Tell You

"For one word a man is often deemed to be wise, and for one word he is often deemed to be foolish. We should be careful indeed of what we say.
-- Confucius

"Be straightforward in the way we dodge issues."
-- Anonymous

Perhaps the title of this chapter is a little strong. As I have stated earlier I have a number of stock broker friends who are totally honest and would never deliberately mislead a client ... but too often too many stock brokers *fail to emphasize the historical significance of past stock market time frames.* This may be because they simply do not know of this history. It may be because they feel that what has happen over the past five, ten, fifteen or even twenty years is all that really matters. But,

I strongly feel that past stock market history is very significant and to imply that we may not see similar re-runs of past patterns emerging in the future may indeed be presenting a false sense of security for the would-be investor.

I am often asked "What mutual fund should I invest in?" My answer usually is, "I need to know more about *you*."

"Why do you need to know anything about me? My broker doesn't ask questions about me. He simply gives me information about stocks or mutual funds," he replies.

"First, for me to give you any kind of advice, I'd want to know how long will it be before you'll need to draw out any of your investment money?"

"Oh, I can be in the market quite a while. I don't think I will need this money for two years," he answers.

"In that case, you need your money too soon and you'll be safer in a good money fund or CDs. I really don't look at two-year money as being an investment. You're just looking for a safe parking place." My answer he probably won't like. However if the market had been down for the previous three years in a row then I would be advising him to go into the market with the upcoming year.

If the inquiry is coming from someone who really has *investment* money that can be tied up for ten years or so then we can go from there. I'll also want to know how he'll respond emotionally if his investment shows a loss for a year or two? Will he panic and get all upset or is he the type of person who has patience and is well disciplined? There are so many things I think one should know about the potential investor before handing out advice. What is their age, approximate income, plans for the future, etc. After the necessary information about the investor is obtained then he should be shown what I think is rarely presented to the potential client ... and that is *all the possible five-year, ten-year, fifteen-year and twenty-year time period growth comparison of various investment strategies.* You are about to receive this information very shortly.

Actually if the market had been down two or three years in a row its doubtful anyone would be asking about "... going into the market," advice. These questions for market advice almost always come after the market has had a good year or two and the individual feels he's missed out on something or CD and money fund rates are so low that he thinks there has to be a better deal somewhere.

The historical fact is that most new investors and many other individuals invest in the stock market when historical patterns show that the market may be over-valued and ready for a down-turn correction and that they tend to sell out after the down-turn correction has occurred and the market may be ready to enter a bull period. This is why so many contrarian strategies work so well. And to a large extent Hits-Plus and Super Hits-Plus is a contrarian approach too. Unlike some contrarian strategies Hits-Plus and Super Hits-Plus usually do not keep you in the market for long hauls (almost buy-and-hold positions), nor do they try to fine-tune you in-and-out of the market four or five times a year as many timing strategies do.

The Truth Is In The Tables

In any event the investor should know how past markets have performed in various time frames so they are fully aware of what may take place again in future time frames.

First we'll look at Table 12.1 to see how all possible five-year periods (from 1950 through 1993) performed comparing Super Hits-Plus, Hits-Plus, the S&P 500 Buy-and-Hold and the Small Company Stock Index Buy-and-Hold. With five-year time periods we will always see some periods that were fantastically high performers and others that were disastrous.

We will note (by the little "frown faces") that Super Hits-Plus' worst five-year periods were an average annual compounded growth of +5.83%, +6.71% and +10.12%. This performance compares favorable with Hits-Plus with its worst five-year periods of +6.39%, +6.49% and +8.28%.

When we turn to the S&P 500 buy-and-hold approach the worst five-year time periods were (-2.37%), (-0.24%) and

Table 12.1

All Possible Five-Year Periods 1950 Thru 1993
Average Annual Compounded % Growth Comparison Table

Years	*Super Hits-Plus (no margin)* % Growth	Hits-Plus (w/margin) % Growth	*S&P 500 B & H** % Growth	S.C.S.I B & H* %Growth
1950-1954	+20.47	+24.80☺	+23.90☺	+18.27
1951-1955	+17.10	+24.77☺	+23.90☺	+14.97
1952-1956	+15.60	+19.75	+20.19	+14.21
1953-1957	+16.37	+15.74	+13.58	+10.01
1954-1958	+27.97☺	+27.00☺	+22.32☺	+23.22
1955-1959	+20.00	+19.35	+14.98	+15.54
1956-1960	+17.24	+14.57	+ 8.94	+10.58
1957-1961	+23.70	+19.92	+12.81	+15.93
1958-1962	+23.50	+20.07	-13.33	+16.65
1959-1963	+16.57	+13.45	+ 9.87	+10.11
1960-1964	+17.97	+14.35	+10.74	+11.43
1961-1965	+16.91	+13.33	+13.27	+20.28
1962-1966	+11.60	+ 9.05	+ 5.72	+12.13
1963-1967	+24.63	+13.74	+12.40	+29.86
1964-1968	+19.83	+ 9.05	+10.17	+32.37
1965-1969	+15.43	+ 6.39☹	+ 4.97	+19.78
1966-1970	+15.98	+ 6.49☹	+ 3.34	+ 7.51
1967-1971	+18.48	+ 9.18	+ 8.42	+12.47
1968-1972	+ 5.83☹	+ 8.28☹	+ 7.53	+ 0.44☹
1969-1973	+ 6.71☹	+ 9.61	+ 2.00☹	(-12.28)☹
1970-1974	+10.12☹	-10.16	(- 2.37)☹	(-11.11)☹
1971-1975	+13.30	+15.42	+ 3.19	+ 0.53
1972-1976	+20.33	+16.42	+ 4.85	+ 6.76
1973-1977	+20.06	+13.17	(- 0.24)☹	+10.76
1974-1978	+19.43	+11.63	- 4.31	+24.40
1975-1979	+23.66	+14.78	+14.75	+39.80☺
1976-1980	+27.43☺	+15.20	+13.93	+37.35☺
1977-1981	+19.04	+12.92	+ 8.08	+28.74
1978-1982	+22.00	+15.80	+14.04	+29.28
1979-1983	+29.65☺	+20.90	-17.26	+32.51☺
1980-1884	+23.35	+18.97	+14.76	+21.59
1981-1985	+20.54	+18.92	+14.72	+18.82
1982-1986	+19.41	+20.25	+19.88	+17.32
1983-1987	+16.73	+17.47	+16.50	+ 9.51
1984-1988	+13.77	+16.35	-15.39	+ 6.73
1985-1989	+13.44	+20.16	+20.41	+10.34
1986-1990	+10.39	+15.57	+13.13	+ 0.57
1987-1991	+17.28	+17.84	+15.35	+ 6.85
1988-1992	+20.07	+17.69	+15.89	+13.63
1989-1993	+19.70	+16.28	+14.51	+13.28

* Buy & Hold
☹The worst three 5 year time periods
☺The best three 5 year time periods

168

+2.00% average annual compounded return. This, of course, means in two of those five-year periods you would have ended up with less money than you started with (the worst dropping $10,000 to $8,869). In twelve other five-year time periods your gains would have been in single digits, ie +9.61% or less whereas with Super Hits-Plus, thirty eight out of the forty five-year periods from 1950 through 1993 gave us double digit compounded returns (+10.12% or more).

Now when we take a look at the Small Companies Stock Index we really see how high highs can be and how low lows can be. This is why most mutual funds that seek to mirror a Small Companies Index will carry a high risk rating by most mutual fund rating services.

The three worst five-year periods with a SCSI Buy-and-Hold strategy are (-12.28%), (-11.11%), and +0.44%. Look a little closer and we'll find there are several additional five-year time periods that produced average annual compounded growth in single digits or less. We all should ask ourselves how we would have reacted emotionally if our portfolio had performed in such a poor manner. "Oh, but look at those seven five-year periods in a row (1974 through 1985) with all those great returns." They certainly were terrific performance periods but how do you know when they're coming. We already know that for the entire 44 years (1950 through 1993) Super Hits-Plus greatly outperformed the SCSI Buy-and-Hold approach (over ten times the end-of-time results).

Going now to Table 12.2 we look at all possible ten-year periods from 1950 through 1993 and we see the return curve is flattened a bit. The highs are not as high but the lows are not as low. *The great news with the Super Hits-Plus system is the lowest average annual compounded return in a ten-year period is +12.72% and most mutual funds would never put a "frown face" on this kind of results.*

Regular Hits-Plus (with margin) had a low ten-year period return of +8.26% but greatly exceeded the performance of the S&P 500 Buy-and-Hold strategy.

Table 12.2

All Possible Ten-Year Periods 1950 Thru 1993
Average Annual Compounded % Growth Comparison Table

	Super Hits-Plus (no margin)	Hits-Plus (w/margin)	*S&P 500 B & H**	S.C.S.I. B & H*
Years	% Growth	%Growth	%Growth	%Growth
1950-1959	+20.23	+22.04©	+19.36©	+16.90
1951-1960	+17.17	+19.56	+16.18	+12.75
1952-1961	+19.57	+19.83©	+16.44	+15.07
1953-1962	+19.88	+17.88	+13.46	+13.28
1954-1963	+22.14	+20.03©	+15.93	+16.48
1955-1964	+18.98	+16.83	+12.84	+13.46
1956-1965	+17.07	+13.94	+11.09	+15.33
1957-1966	+17.49	+14.36	− 9.21	+14.01
1958-1967	+23.96©	+16.86	− 12.87	+23.08
1959-1968	+18.19	+11.23	+10.02	+20.73
1960-1969	+16.75	+10.30	+ 7.82	+15.53
1961-1970	+16.44	+ 9.85	+ 8.19	+13.71
1962-1971	+14.99	+ 9.11⊗	+ 7.06	+12.30
1963-1972	+14.85	+10.97	+ 9.94	+14.21
1964-1973	+13.08	+ 9.33⊗	+ 6.01	+ 7.75
1965-1974	+12.80⊗	+ 8.26⊗	+ 1.23⊗	+ 3.18⊗
1966-1975	+14.63	+10.87	+ 3.26⊗	+ 3.96⊗
1967-1976	+19.40	+12.74	+ 6.62	+ 9.58
1968-1977	+12.72⊗	+10.70	+ 3.57	+ 5.48
1969-1978	+12.89⊗	+10.61	+ 3.15⊗	+ 4.46⊗
1970-1979	+16.70	+12.45	+ 5.18	+11.47
1971-1980	+20.16	+15.31	+ 8.43	+17.50
1972-1981	+19.68	+14.66	+ 6.45	+17.24
1973-1982	+20.02	+14.48	+ 6.66	+19.66
1974-1983	+24.43©	+16.17	+10.60	+28.39©
1975-1984	+23.50	+16.86	+14.75	+30.38©
1976-1985	+23.93©	+17.05	+14.33	+27.75©
1977-1986	+19.23	+16.53	+13.83	+22.90
1978-1987	+19.33	+16.63	+15.26	+18.98
1979-1988	+21.45	+18.61	+16.32	+18.93
1980-1989	+18.29	+19.56	+17.75©	+15.83
1981-1990	+15.35	+17.74	+13.93	+ 9.32
1982-1991	+18.34	+19.04	− 17.60©	+11.96
1983-1992	+18.39	+17.67	+13.86	+11.55
1984-1993	+16.20	+16.41	+14.25	+ 9.96

*Buy & Hold
⊗The worst three 10 year time periods
©The best three 10 year time periods

This is as good a time as any to address a question that may be coming up with many readers. "O.K," they might ask. "So Super Hits-Plus and Hits-Plus produced superior performance over the S&P 500 Index and the SCSI but these are unmanaged indexes. Just how would Super Hits-Plus and Hits-Plus compare with the best mutual funds with great management?"

There's no doubt if we look back at the past performance records of the *very* *best* managed mutual funds we will see that several have out performed Super Hits-Plus *in* *certain* *time* *frames*. However we have the benefit of hind sight to pick which managed funds were the absolute best during those time frames.

For example we know now that the all time champion for the *longest* duration is Fidelity Magellan under the management of Peter Lynch (and in my opinion he was the very best). If we had the foresight, at the beginning of 1976, to have invested $10,000 in Fidelity Magellan at the end of 1985 (ten years) we would have $187,516 for an average annual compounded return of +34.06%. What a performance!

But if one had bought the SCSI at the beginning of 1976 and held this un-managed index until the end of 1985 the average annual return would have been +27.75%. Not bad either but who could have predicted such a great consistent run by small companies stocks. Another catch is ... if we had waited until 1977 to have bought Fidelity Magellan it would have been too late as the fund was closed to new investors from 1977 through 1980.

Actually Fidelity Magellan wasn't looked on as such a champion in the late sixties and through 1974. Fidelity Magellan drifted down from being a $20 million fund in 1966 to the level of just $6 million by 1976. This happened to most aggressive growth funds as the late sixties and the Grizzly Bear of 1973 and 1974 took its toll. Peter Lynch took over the management of Fidelity Magellan in 1977 and until his retirement in 1990 he did a magnificent job.

But another mutual fund was looked on by many mutual fund newsletter publishers as being the best buy for the aggressive investor. That was the 44 Wall Street Fund. After a big +72.8% year in 1971 it had crashed and burned in 1973 and 1974 but with a +184.1% rebound performance in 1975 many pundits were again saying 44 Wall Street would be the champ (not much mention of Fidelity Magellan). And if we had invested our $10,000 in 44 Wall Street at the beginning of 1976 we would have been pretty happy for the next five years as 44 Wall Street would have given you an average annual compounded return of +39.95%. Of course the un-managed SCSI returned an average of +37.35% over the same period.

But then something happened to the would be champ. As more and more advisors recommended 44 Wall Street it took a -22.55% loss in 1981. It went on to make just single digit gains in 1982 and 1983 and then took a big -58.62% hit in 1984 followed by a -20.13% drop in 1985. The end results is an average annual compounded return of just +4.97% for this ten-year period while most everyone else is doing great.

The point is can we really say which managed mutual fund we would have chosen back in 1976 as our investment vehicle? Do we really know today which funds may be the future Fidelity Magellans and which funds may be the future 44 Wall Streets? I kind of doubt it.

The Worst of Super Hits-Plus is Great

Now we look at Table 12.3 for all possible fifteen-year periods from 1950 through 1993 and again we see the return curve flattens a little more with lower highs and higher lows.

The best performing fifteen-year period represented on Table 12.3 is 1975 through 1989 with the SCSI Buy-and-Hold producing an average annual compounded growth of +23.32%. But, I don't think many of us would want to risk a buy-and-hold commitment to the SCSI when we see there were three such periods that only gave you a single digit return. *The big news,*

Table 12.3

All Possible Fifteen-Year Periods 1950 Thru 1993
Average Annual Compounded % Growth Comparison Table

Years	Super Hits-Plus (no margin) %Growth	Hits-Plus (w/margin) %Growth	S&P 500 B & H* %Growth	S.C.S.I. B & H* %Growth
1950-1964	+19.46	+19.43☺	+16.42☺	+15.04
1951-1965	+17.07	+17.45	+15.20	+15.21
1952-1966	+16.85	+16.13	+12.75	+14.08
1953-1967	+21.43☺	+16.48	+13.10	+18.55
1954-1968	+21.36☺	+16.25	+13.98	+21.55☺
1955-1969	+17.81	+13.24	+10.15	+15.53
1956-1970	+16.70	+11.40	+ 8.44	+12.66
1957-1971	+17.81	+12.60	+ 8.95	+13.50
1958-1972	+17.64	+13.93	+11.06	+15.01
1959-1973	+14.21☹	+10.68	+ 7.28	+ 8.53☹
1960-1974	+14.48☹	+10.25☹	+ 4.31☹	+ 5.86☹
1961-1975	+15.37	+11.68	+ 6.50	+ 9.14☹
1962-1976	+16.73	+11.50	+ 6.32	+10.42
1963-1977	+16.54	+11.70	+ 6.44	+13.05
1964-1978	+15.14☹	+10.09☹	+ 5.44☹	+13.04
1965-1979	+16.30	+10.39☹	+ 5.55☹	+14.17
1966-1980	+18.73	+12.29	+ 6.70	+14.07
1967-1981	+19.27	+12.80	+ 7.10	+15.46
1968-1982	+15.72	+12.37	+ 6.95	+12.88
1969-1983	+18.21	+13.94	+ 7.65	+13.08
1970-1984	+18.86	+14.58	+ 8.73	+14.75
1971-1985	+20.27	+16.50	+10.49	+17.94
1972-1986	+19.58	+16.49	+10.75	+17.26
1973-1987	+19.57	+15.47	+ 9.85	+16.18
1974-1988	+20.77	+16.23	+12.17	+20.72☺
1975-1989	+20.05	+17.95☺	+16.61☺	+23.32☺
1976-1990	+19.24	+16.55	+13.93	+17.96
1977-1991	+18.57	−16.96	−14.33	+17.30
1978-1992	+19.58	+16.98	+15.47	+17.17
1979-1993	+20.87☺	+17.83☺	+15.71☺	+17.01

*Buy & Hold
☹The worst three 15 year time periods
☺The best three 15 year time periods

Table 12.4

All Possible Twenty-Year Periods 1950 Thru 1993
Average Annual Compounded % Growth Comparison Table

Years	*Super Hits-Plus (no margin)* %Growth	Hits-Plus (w/margin) %Growth	*S&P 500 B & H** %Growth	S.C.S.I. B & H* %Growth
1950-1969	+18.47	+16.02	+13.41☺	+16.21
1951-1970	+16.80	+14.60	+12.11☺	+13.23
1952-1971	+17.25	+14.35	+11.66	+13.67
1953-1972	+17.32	+14.38	+11.68	+13.74
1954-1973	+17.62	+14.56	+10.86	+12.03
1955-1974	+15.83⊗	+12.46	+ 6.88	+ 8.20⊗
1956-1975	+15.83⊗	+12.39	+ 7.10	+ 9.50⊗
1957-1976	+18.43	+13.55	+ 7.91	+11.77⊗
1958-1977	+18.25	+13.74	+ 8.12	+13.94
1959-1978	+15.50⊗	+10.92⊗	+ 6.53⊗	+12.30
1960-1979	+16.71	+11.37⊗	+ 6.83⊗	+13.48
1961-1980	+18.27	+12.55	+ 8.31	+15.59
1962-1981	+17.30	+11.85⊗	+ 6.76⊗	+14.74
1963-1982	+17.88	-12.71	+ 8.29	+16.90☺
1964-1983	+18.61	+12.70	+ 8.28	+17.62☺
1965-1984	+18.02	+12.47	+ 7.78	+15.98
1966-1985	+19.18	+13.91	+ 8.65	+15.24
1967-1986	+19.30☺	-14.62	+10.16	+16.05
1968-1987	+15.97	+13.63	+ 9.26	+12.03
1969-1988	+17.08	+14.54	+ 9.54	+11.46
1970-1989	+17.48	-15.95	+11.54	+13.63
1971-1990	+17.72	+16.27☺	+11.14	+13.34
1972-1991	+19.00	+16.83☺	+11.89	+14.57
1973-1992	+19.70☺	+16.02	+11.33	+15.53
1974-1993	+20.50☺	+16.24☺	+12.75☺	+18.82☺

*Buy & Hold
⊗The worst three 20 year time periods
☺The best three 20 year time periods

174

to me, is the average return for the worst three, fifteen-year periods for Super Hits-Plus was an average annual compounded return of +14.69%, which will almost increase your portfolio 8-fold in fifteen years.

The regular Hits-Plus is still doing fine with all fifteen-year periods giving double digit returns as opposed to fifteen time periods in single digits with the S&P 500 Buy-and-Hold strategy.

Looking over Table 12.4 representing all possible twenty-year periods from 1950 through 1993, and we see that the lowest Super Hits-Plus return is an average annual compounded return of 15.5% which would increase the value of your portfolio 17.85 times. That's turning $10,000 into $178,500 or $100,000 into $1,785,000 (taxes not figured). *The average annual compounded return for all twenty-year periods (from 1950 through1993) with Super Hits-Plus was +17.76% which would increase the value of your portfolio over 26-fold.*

Regular Hits-Plus's worst twenty-year periods produced average annual compounded returns of +10.92%, +11.37% and +11.85%, with the average twenty-year period earning an average annual compounded return of +13.94%.

The S&P 500 Buy-and-Hold investor's best twenty-year period was less than the Hits-Plus average twenty-year period. The S&P 500 Buy-and-Hold portfolio featured 14 out of 25 twenty-year periods with single digit compounded interest results and an average of compounded returns of +9.55%. As we would expect the SCSI Buy-and-Hold strategist would have had superior performance over the S&P 500 Buy-and-Hold position (although with more volatility). Still the SCSI Buy-and-Hold approach had two twenty-year periods with single digit compounded returns and an average of +13.98% compounded growth.

For those who want to see how Super Hits-Plus, Hits-Plus, S&P 500 Buy-and-Hold and SCSI Buy-and-Hold compared during the chaotic times from 1929 through 1949, take a look at Table's 12.5, 12.6, 12.7 and 12.8. Surprisingly,

175

Table 12.5

All Possible Five-Year Periods 1929 Thru 1949
Average Annual Compounded % Growth Comparison Table

Super Hits-Plus (no margin)		Hits-Plus (w/margin)	S&P 500 B & H*	S.C.S.I. B & H*
Years	%Growth	%Growth	%Growth	%Growth
1929-1933	+ 7.88②	+ 9.74	(-11.24)②	(-19.06)②
1930-1934	+11.50	+ 8.41	(- 9.93)②	(- 2.37)
1931-1935	+35.03	+25.98①	+ 3.12	+14.99
1932-1936	+49.25①	+33.59①	+22.47①	+45.83①
1933-1937	+47.67①	+28.75①	+14.29	+23.96
1934-1938	+29.03	+18.63	+10.67	+ 9.86
1935-1939	+21.85	+17.72	+10.91	+ 5.27
1936-1940	+14.26	+ 8.48	+ 0.50	(- 2.64)②
1937-1941	+ 1.46②	(- 1.69)②	(- 7.51)②	(-13.55)②
1938-1942	+ 9.02①	+ 4.92②	+ 4.62	+10.70
1939-1943	+18.41	+ 6.13①	+ 3.77	+18.71
1940-1944	+31.09	+10.99	+ 7.67	+29.28
1941-1945	+45.90	+18.60	+16.96①	+45.90①
1942-1946	+48.90①	+23.61	+17.87①	+45.05①
1943-1947	+38.57	+16.92	+14.86	+35.00
1944-1948	+21.56	+13.24	+10.87	+18.43
1945-1949	+15.64	+16.22	+10.69	+12.66

*Buy & Hold
②The worst three 5 year time periods
①The best three 5 year time periods

176

Table 12.6

All Possible Ten-Year Periods 1929-1949
Average Annual Compounded %Growth Comparison Table

Super Hits-Plus (no margin)		Hits-Plus (w/margin)	S&P 500 B & H*	S.C.S. I.B & H*
Years	% Growth	% Growth	% Growth	% Growth
1929-1938	+17.99⊗	+14.10	(-0.09)⊗	(-5.70)⊗
1930-1939	+16.56⊗	+12.97	(-0.05)⊗	+1.38⊗
1931-1940	-24.21	+16.90⊙	+1.80⊗	+5.81⊗
1932-1941	+23.05	+14.60⊙	+6.43	+12.28
1933-1942	+26.88⊙	+16.23⊙	+9.35⊙	+17.14
1934-1943	+23.72	+12.21	+7.17	+14.20
1935-1944	+26.38⊙	+14.30	+9.28⊙	+16.66
1936-1945	+29.11⊙	+13.43	+8.42	+19.18⊙
1937-1946	+22.91	+10.24⊗	+4.41	+11.98
1938-1947	+22.91	+10.75⊗	+0.62	+22.24⊙
1939-1948	-19.97⊗	+9.63⊗	+7.26	+18.57
1940-1949	+23.12	+13.58	+9.17⊙	+20.69⊙

*Buy & Hold
⊗The worst three 10 year time periods
⊙The best three 10 year time periods

Table12.7

All Possible Fifteen-Year Periods 1929-1949
Average Annual Compounded % Growth Comparison Table

Super Hits-Plus (no margin)		Hits-Plus (w/margin)	*S&P 500 B & H**	S.C.S.I B & H*
Years	%Growth	%Growth	%Growth	%Growth
1929-1943	+18.20⊗	+11.38⊗	+ 6.44⊗	+ 1.81☺
1930-1944	+21.21⊗	+12.31⊗	+ 2.46⊗	+ 9.93⊗
1931-1945	+31.06☺	+17.47☺	+ 6.62⊗	+17.76☺
1932-1946	+31.13☺	+17.53☺	+10.11☺	+22.28☺
1933-1947	+30.67☺	+16.46☺	+11.15☺	+22.80☺
1934-1948	+23.00	+12.55⊗	+ 8.39	+15.59
1935-1949	+22.70⊗	+14.94	+ 9.74☺	+15.31⊗

*Buy & Hold
⊗The worst three 15 year time periods
☺The best three 15 year time periods

Table 12.8

All Possible Twenty-Year Periods 1929-1949
Average Annual Compounded % Growth Comparison Table

Super Hits-Plus (no margin)		Hits-Plus (w/margin)	*S&P 500 B & H**	S.C.S.I. B & H*
Years	%Growth	%Growth	%Growth	%Growth
1929-1948	+19.03	+11.84	+ 3.11	+ 5.74
1930-1949	+19.79	+13.27	+ 4.46	+10.61

considering the overall time frame, Super Hits-Plus only had one really bad five-year period (1937 through 1941). Even medium to high single digit performance (during this time of depression, virtual no inflation and low interest rates) would have been considered excellent.

When we move to Table 12.6 (ten-year periods) the very idea of putting a "frown face" beside an average annual compounded return of +16.56% seems ridiculous, but that was the worst ten-year period for Super Hits-Plus. Actually the high volatility of these times seemed to help Super Hits-Plus. Both buy-and-hold approaches put "frown faces" beside some pretty bad performance time periods.

Sorry, No Crystal Ball

So what can we properly surmise from all these tables? Since no one has a fool-proof crystal ball we just can't predict the future. The future could bring forth some record breaking time periods both with higher highs or lower lows in average annual compounded returns. However I certainly wouldn't count on future higher performing five-year periods for Super Hits-Plus as we saw from 1932 through 1936, 1933 through 1937, 1942 through 1946 and 1943 through 1947. If we do have another high producing nine-year run with the SCSI as we had from 1975 through 1983 I doubt anyone can predict when and how it will happen.

We can't rule out that Super Hits-Plus won't have a lower producing five-year period than 1968 through 1972 or 1937 through 1941. The same is true of all other strategies one might employ. But, historically the odds would be that we hopefully can expect future performances similar to the past. If I was going to predict the future (which I absolutely will not do) I would invest for a ten-year time period, or more, and count on it producing the lowest return that has occurred for a ten-year period in the past, while hoping that I would experience performance of the past averages or better.

Some investors might wish to have one investment portfolio follow the regular Hits-Plus system while having another utilizing the Super Hits-Plus strategy. Why? If you go back and look at all possible five-year periods (there were a total of forty) you will find that with these shorter time spans regular Hits-Plus did out-perform Super Hits-Plus very nicely in ten five-year periods and was about even in three others. A 50/50 balance in strategies would have evened things out a bit due to the higher volatility of the Super Hits-Plus approach.

When we look at the ten-year time periods (there were a total of thirty six) there were five ten-year periods when regular Hits-Plus out-performed Super Hits-Plus in a good manner and two others when it was better but just barely.

However when we look at all possible fifteen-year time periods (there were a total of thirty), from 1950 through 1993, Super Hits-Plus is the winner in all but one time period (1951 through 1964) and that was very close. 1950 through 1963 was also virtually a tie. But after that it was no contest in all twenty-year time periods with Super Hits-Plus beating everything without a problem.

While we can't correctly predict the future, from past historical performance, an investor might consider splitting his/her investment portfolios between regular Hits-Plus and Super Hits-Plus unless they are sure they won't need to touch their investment money for a long time frame and volatillity will not over tax their patience and discipline. This would have to be a judgment decision by the individual investor.

Chapter Thirteen covers the power of compounded interest with various tables on compounded return results. Some additional exploration of this is brought out in Chapter Fourteen and Chapter Eighteen, but you might like to study Table 12.9 here to see what sort of average annual com

Table 12.9
Annual Compounded% Return Needed to Increase Your Portfolio

Years Needed	2-Fold	3-Fold	4-Fold	5-Fold	6-Fold	7-Fold	8-Fold	9-Fold	10-Fold	11-Fold	12-Fold	13-Fold	14-Fold	15-Fold	16-Fold
8	9.05%	14.72%	18.92%	22.28%	25.10%	27.54%	29.68%	31.61%	33.35%	34.95%	36.43%	37.80%	39.08%	40.28%	41.42%
9	8.00%	12.98%	16.65%	19.58%	22.03%	24.14%	26.00%	27.65%	29.15%	30.53%	31.80%	32.97%	34.07%	35.11%	36.08%
10	7.18%	11.61%	14.87%	17.46%	19.62%	21.48%	23.11%	24.57%	25.89%	27.10%	28.21%	29.24%	30.20%	31.10%	31.95%
11	6.50%	10.50%	13.43%	15.76%	17.69%	19.35%	20.81%	22.11%	23.28%	24.36%	25.34%	26.26%	27.11%	27.91%	28.67%
12	5.95%	9.59%	12.25%	14.35%	16.10%	17.60%	18.92%	20.09%	21.15%	22.12%	23.01%	23.83%	24.60%	25.32%	25.99%
13	5.47%	8.82%	11.25%	13.18%	14.78%	16.15%	17.35%	18.41%	19.38%	20.26%	21.06%	21.81%	22.51%	23.16%	23.77%
14	5.07%	8.16%	10.41%	12.18%	13.65%	14.91%	16.01%	16.99%	17.88%	18.68%	19.42%	20.11%	20.74%	21.34%	21.90%
15	4.73%	7.60%	9.68%	11.33%	12.69%	13.85%	14.87%	15.78%	16.59%	17.33%	18.02%	18.65%	19.24%	19.79%	20.30%
16	4.43%	7.11%	9.05%	10.58%	11.85%	12.93%	13.88%	14.72%	15.47%	16.17%	16.80%	17.39%	17.93%	18.44%	18.92%
17	4.16%	6.68%	8.50%	9.93%	11.11%	12.13%	13.01%	13.80%	14.50%	15.14%	15.74%	16.29%	16.79%	17.27%	17.71%
18		6.29%	8.00%	9.35%	10.47%	11.42%	12.24%	12.98%	13.65%	14.25%	14.80%	15.31%	15.79%	16.24%	16.65%
19		5.95%	7.57%	8.84%	9.89%	10.78%	11.57%	12.26%	12.88%	13.45%	13.97%	14.45%	14.90%	15.32%	15.71%
20		5.65%	7.18%	8.38%	9.37%	10.22%	10.96%	11.61%	12.20%	12.74%	13.23%	13.68%	14.11%	14.50%	14.87%
21		5.37%	6.82%	7.91%	8.91%	9.71%	10.41%	11.03%	11.59%	12.09%	12.56%	12.99%	13.39%	13.76%	14.11%
22		5.12%	6.50%	7.59%	8.48%	9.25%	9.91%	10.50%	11.03%	11.52%	11.96%	12.37%	12.74%	13.10%	13.43%
23		4.89%	6.21%	7.25%	8.10%	8.83%	9.46%	10.02%	10.53%	10.99%	11.41%	11.80%	12.16%	12.50%	12.81%
24			5.95%	6.93%	7.75%	8.44%	9.05%	9.59%	10.07%	10.51%	10.91%	11.28%	11.62%	11.94%	12.25%
25			5.70%	6.69%	7.43%	8.09%	8.67%	9.18%	9.65%	10.06%	10.45%	10.80%	11.13%	11.44%	11.73%

pounded return you would need to grow your portfolio to a certain level. For example if your goal is to triple (3-fold) your portfolio's value in five years you'll see you will need to earn an average annual compounded return of 24.57%.

To increase the value of your portfolio by five times (5-fold) its current value in ten years you would need an average annual compounded return of 17.46%.

Basically the investor should be aware of past performance history covering many different types of time frames and he should set return goals in keeping with logical expectations.

PART THREE
Other Stuff, Some Important

CHAPTER THIRTEEN
The Power of
Compounded Interest

"Money makes money. And the money that money makes makes more money."

-- Benjamin Franklin

I could stop right there with that Benjamin Franklin quote as it really explains quite well what compounded interest is all about.

At various times I have heard of compounded interest being referred to as "The *Magic* of Compounded Interest" or "The *Mystery* of Compounded Interest." I don't like either of these references since there's nothing magical or mysterious about it. It's just like Ben Franklin said: Money that makes money makes more money. And it all continues to add up. I prefer to call it "The *Power* of Compounded Interest."

So much has been written about the power of compounded interest that you may feel you are thoroughly drenched with the subject by now. As such, this chapter will be rather brief, but you might just discover a little something new about compounded interest.

An Ideal Thirty-Day Job

My first brush with the idea (and power) of compounded interest came when I was a youngster and someone asked me, "You are offered a job by two people doing the same type work, and the job is to last thirty days. Offer "A" is going to pay you $1,000 per day for the thirty days, and offer "B" is going to pay you one cent the first day but would double that daily pay each day. Which job would you take?"

My first response was that $30,000 for thirty days work would really be great, and a penny a day even doubling it daily sounded mighty cheap. Even in my head, I could calculate that after ten days I would have earned just a little over $10.00. What I did do was go home and work it out (in those days without a calculator), and when I saw the results, I thought in terms of <u>Magic</u>, <u>Mystery</u>, and <u>Unbelievable</u>.

Table 13.1 shows my tabulations.

You know and I know that we won't be receiving any such job offer and we won't find any kind of investment vehicle that will double our money every day. But we also know that we can double our money every five years with an average annual compounded return of +15%, and we can double our money every four years with an average annual compounded return of +19%. We know that this is very much in the range of probability with Hits-Plus or Super Hits-Plus and hopefully we will be working with more than just doubling

Table 13.1

$1000 a Day Vs. 1 Cent a Day Compounded

	Offer A		Offer B
Day	**Amount in $**	**Day**	**Amount in $**
1	1,000	1	.01
2	1,000	2	.02
3	1,000	3	.04
4	1,000	4	.08
5	1,000	5	.16
6	1,000	6	.32
7	1,000	7	.64
8	1,000	8	1.28
9	1,000	9	2.56
10	1,000	10	5.12
11	1,000	11	10.24
12	1,000	12	20.48
13	1,000	13	40.96
14	1,000	14	81.92
15	1,000	15	163.84
16	1,000	16	327.68
17	1,000	17	655.00
18	1,000	18	1,310
19	1,000	19	2,620
20	1,000	20	5,240
21	1,000	21	10,480
22	1,000	22	20,960
23	1,000	23	41,920
24	1,000	24	83,840
25	1,000	25	167,680
26	1,000	26	335,360
27	1,000	27	670,720
28	1,000	28	1,341,440
29	1,000	29	2,682,880
30	1,000	30	5,365,760
Total	**$30,000**		**$10,731,520**

Table 13.2

$10,000 One Lump Invested at Various Compounded Interest Rates

Interest Rate	5 Years	10 Years	15 Years	20 Years	25 Years	30 Years
8%	$14,693	$21,589	$31,722	$46,610	$68,485	$100,627
9%	$15,386	$23,674	$36,425	$56,044	$86,231	$132,677
10%	$16,105	$25,937	$41,772	$67,275	$108,347	$174,494
11%	$16,851	$28,394	$47,846	$80,623	$135,855	$228,923
12%	$17,623	$31,058	$54,736	$96,463	$170,001	$299,599
13%	$18,424	$33,946	$62,543	$115,231	$212,354	$391,159
14%	$19,254	$37,072	$71,379	$137,435	$264,619	$509,501
15%	$20,114	$40,455	$81,371	$163,665	$329,189	$662,118
16%	$21,003	$44,114	$92,655	$194,608	$408,742	$858,499
17%	$21,924	$48,068	$105,387	$231,056	$506,578	$1,110,646
18%	$22,877	$52,338	$119,737	$273,930	$626,686	$1,433,706
19%	$23,863	$56,947	$135,895	$324,294	$773,881	$1,846,531
20%	$24,863	$61,917	$154,070	$383,376	$953,962	$2,373,763
21%	$25,937	$67,275	$174,494	$452,592	$1,173,908	$3,004,816
22%	$27,027	$73,046	$197,423	$533,576	$1,442,101	$3,897,579
23%	$28,153	$79,259	$223,139	$628,206	$1,768,592	$4,979,128
24%	$29,316	$85,944	$251,956	$738,641	$2,165,420	$6,348,199

the value of a penny.

We have already seen excellent examples of the results of compounded interest with the tracking of Hits-Plus and Super Hits-Plus over the years with the starting sum of $10,000. However, it might be good to look at Table 13.2 to grasp again how various compounded interest rates will cause your investment to grow.

Two things should become very obvious to us when we look back over the above $10,000 one lump compounded interest table. First, time is important to really make the big dollars come about through compounded earning power. Even at just an 8% return you more than double your money in ten years and you reach the tenth multiple after thirty years. Second, you will note how much difference a few more percentage points in growth will make in your level of achievement.

Remember in the 44-year period from 1950 thorough 1993, Hits-Plus gave us an average annual compounded return of over +16%. This would almost put us to the tenth multiple in fifteen years. With Super Hits-Plus you would have reached the tenth multiple in thirteen and a half years. The longer the time period the more just one or two percentage points makes in what multiple levels of growth you achieve.

A simple conclusion would be that one should strive to earn more in compounded return and hang in there for the long duration to achieve a really nice multiple level reward.

Watch Out for "Mr. Slick"

A dangerous conclusion would be for us to decide that we're going to put all our investment in high risk areas in an effort to leap to a really big multiple level in a relatively short time period. It's the people who are in this frame of mind that are most susceptible to the unsolicited telephone calls from "Mr. Slick" who's going to double your money in just a year or less with options or futures in some uranium mines or high flying penny stocks.

Math with Washington's Smoke and Mirrors

I am convinced that one reason the politicians in Washington can put so much over on us taxpayers is that too many of us lack a basic understanding of simple math. I remember when the capital gains tax was raised from a maximum of 20% to 28% plus. I gave the general argument to friends of mine that this put the U.S.A. in a position of taxing capital gains much higher than the other industrial nations that were our main competitors and would result in a lesser incentive to invest and hurt the American economy a few years down the road. Plus the capital gains tax contained many unfair factors. For example, the money you are investing has already been earned and taxed, only to be taxed again when and if it earns more. At the time of this writing inflation is not indexed into capital gains so if you only earned 8% on your investment and inflation ran 8% over that same time period, you are then being taxed on a gain that never really took place. If your investment lost money, you could face-off those losses against possible gains in the future over a long period of time, but you might die first, and your tax credit would die with you—bad for your heirs, good for Washington.

"You may be right," some of my liberal friends would reply. "But, after all, we're only talking about an 8% increase in the capital gains tax."

"Not so," I would say. "Look again. The tax rate went up eight percentage points but its a whopping forty percent increase in taxes paid." I would then go on to explain that eight is 40% of twenty. If you had achieved a capital gains of $100,000 at a 20% tax rate you would pay $20,000 in taxes. At a 28% tax rate you would pay $28,000. That's $8,000 more paid in taxes, i.e., 40% more than $20,000. Now, this is so very simple, and I'm sure most of you readers knew this all along, but you would be astounded at how many of our fellow citizens never even think in these terms.

In any event, I don't want this to be a political book and we will need to save and invest on our own, regardless of the national political climate, to ever hope to enjoy a decent standard of living in retirement. If you think Washington is going to take care of you during your golden years then you still might be the perfect candidate to buy some swamp land. Oh well, let's get rid of the soap box and get on with our study of compounded interest.

No One Lump; Go by the Month

Table 13.3 gives us the results of compounded interest at various rates of return from $200 per month being invested.

This would be like "dollar cost averaging" investing, which we will cover in a later chapter, except in this case we are assuming a fixed interest rate return or an average of that percentage return compounded monthly.

I have chosen the monthly savings and investment figure to be $200 per month. Of course, if you plan to save and invest $100 per month, divide the results by two. If you can save and invest $600 per month, multiply the results by three. You will also note that I have selected different terms of years for Table 13.3: 5 years, 8 years, 10 years, 15 years, 20 years, and 25 years. I will explain the reason for this shortly.

The $200 per month saving and investment table shows us that we can achieve excellent results even if we don't have $10,000 in a one lump sum to start out with. It shows that if we only receive an +8% compounded return, our $200 per month investment will catch up with the $10,000 one lump +8% return investor in just five years.

Various Time Frames; Various Goals

I decrease the number of years on the $200 per month investment chart for several reasons. If you are married with young children you may decide that your monthly investment will be to build a college fund for your children's education

Table 13.3

$200 Per Month Invested at Various Monthly Compounded Interest Rates

Interest Rate	5 Years	8 Years	10 Years	15 Years	20 Years	25 Years
8%	$14,695	$26,774	$36,589	$ 69,208	$ 117,804	$ 190,205
9%	$15,085	$27,971	$38,703	$ 75,681	$ 133,577	$ 224,224
10%	$15,487	$29,236	$40,969	$ 82,894	$ 151,873	$ 265,367
11%	$15,904	$30,573	$43,400	$ 90,938	$ 173,128	$ 315,227
12%	$16,334	$31,985	$46,008	$ 99,916	$ 197,851	$ 375,769
13%	$16,779	$33,479	$48,807	$109,945	$ 226,648	$ 449,418
14%	$17,239	$35,058	$51,813	$121,157	$ 260,233	$ 539,165
15%	$17,715	$36,728	$55,043	$133,701	$ 299,448	$ 648,706
16%	$18,207	$38,495	$58,514	$147,746	$ 345,288	$ 782,609
17%	$18,716	$40,365	$62,245	$163,482	$ 398,932	$ 946,525
18%	$19,243	$42,344	$66,258	$181,125	$ 461,771	$1,147,451
19%	$19,788	$44,439	$70,574	$200,919	$ 535,453	$1,394,049
20%	$20,352	$46,657	$75,219	$223,140	$ 621,930	$1,697,057
21%	$20,935	$49,007	$80,219	$248,101	$ 723,512	$2,069,788
22%	$21,539	$51,497	$85,603	$276,157	$ 842,936	$2,528,756
23%	$22,164	$54,134	$91,403	$307,707	$ 983,445	$3,094,459
24%	$22,810	$56,929	$97,652	$343,208	$1,148,887	$3,792,345

and you have just five, eight, ten or fifteen years to achieve this goal needed for the education fund. You may feel that when your children reach college age you will be able to pay for their education from your regular income but you need to build up your own retirement fund for the next number of years until they do go off to college. Maybe you're forty-five or fifty years old now and suddenly you realize you're going to need to save and invest over the next fifteen or twenty years in order to have a retirement fund needed to enjoy a decent standard of living when you do retire.

Reaching for the Million Dollars

Even though a million dollars ($1,000,000) is not what it used to be, it's still not a bad level of achievement. By combining Tables 13.2 and 13.3, we will find that if we did have a one lump sum of $10,000 and could also invest $200 per month at a 15% annual compounded return on the $10,000 and a 15% monthly compounded return on the $200 per month, we would reach $977,895 in twenty-five years. Suppose you have the $10,000 one lump but you need to reach as high a multiple level as possible in twenty years and you can invest $450 per month during that time frame. With this scenario you could reach $837,423 in twenty years with the 15% compounded returns.

Then you may not have a one lump sum of capital at all but feel because of your new raise and cutting back on living expenses a bit you could save and invest $600 per month for ten years. But, then you would have to stop and let whatever you had achieved by that time continue to grow for an additional five to fifteen years. By looking at the $200 per month chart and multiplying the results by three ($200 x 3 =$600 per month), you would find that at a monthly compounded growth rate of 15% you would have reached $165,129 in ten years when you would stop your monthly savings and investing program for whatever reason and let the $165,129 one lump grow on into the future. Looking back at the $10,000 one lump table we find this sum is almost identical to where the $10,000 one lump would be in twenty years at an annual 15% compounded growth rate. So, we see that $600 per month saved and invested would reach the same multiple as the $10,000 one lump in half the time. From then on, we can project the growth of our $165,129 from the one lump chart. At an annual 15% compounded return we should have over $330,000 in the next five years, over $660,000 in the next ten years, and over $1,300,000 in the next fifteen years. That's achieving over $1,330,000 in an overall time frame of twenty-five years by saving and investing $600 per month for the first ten years and then stopping.

The Early Bird Gets the Most Money

The important thing is to start a savings and investment programs as soon as possible—like now. Table 13.4 will show you how starting early and then stopping is much better than waiting until later and then starting a savings and investing program.

Table 13.4 is correct. Even though as the early starter, you stopped your $900 per month savings and investing program after just eight years, you have beaten the late starter almost two-to-one and he's put $900 a month away for twenty-two years. Actually, you would still have him beaten after eight additional years (a total of thirty investment years for the late starter), having him down by over $4,000,000 that is. In fact, if the early starter just invested $500 per month for eight years and stopped, he or she would still have more than the $900 per month late starting investor at the end of the total thirty-year period.

Table 13.4
$900 Per Month at 15% a Month Compounded Return

	Starting Early		Starting Late	
Year	Monthly Investment	End-of-Year Value	Monthly Investment	End-of-Year Value
1	$900	$11,574	0	0
2	$900	$25,009	0	0
3	$900	$40,603	0	0
4	$900	$58,705	0	0
5	$900	$79,717	0	0
6	$900	$104,106	0	0
7	$900	$132,416	0	0
8	$900	$165,277	0	0
9	0	$190,069	$900	$11,574
10	0	$218,579	$900	$25,009
11	0	$251,366	$900	$40,603
12	0	$289,071	$900	$58,705
13	0	$332,431	$900	$79,717
14	0	$382,296	$900	$104,106
15	0	$439,640	$900	$132,416
16	0	$505,586	$900	$165,277
17	0	$581,424	$900	$203,120
18	0	$668,638	$900	$257,695
19	0	$768,934	$900	$299,087
20	0	$884,274	$900	$358,742
21	0	$1,016,915	$900	$427,985
22	0	$1,169,452	$900	$508,360
23	0	$1,344,870	$900	$601,655
24	0	$1,546,600	$900	$709,949
25	0	$1,778,590	$900	$835,651
26	0	$2,045,379	$900	$981,560
27	0	$2,352,186	$900	$1,150,924
28	0	$2,705,014	$900	$1,347,515
29	0	$3,110,766	$900	$1,575,708
30	0	$3,577,381	$900	$1,840,585

And then there's progressive dollar cost averaging that we will cover more in Chapter Sixteen. But for now let's say the early starter invested only $300 a month the first year, $400 per month the second year, $500 per month the third year, $600 per month the forth year, $700 per month the fifth, $800 per month the sixth, $900 per month the seventh year, and still $900 per month for the eighth year and then stopped. How would he or she stack up against the $900 per month late starter? The early starter wins again with $398,780 more money at the end of the overall 30-year period.

We will refer back to Table 13.4 in later chapters. It is very important that you start a savings and investing program as soon as possible no matter how young or old you may be at this time.

Of course, we have not figured your personal income taxes, as is the case on all gains in this book because individual tax situations vary so much. You would have to pay Federal Income Tax and probably State Income Tax on this growth each year unless it took place within an IRA account which could be $166.66 per month for you or $333.33 for you and your spouse. This monthly investment is based on $2,000 per year that can be invested in an IRA by each working spouse. In order to invest the annual maximum of $2,000 in a IRA, this $2,000 must be earned (salaries, self-employed income, etc.), not unearned (dividends, etc.) income. Then all of the growth would take place untaxed until you began to withdraw from your IRA account. At the time of this writing, you can start withdrawing at 59 1/2 years old without penalty and mandatory withdrawals are required at the age of 70 1/2.

You might well qualify to invest $900 per month or even more in a self-directed 401(k) program. And then there are variable annuities which we will cover in a later chapter. All of these could grow un-taxed until withdrawal time, but you could not use margin if you followed a Hits-Plus investment program. However, even without margin Hits-Plus and Super Hits-Plus performs quite well.

A savings and investing program is started for many reasons: education for your children; a better future standard of living for you and your family; comfortable and fun-filled retirement years for you and your spouse; and to leave some sort of financial helping hand to your children, grand children, favorite charity, or whatever. Never mind Washington; they will get their pound of financial flesh sooner or later anyway.

But, in the next chapter let's look toward what we would all hope to be golden retirement years.

CHAPTER FOURTEEN

The Golden Retirement Years

"I'm working as hard as I can to get my life and my cash to run out at the same time. If I can just die after lunch Tuesday, everything will be fine."
-- *Doug Sanders, Golf Pro*

Most of us don't even want to think about that ultimate time of dealing with our mortality. A lot of people won't make out their wills because that action in itself admits they are indeed mortal. This is a rather stupid position to take.

There is a story about an old gentleman that once lived in my home town that may tie in some with what Doug Sanders said. The story goes that Harvey came from a fairly well off family that left him a nest egg when Harvey was in his early forties. This was back when life expectancy for males did not exceed the age of 60, and age 65 was considered really old.

Harvey's Plan

Harvey decided he would place his inheritance in fixed income CDs and Government Bonds, and if he withdrew the interest plus a predetermined amount of the principal, his funds wouldn't zero out until he was 65 years old. Harvey figured he wouldn't work any more, he'd just live it up and have a good time until he died sometime before he reached the age of 65. Harvey was wrong in several areas. Actually, the return on some of his rolled over CDs and Bonds increased but inflation increased too.

The main thing, however, was when Harvey reached the age of 65 he was healthy as a horse and stone broke. Harvey worked for the next twenty years running a little run-down tavern. He passed away around the age of 85. I remember him as being a very grouchy individual. Harvey's experience points out how you can't (and shouldn't try) to predict your life span. Neither should most people count on conservative bonds and CDs to be their main source of retirement income.

There is a general consensus that when you reach a certain age (55 or 65??), it's preferable to go real conservative with your investments, putting most of your capital in fixed-income vehicles. I don't agree with this assumption. A little more conservative, perhaps. But, going totally fixed-income conservative could be a big mistake.

As an ex-advertising man and a history buff I have collected a lot of ads from old magazines: *Life*, *Colliers*, *Look*, *Saturday Evening Post*, etc. Among these ads are two from a well known insurance company, each advertising retirement (fixed rate) annuities.

The $250 a Month Retiree

The first ad is from the year 1954. It shows a man happily fishing in the surf and proclaiming "How I retired in 15 years with $250 a month." The ad goes on to say how he answered the insurance company's ad back in 1939 when he was forty years old and started investing in an annuity that led to that happy day in 1954 when he retired at just fifty-five years of age on his monthly check of $250 a month guaranteed for life.

There were several factors that could have influenced this poor man to invest in fixed annuities at that time. In 1939 we were still in perilous economic times and a guaranteed monthly income would sound mighty good. And believe it or not you could live very well on $250 a month back during those times. There was no inflation then. In fact, 1938 and 1939 were deflation years. But, over the next fifteen years, the gentleman should have become aware of inflation as it averaged about 4.5% per year.

I would suppose that the first ten years of this man's retirement went O.K. as inflation from 1954 through 1964 only averaged about 1.5% per year. This did, however, cause the insurance company to change its ad in 1964 to pushing retirement at $300 per month.

The Killer Inflation

I'm sure the next ten years put our $250 a month retiree into a real financial dilemma as from 1964 through 1974 inflation averaged over 5% per year with 1974 itself being a tremendous 12.2%. Our retiree is now 75 years old and still trying to live on $250 a month plus what little he gets from social security. An inflation rate of only 5% per year would call for our retiree to need $428 a month in eleven years, so by now he would need that much just to tread water and I know this sounds very small by today's standards.

The next five years, from 1974 through 1979, saw inflation average over 8% per year. I don't know what our $250 a month retiree, now at eighty years old, would be doing. With inflation averaging over 6% for fifteen years, our retiree would need almost $800 a month or more to live real cheap. I expect he would have had to have started operating a little run-down tavern like Harvey did sometime around his seventieth birthday..

The $300 a Month Retiree

The case of the 1964 retiree would be even worse. That 1964 insurance company ad showed a man and his wife living it up on a Florida beach bragging about how he started investing in the insurance annuity fifteen years prior, in 1949, and was now enjoying his golden years on $300 a month. There wasn't a great deal of inflation in the United States from 1949 through 1964 but after that we saw inflation like never before.

You guessed it, I want to run a little comparison with Hits-Plus and Super Hits-Plus from 1949 through 1963 and lets see how the Hits-Plus or Super Hits-Plus retiree would compare.

The Hits-Plus Build-Up Time

I will have our Hits-Plus man invest $2,000 per year at the beginning of each year starting in January 1949 and ending in December 1963 when he retires (See Table 14.1). I believe this would represent a smaller investment than the insurance annuity candidate who began his retirement investment at the same time and stopped to retire at the same time on his $300 per month check.

Our Hits-Plus retiree has accumulated $158,697 in fifteen years by just investing $2,000 at the beginning of each year. I admit that this fifteen-year period represents a pretty good time frame for Hits-Plus, but we will examine other time frames as well.

The Hits-Plus 8% Retiree

Now we will have our Hits-Plus retiree stay with the Hits-Plus program but he will withdraw 8% of the total value balance from his S&P 500 Index Fund or T-Bill/Bonds Funds at the beginning of each year and put it in a money fund to write his monthly retirement checks on (See Table 14.2). In reality

Table 14.1

"Hits-Plus" Retirement Program 1949 Through 1963

Year	Investment	Year's Performance	End-of-Year Value	$ Added for Next Year
1949	$ 2,000	+35.9%	$ 2,718	$2,000
1950	$ 4,718	+31.7	$ 6,214	$2,000
1951	$ 8,214	+24.0	$ 10,185	$2,000
1952	$ 12,185	+18.4	$ 14,427	$2,000
1953	$ 16,427	+ 2.5	$ 16,838	$2,000
1954	$ 18,838	+52.6	$ 28,747	$2,000
1955	$ 30,747	+31.6	$ 40,463	$2,000
1956	$ 42,463	+ 1.0	$ 42,888	$2,000
1957	$ 44,888	- .02	$ 44,798	$2,000
1958	$ 46,798	+63.1	$ 76,328	$2,000
1959	$ 78,328	+12.0	$ 87,727	$2,000
1960	$ 89,727	+ 7.2	$ 96,187	$2,000
1961	$ 98,187	+26.9	$124,599	$2,000
1962	$126,599	+ .05	$127,232	$2,000
1963	$129,232	+22.8	$158,697	

Table 14.2

	"Hits-Plus" 8% Retirement Withdrawal			
Year	8% Withdrawal	$ After Withdrawal	Year's Performance	End-of-Year Value
1964	$12,740	$146,508	+16.5%	$170,682
1965	$13,655	$157,027	+ 2.5	$160,953
1966	$12,876	$148,077	+ 4.7	$155,037
1967	$12,403	$142,634	+24.0	$176,886
1968	$14,149	$162,717	- .05	$161,903
1969	$12,952	$148,951	+ 2.9	$153,271
1970	$12,262	$141,009	+ 2.9	$145,098
1971	$11,608	$133,490	+18.6	$158,319
1972	$12,666	$145,653	+19.0	$173,327
1973	$13,866	$159,461	+ 5.8	$168,710
1974	$13,497	$155,213	+ 5.6	$163,905
1975	$13,112	$150,793	+30.0	$196,031
1976	$15,682	$180,349	+23.8	$223,272
1977	$17,862	$205,410	+ 3.3	$212,189
1978	$16,975	$195,014	- 1.2	$192,871
1979	$15,430	$177,441	+21.3	$215,236
1980	$17,219	$198,017	+32.4	$262,175
1981	$20,974	$241,201	+12.1	$270,386
1982	$21,631	$248,755	+17.1	$291,292
1983	$23,202	$267,989	+22.5	$328,287
1984	$26,263	$302,024	+11.9	$337,965
1985	$27,037	$310,928	+32.2	$411,047
1986	$32,884	$378,163	+18.5	$448,123
1987	$35,850	$412,273	+ 4.2	$429,588
1988	$34,367	$395,221	+16.8	$461,618
1989	$36,929	$424,689	+31.5	$558,466
1990	$44,677	$513,789	+ 8.8	$558,466
1991	$44,720	$514,282	+30.6	$671,652
1992	$53,732	$617,920	+ 4.2	$643,873
1993	$51,510	$592,363	+10.0	$651,160

he could choose to simply write checks on the mutual funds themselves but I have chosen to handle it this way for the simplicity of tabulation. Bare in mind our Hits-Plus retiree continues to manage his or her retirement portfolio via the Hits-Plus System, i.e., switching from the S&P 500 Index Fund to a money fund and bond funds as called for and back again, etc. Table 14.2 shows that while your annual 8% withdrawal will vary from year to year it will increase, in general, over the years to more than keep up with inflation. You will also note that the end-of-year value of your retirement fund also varies, but increases, in general, to a very nice level as time passes.

I don't think there's any question about how much better our Hits-Plus retiree fared compared to the $300 a month insurance annuity gentleman. *We see at once that the Hits-Plus retiree starts off drawing over three times more per month than the annuitant.*

To see how the Super Hits-Plus (without the use of margin) 8% retiree made out look at Tables 14.3 and 14.4.

The Big Benefits of the IRA

Of course, we have not figured personal taxes, and this Hits-Plus program did use margin in the years 1949, 1958, 1971,1975 and 1979. However, let's assume your $2,000 per year savings and investment program had been carried out within a self-directed IRA. Then you could not have used margin, but all other aspects of Hits-Plus could have been used and your fund would have grown under the IRA untaxed shelter. Only when you started your retirement withdrawal would you be taxed and then only on the amount you withdrew. In this case, your withdrawals would be taxed at just a little less than ordinary income rates. Remember though, with an IRA you cannot start your retirement withdrawal without penalty until you're 59 1/2 years of age.

If the Hits-Plus retirement program had been utilized within a self-directed IRA (and therefore without the use of

Table 14.3

"Super Hits-Plus" Retirement Program 1949 Through 1963

Year	Investment	Year's Performance	End-of-Year Value	$ Added for next Year
1949	$2,000	+19.73%	$2,395	$2,000
1950	$4,395	+38.74%	$6,098	$2,000
1951	$8,098	+ 7.80%	$8,730	$2,000
1952	$10,730	+ 3.02%	$11,054	$2,000
1953	$13,054	+ 2.50%	$13,380	$2,000
1954	$15,380	+60.57%	$24,696	$2,000
1955	$26,696	+20.43%	$32,150	$2,000
1956	$34,150	+ 1.02%	$34,498	$2,000
1957	$36,498	+ 6.56%	$38,892	$2,000
1958	$40,892	+64.88%	$67,423	$2,000
1959	$69,423	+16.39%	$80,801	$2,000
1960	$82,801	+ 7.20%	$88,763	$2,000
1961	$90,763	+32.08%	$119,880	$2,000
1962	$121,880	+ 5.70%	$128,827	$2,000
1963	$130,827	+23.56%	$161,650	

204

Table 14.4

		$ After	**Year's**	**End-of-Year**
Year	**8% Withdrawal**	**Withdrawal**	**Performance**	**Value**
1964	$12,932	$148,718	+23.52%	$183,696
1965	$14,696	$169,000	+ 2.47%	$173,174
1966	$13,854	$159,320	+ 4.70%	$166,808
1967	$13,345	$153,463	+83.56%	$281,697
1968	$22,536	$259,161	+ 5.52%	$273,467
1969	$21,877	$251,590	+ 2.96%	$259,012
1970	$20,721	$238,291	+ 4.42%	$248,823
1971	$19,906	$228,917	+16.49%	$266,665
1972	$21,333	$245,332	+ 4.43%	$256,200
1973	$20,496	$235,704	+ 5.76%	$249,280
1974	$19,942	$229,338	+20.57%	$276,513
1975	$22,121	$254,392	+20.36%	$306,186
1976	$24,495	$281,691	+57.37%	$443,297
1977	$35,464	$407,833	+ 3.26%	$421,128
1978	$33,690	$387,438	+ 3.02%	$399,139
1979	$31,931	$367,208	+43.46%	$526,796
1980	$42,144	$484,652	+39.87%	$677,883
1981	$54,231	$623,653	+12.08%	$698,990
1982	$55,919	$643,071	+16.72%	$750,592
1983	$60,047	$690,544	+39.66%	$964,414
1984	$77,153	$887,261	+11.94%	$993,200
1985	$79,456	$913,744	+24.66%	$1,139,073
1986	$91,126	$1,047,947	+ 6.85%	$1,119,731
1987	$89,578	$1,030,152	+ 4.18%	$1,073,212
1988	$85,857	$987,355	+22.87%	$1,213,163
1989	$97,053	$1,116,110	+10.17%	$1,229,618
1990	$98,369	$1,131,249	+ 8.77%	$1,230,459
1991	$98,437	$1,132,022	+44.63%	$1,637,243
1992	$130,979	$1,506,263	+17.21%	$1,765,491
1993	$141,239	$1,624,252	+21.00%	$1,965,345

"Super Hits-Plus" 8% Retirement Withdrawal

margin) you would have had $137,624 in your retirement fund instead of $158,697. With the same 8% of total fund value withdrawal at the beginning of each retirement year, the first ten years from your IRA account would have averaged $10,411 ($867 per month) per year, and your 1993 withdrawal would have been $51,539 ($4,295 per month).

It would be more than worth giving up the use of margin in order to have the tax-free build-up benefit of the IRA account. We will take another look at IRS's, 401(k)'s and annuities in another chapter. Of course the Super Hits-Plus program was conducted without the use of margin so Table 14.3 and Table 14.4 would still be correct for the performance of the Super Hits-Plus IRA fund.

Imagine how your retirement picture would have been if you and your spouse both had invested $2,000 (total of $4,000 together) per year in a Hits-Plus or Super Hits-Plus IRA for fifteen years?

Actually, whereas I highly recommend the use of an IRA program, I do not think this should be your only avenue of savings and investing. I would hope that with the above scenario we would find that a married couple would have been able to save and invest $4,000 each for fifteen years. In this case, I think I would have recommended that each would have invested $2,000 per year in a Super Hits-Plus IRA program, $1,000 each in the regular Hits-Plus (with or without margin depending on their comfort zone) and $1,000 each in a Super Hits-Plus program (again with or without margin depending on the individual). Such an investment approach as this could deliver fantastic results.

Although the first fifteen years (1949 through 1963) were pretty good investment years in the market, the next eleven year period (when you were withdrawing from your retirement fund) was one of the worst investment time frames. This is why I believe 8% is the best percentage figure to use for a retirement withdrawal. This should allow you to go through a long stretch of a poor performance market period, and, in the long run, you would more than keep up with inflation and all the while be building up a very nice estate for your heirs, charity, or whatever. With the $250 a month and $300 a month insurance annuity retirement cases, I doubt that even the man's wife was covered with insurance death benefits unless he had additional insurance at additional cost. In any event, with your Hits-Plus or Super Hits-Plus program, you could afford a lot more term life insurance than he could, if you so desired.

As I have stated before, I strongly believe in starting early even if you have to stop for a period of time some years later.

In this case I would hope the individual or couple would be able to keep up the program for at least eight years and then if they had to stop the systematic investment program they would still have a number of years before they would have to start withdrawing from the fund.

In Chapter Thirteen we saw how a $900 per month investment at 15% a month compounded return would grow for eight years and then continue to grow after the investment program had stopped.

The Saga of Helen and Henry

Let's take a look at the saving and investment life of a hypothetical couple, Helen and Henry. At the beginning of 1971, Helen is thirty years old and Henry is thirty-four years old. They have two children ages five and seven. Henry is a college graduate with a good job. Helen stayed out of the work market until the five-year-old reached kindergarten age. She has just now started back to work.

Helen and Henry are fairly conservative, but they do not want to sacrifice to the point of denying themselves and the children many of the pleasures of life that do call for monetary spending. And yet, they have started thinking about the future college years for their children and their own retirement years, too.

They feel that from their total family income, they can save and invest $8,000 per year ($4,000 each). Now I will beg the reader to suspend the realities, to some extent, that were in effect in 1971, and let's assume that IRAs as they are set up today existed in the same manner in 1971. I do believe this is important in order for us to use this admitted hypothetical case as a possible guidepost for the future.

Helen and Henry both will invest $2,000 at the beginning of each year in their own self-directed IRA and use the Super Hits-Plus program without margin, since margin can't be used with IRA investing anyway (See Table 14.5 for Henry's investment program performance). They will also invest $1,000 each in an untax- sheltered Hits-Plus program at the beginning of each year and use margin as Hits-Plus directs. In addition, it's decided that Henry will invest $1,000 at the beginning of each year with the regular Hits-Plus program but without the use of margin. While Helen elects to be more aggressive and go with Super Hits-Plus and use margin (refer to Chapter 16 on using margin with Super Hits-Plus). They both plan to stop all investing after eight years and concentrate on preparing for their oldest (who will then be sixteen years old) to enter college two years later to be followed by the youngest two years from that time.

Helen and Henry's Super Hits-Plus programs had four poor performing years out of the eight. But, with four good years at the end of 1978 they each have $33,182 in their own IRA account, for a total of $66,364 together.

Henry's more conservative approach, with an untax-sheltered portfolio, investing $1,000 per year for eight years with the regular Hits-Plus program (without the use of margin) resulted in a value of $12,602 (taxes not figured) at the end of 1978 (see second part of Table 14.5).

Table 14.5

Henry's $2,000 Per Year "Super Hits-Plus" IRA Program

Year	Investment	Year's Performance	End-of-Year Value	Next Year's Investment
1971	$ 2,000	+16.49%	$ 2,330	$2,000
1972	$ 4,330	+ 4.43%	$ 4,522	$2,000
1973	$ 6,522	+ 5.76%	$ 6,898	$2,000
1974	$ 8,898	+20.57%	$10,728	$2,000
1975	$12,728	+20.36%	$15,319	$2,000
1976	$17,319	+57.27%	$27,255	$2,000
1977	$29,255	+ 3.26%	$30,209	$2,000
1978	$32,209	+ 3.02%	$33,182	

Henry's $1,000 Per Year "Hits-Plus" (without margin) Program

Year	Investment	Year's Performance	End-of-Year Value	Next Year's Investment
1971	$ 1,000	+14.30%	$ 1,143	$1,000
1972	$ 2,143	+19.00%	$ 2,550	$1,000
1973	$ 3,550	+ 5.80%	$ 3,756	$1,000
1974	$ 4,756	+ 5.60%	$ 5,022	$1,000
1975	$ 6,022	+22.62%	$ 7,384	$1,000
1976	$ 8,384	+23.80%	$10,379	$1,000
1977	$11,379	+ 3.30%	$11,755	$1,000
1978	$12,755	- 1.20%	$12,602	

Henry's $1,000 Per Year "Hits-Plus" (with margin) Program

Year	Investment	Year's Performance	End-of-Year Value	Next Year's Investment
*1971	$ 1,000	+18.60%	$ 1,186	$1,000
1972	$ 2,186	+19.00%	$ 2,601	$1,000
1973	$ 3,601	+ 5.80%	$ 3,810	$1,000
1974	$ 4,810	+ 5.60%	$ 5,079	$1,000
*1975	$ 6,079	+30.00%	$ 7,903	$1,000
1976	$ 8,903	+23.80%	$11,022	$1,000
1977	$12,022	+ 3.30%	$12,419	$1,000
1978	$13,419	- 1.20%	$13,258	

*Years margin was used.

Henry's "Super Hits-Plus" IRA Fund:	$33,182
Henry's "Hits-Plus" (without margin) Program:	$12,602
Henry's "Hits-Plus" (w/margin) Program:	$13,258
Total Value of Portfolio:	$59,042

Table 14.6

Helen's $2,000 Per Year "Super Hits-Plus" IRA Program

Year	Investment	Year's Performance	End-of-Year Value	Next Year's Investment
1971	$ 2,000	+16.49%	$ 2,330	$2,000
1972	$ 4,330	+ 4.43%	$ 4,522	$2,000
1973	$ 6,522	+ 5.76%	$ 6,898	$2,000
1974	$ 8,898	+20.57%	$10,728	$2,000
1975	$12,728	+20.36%	$15,319	$2,000
1976	$17,319	+57.37%	$27,255	$2,000
1977	$29,255	+ 3.26%	$30,209	$2,000
1978	$32,209	+ 3.02%	**$33,182**	

Helen's $1,000 Per Year "Super Hits-Plus" (with margin) Program

Year	Investment	Year's Performance	End-of-Year Value	Next Year's Investment
*1971	$ 1,000	+21.81%	$ 1,218	$1,000
1972	$ 2,218	+ 4.30%	$ 2,313	$1,000
1973	$ 3,313	+ 5.76%	$ 3,504	$1,000
1974	$ 4,504	+20.57%	$ 5,430	$1,000
*1975	$ 6,430	+26.15%	$ 8,112	$1,000
1976	$ 9,112	+57.37%	$14,339	$1,000
1977	$15,339	+ 3.26%	$15,839	$1,000
1978	$16,839	+ 3.02%	**$17,348**	

Helen's $1,000 Per Year "Hits-Plus" (with margin) Program

Year	Investment	Year's Performance	End-of-Year Value	Next Year's Investment
*1971	$ 1,000	+18.60%	$ 1,186	$1,000
1972	$ 2,186	+19.00%	$ 2,601	$1,000
1973	$ 3,601	+ 5.80%	$ 3,810	$1,000
1974	$ 4,810	+ 5.60%	$ 5,079	$1,000
*1975	$ 6,079	+30.00%	$ 7,903	$1,000
1976	$ 8,903	+23.80%	$11,022	$1,000
1977	$12,022	+ 3.30%	$12,419	$1,000
1978	$13,419	- 1.20%	**$13,258**	

* Years margin was used.

Helen's "Super Hits-Plus" IRA Fund:	$33,182
Helen's "Super Hits-Plus" (w/margin) Program:	$17,348
Helen's "Hits-Plus" (w/margin) Program:	$13,258
Total Portfolio:	$63,788

Both Henry and Helen elected to invest $1,000 per year with the regular Hits-Plus system, using margin when called for. This resulted in a value of $13,258 for each portfolio ($26,516 for both) at the end of 1978 (see third part of Table 14.5).

Helen became the more aggressive investor with her election to invest $1,000 per year utilizing the Super Hits-Plus program complete with the use of margin, which she can, since this is an untax-sheltered portfolio. The results gave Helen bragging rights over Henry by achieving $17,348 vs. Henry's, non-margin regular Hits-Plus approach, with a $12,602 value at the end of 1978 (see Table 14.6 for Helen's investment program performance).

Helen's decision does not seem so bold if she was confident she would not need to draw any funds from this portfolio and she's looking to keep this investment approach for a long term duration.

Here's the situation for both Henry and Helen after the 1971 through 1978, eight-year save and invest period.

Henry's Portfolio End of 1978

Super Hits-Plus IRA Fund	$33,182
Regular Hits-Plus With Margin	$13,258
Regular Hits-Plus Without Margin	$12,602
Total:	$59,042

Helen's Portfolio End of 1978

Super Hits-Plus IRA Fund	$33,182
Regular Hits-Plus With Margin	$13,258
Super Hits-Plus With Margin	$17,348
Total:	$63,788

Henry and Helen did very well with their eight year period of saving and investing with combined portfolios totaling $122,830 (not figuring taxes on the non-IRA untax-sheltered portfolios).

Table 14.7

Henry's "Super Hits-Plus" IRA Fund

Year	Performance	End-of-Year Value
1979	+43.46%	$ 47,603
1980	+39.87%	$ 66,582
1981	+12.00%	$ 74,572
1982	+16.72%	$ 87,040
1983	+39.66%	$121,560
1984	+11.80%	$135,904
1985	+24.66%	$169,418
1986	+ 6.85%	$181,023
1987	+ 4.18%	$188,590
1988	+22.66%	$231,720
1989	+10.17%	$255,286
1990	+ 8.77%	$277,675
1991	+44.63%	$401,601
1992	+17.21%	$470,717
1993	**+21.00%**	**$569,567**

Henry's "Hits-Plus" (without margin) Program

Year	Performance	End-of-Year Value
1979	+18.40%	$ 14,921
1980	+32.40%	$ 19,755
1981	+12.10%	$ 22,145
1982	+17.10%	$ 25,932
1983	+22.50%	$ 31,767
1984	+11.90%	$ 35,547
1985	+32.20%	$ 46,993
1986	+18.50%	$ 55,687
1987	+ 4.20%	$ 58,026
1988	+16.80%	$ 67,774
1989	+31.50%	$ 89,123
1990	+ 8.80%	$ 96,966
1991	+30.60%	$126,637
1992	+ 4.26%	$132,032
1993	**+10.00%**	**$145,235**

Henry's "Hits-Plus" (w/margin) Program

Year	Performance	End-of-Year Value
1979	+21.30%	$ 16,082
1980	+32.40%	$ 21,293
1981	+12.10%	$ 23,869
1982	+17.10%	$ 27,951
1983	+22.50%	$ 34,268
1984	+11.90%	$ 38,346
1985	+32.20%	$ 50,693
1986	+18.50%	$ 60,071
1987	+ 4.20%	$ 62,594
1988	+16.80%	$ 73,110
1989	+31.50%	$ 96,140
1990	+ 8.80%	$104,600
1991	+30.60%	$136,608
1992	+ 4.26%	$142,427
1993	**+10.00%**	**$156,670**

Total All of Henry's Portfolios: $871,472

Table 14.8

Helen's "Super Hits-Plus" IRA Fund		
Year	Performance	End-of-Year Value
1979	+43.46%	$ 47,603
1980	+39.87%	$ 66,582
1981	+12.00%	$ 74,572
1982	+16.72%	$ 87,040
1983	+39.66%	$121,560
1984	+11.80%	$135,904
1985	+24.66%	$169,418
1986	+ 6.85%	$181,023
1987	+ 4.18%	$188,590
1988	+22.66%	$231,720
1989	+10.17%	$255,286
1990	+ 8.77%	$277,675
1991	+44.63%	$401,601
1992	+17.21%	$470,717
1993	+21.00%	$569,567

Helen's "Super Hits-Plus" (with margin) Program		
Year	Performance	End-of-Year Value
1979	+58.86%	$ 27,559
1980	+39.87%	$ 38,547
1981	+12.00%	$ 43,173
1982	+16.72%	$ 50,391
1983	+39.66%	$ 70,376
1984	+11.80%	$ 78,680
1985	+24.66%	$ 98,083
1986	+ 6.85%	$104,802
1987	+ 4.18%	$109,183
1988	+22.87%	$134,153
1989	+10.17%	$147,796
1990	+ 8.77%	$160,758
1991	+44.63%	$232,504
1992	+17.21%	$272,518
1993	+21.00%	$329,746

Helen's "Hits-Plus" (w/margin) Program		
Year	Performance	End-of-Year Value
1979	+21.30%	$ 16,082
1980	+32.40%	$ 21,293
1981	+12.10%	$ 23,869
1982	+17.10%	$ 27,951
1983	+22.50%	$ 34,268
1984	+11.90%	$ 38,346
1985	+32.20%	$ 50,693
1986	+18.50%	$ 60,071
1987	+ 4.20%	$ 62,594
1988	+16.80%	$ 73,110
1989	+31.50%	$ 96,140
1990	+ 8.80%	$104,600
1991	+30.60%	$136,608
1992	+ 4.26%	$142,427
1993	+10.00%	$156,670

Total All of Helen's Portfolios: $1,055,983

Now we enter the period from the beginning of 1979 through 1993 when neither Henry nor Helen will invest anymore in their portfolios, but, of course, they must continue to track their performance monthly and follow the Hits-Plus and Super Hits-Plus trading directives (see Tables 14.7 and 14.8).

Although the 1971 through 1978 saving and invest period for Henry and Helen was not a very good investment time frame, 1979 through 1993 proved to be a great growth period. *Their Super Hits-Plus IRAs grew by an average annual compounded return of +20.87%. That's an IRA Fund of $569,567 for a total of $1,139,134 together.* They both have $156,670 each in their   untax-sheltered Hits-Plus (w/margin) account for a total of $313,340 together (taxes not figured). But Helen's Super Hits-Plus (w/margin) choice greatly out performed Henry's more conservative regular Hits-Plus (without margin). **All told, the family's portfolios total $1,927,455.** Their entire investments look like this:

Henry's Portfolio End of 1993

Super Hits-Plus IRA Fund	$569,567
Hits-Plus (without margin)	$145,235
Hits-Plus (w/margin)	$156,670
Total:	$871,472

Helen's Portfolio End of 1993

Super Hits-Plus IRA Fund	$569,567
Super Hits-Plus (w/margin)	$329,746
Hits-Plus (with margin)	$156,670
Total:	$1,055,983

Helen and Henry have achieved great investment results by just investing $4,000 each for eight years. With Henry now being 57 years old and Helen 53, they would have to wait until they are 59 1/2 years old in order to start withdrawals from their IRA Funds without penalties. But they wouldn't need to withdraw from their IRAs if they did choose to retire at this time, because of the success they have had with their other unsheltered programs. Of course these programs would not be as strong as the tables indicate because taxes are not figured but there would be no tax penalty for withdrawal at any time.

Another good reason to have separate portfolios outside of IRAs (or other tax-sheltered programs) is that bad things sometimes do happen. Jobs are lost, recessions occur, and people get sick. If and when bad things do happen, it's better to have outside of IRA investments you can draw from rather than dipping into your IRA and paying the penalty.

Another thing that I think is very important with married couples is a sense of cooperative teamwork as a family unit. The husband needs some money of his own from the family budget for his golf or fishing hobbies, etc.; the same for the wife for her own personal pursuits. But after that the budget should be a family unit. Of course, their IRAs must be separate investments by law. But more about this in the last chapter.

The main general points to remember from this chapter are:

1. Don't try to time when your money and your life will run out.
2. Start a savings and investment program as early as possible, even if you have to stop it some years later. But, do keep investing as long as you can; after all, the longer you can keep it up, the greater the reward will be.
3. Don't try to overreach when withdrawal time comes. You should try to live within an 8% withdrawal yearly from the total value of your funds.
4. You should not go mostly with conservative fixed income investments just because you're 55 or 65 years old. If you're 55 years old your life expectancy would be 22 more years. But when you reach 77 years old your life expectancy would then be over eight

more years. These are male life expectancy figures. The female normally can expect to live from two to five years longer. Remember too, that if inflation averages 5.25%, today's $18,000 automobile will cost $30,000 ten years from now and a $30 restaurant check would go to $50.

I know of a number of 85 year olds who still enjoy golf, travel, good food, and good times. The key is to take good care of your physical health and your financial health and to start paying attention to both at an early age. But it's never too late to start. Do it now.

CHAPTER FIFTEEN

IRA's, SEP-IRA's, Keoghs, Variable Annuities, 401(k)s, etc.

"Death and taxes may always be with us, but death at least doesn't get any worse."

-- Unknown

"Never put off until tomorrow what you can do the day after tomorrow."

-- Mark Twain

The Mark Twain quote refers to paying taxes, not as an excuse to procrastinate in other areas. You are going to have to pay your taxes today or sometime later, or your heirs will have to pay them. All other things being equal it is usually better to postpone paying your taxes as long as you can, if it's clear that its not going to ultimately cost you more by doing so.

Except for the possible psychological benefit of discipline in saving and investing, the key advantage of all IRAs, SEP-IRAs, Keogh plans, Variable Annuities, 401(k)s, and all other similar retirement plans is the fact that your savings and investing is sheltered from the tax collector until the time comes when you begin to make withdrawals.

In some respects, this chapter is the toughest to write because with some retirement vehicles, there is controversy and some end up appearing to be on-the-bubble as far as the benefits are concerned. Also, Congress is subject to change the tax laws affecting many of these plans at any time. From the tax law stand point, we must look at all the plans as the tax law is today. Rest assured that the stock market is much easier to predict than the future actions of the U.S. Congress.

IRAs

First, the Individual Retirement Accounts (IRAs) should, without a doubt, be a part of your overall savings, investing and retirement plans. If you plan to follow a Hits-Plus type investment program with your IRA you can easily set up the account directly with the mutual fund family you wish to deal with such as Vanguard, Fidelity, etc., or you could go through Charles Schwab & Co. (as I do) or with any other broker that deals with no-load mutual funds. You can direct the investing and shifting of your IRA investments, as Hits-Plus might call for usually with just a telephone call.

To set up a self-directed IRA, simply call the broker (See Appendix B) or the mutual fund family you wish to deal with (See Appendix A) and ask them to send you the appropriate IRA forms. You may ask the customer service representative, on the phone, any questions you wish. You will find them to be very courteous and helpful.

In the early years, Congress had established IRAs so your $2,000 maximum annual investment was not taxed up front; i.e., you invested the $2,000 from your salary and insofar as tax was concerned, it was as if you never were paid the $2,000. Of course, the tax collector would get you on that great day when you started to withdraw from your IRA. At the time of this writing your $2,000 annual contribution may or may not be with after-taxed dollars, but the growth build-up of your individual retirement account is not taxed; therefore, you get a free tax ride until withdrawal time.

When Congress greatly limited the advantage of you being able to invest pre-taxed dollars instead of after-taxes dollars in your IRA program many Americans stopped their contributions altogether. They shouldn't have. Although Congress had turned a good deal into less of a good deal, it was still a good deal and more of us should be utilizing the tax sheltered growth offered by IRAs. Also, at the time of this writing Congress may again take a look at re-establishing the pre-taxed advantage for IRAs. Or, they might not.

Simply put, the gains you make in your IRA contributions are not taxed (while they're growing), therefore the portfolio will grow much faster than an identical taxed portfolio. In all of my tables I have not figured taxes although we know that taxes must be paid in untax-sheltered accounts. Projecting hypothetical individual tax payments is difficult at best. We would need to know one's salary or how else they achieved their income. We would need to know about their tax deductions such as mortgage interest, carry forward tax loses from previous years, etc. In any event, taxes always hurt, but if we use taxes as an excuse for not saving and investing we will hurt even more in the future. Remember, with some portfolios, we might have used margin and the interest paid on the margin loan would have been tax deductible.

However there are two important points to remember. First, if there are no other negative factors, the tax sheltering advantage of an IRA is obviously a great advantage in building up a nice retirement nest egg. Second, in a untax-sheltered portfolio it would have been nice if our hypothetical couple (refer back to Chapter 14) Henry and Helen could have invested a little more to offset the tax problem. Actually, $25 to $50 more per month invested in the non-sheltered Hits-Plus or Super Hits-Plus program would have given Henry and Helen a much stronger position if this $25 to $50 per month continuing on past the eight-year stopping point (the entire 23-year period).

If Henry and Helen didn't have to draw out all their IRA money in one lump it would be much better for them to simply draw 8% of the total value per year for the rest of their lives and make the IRS wait until their ultimate departure from this life to get their full pound of tax flesh. Of course when one reaches 70 1/2 years old you must start withdrawal from your IRA and the amount you must withdraw is based on life expectancy and is dictated by the IRS. You would need to confer with your accountant concerning this. Also you should ask your attorney's advice on how you should handle your IRA in your will with estate planning.

The bottom line is use an IRA as a part of your savings, investment, and retirement program. The only real disadvantage is that if you desperately need funds before you reach the age of 59 1/2 you will pay a 10% penalty on the amount of money you withdraw from the IRA, plus you will have to pay ordinary income tax on a portion of that withdrawal.

How Much in an IRA?
How Much Outside?

Because of the penalty and tax factor for early withdrawal I would always recommend you have outside unsheltered investments the same way Henry and Helen did. If $2,000 a year is the maximum you can save and invest, I would only put half in an IRA until you had built up an outside-of-an-IRA nest egg or your savings ability had grown, to say $3,000 per year. If you can save and invest a total of $3,000 or more per year then I would use full advantage of the IRA. Remember too, your IRA investment can be in the form of $166.67 per month, $500 per quarter, or any other amount at any time during the year for a specified calendar year. The amount cannot exceed $2000 per year per person and must come from earned income. You cannot go back and invest for past missed years, but you do have until April 15th to invest for the preceding calendar year.

Keoghs

If you are self-employed you should look into the possibilities of setting up a Keogh plan or a SEP-IRA. I will not attempt to advise you about your setting up a Keogh plan other than to say if you are self-employed you should certainly look into it. There are money-purchase, defined benefit, and profit-sharing Keoghs, and they can be complicated with various rules you must follow. It is possible that you could be eligible for both a Keogh plan and still invest in an IRA. If you have a very successful business you could contribute a lot more money (up to $30,000 per year) in a tax-sheltered Keogh plan than you could ever approach with an IRA. The answer here is to go to an independent Certified Public Accountant (CPA) who is very knowledgeable in this area. This advice will cost you a little, but if you have a successful business it could be well worth it. Don't ultimately take your advice from someone who will monetarily benefit from your setting up a Keogh plan through the services they offer. The regulations stated here are as they exist at the time of this writing and are subject to change at any time.

SEP-IRAs

If your business is young but growing you'll also want to look into the SEP-IRA, (simplified employee pension plans-individual retirement accounts). Again, you'll want unbiased advice from a knowledgeable CPA. You will find that the SEP-IRA can allow you to contribute 15% of your income (up to $30,000 with possible age-weighted or title-weighted plans that could allow a $30,000 contribution) a year that will be tax deferred until the time of withdrawal with retirement. Imagine how much a man and his wife, operating a small but highly

221

profitable business, could build up over the years by contributing the maximum each in a SEP-IRA and by utilizing mutual funds and the Hits-Plus strategy. Again regulations on SEP-IRAs and other such plans are always subject to change at any time. Remember, you cannot use margin with any tax-deferred plan but this certainly should not deter you. However, I wouldn't go out and start a self-employed business in hopes of gaining the advantages of setting up a SEP-IRA or Keogh plan. Financing, establishing, and building up a self-employed business can be very difficult.

401(k)s

401(k)s also have similarities to Keoghs and SEP-IRAs, and, once again, it calls for some expert objective advice about setting one up if you are the owner of a successful company. If, however, you are an employee with a company that offers a 401(k) plan, you should certainly give it full consideration.

Some 401(k)s will offer you almost the full scope (except for the use of margin) of the advantages of using Hits-Plus and Super Hits-Plus: a wide variety of mutual fund choices, including money funds and bond funds, and the ability to shift your funds around from one fund to another. Other 401(k)s, with some companies, offer a narrow range of choices that would prohibit the utilization of Hits-Plus but still may be worth consideration, especially if they offer a company matching contribution feature. Some very successful companies may offer to match your 401(k) contribution with a 10% to 25% matching contribution of their own. Unless there are some unusual tough restrictions, these matching contribution plans are very attractive.

Now comes the toughest tax-deferred vehicle to call: the variable annuities.

Variable Annuities: A Tough Call

Many variable annuity salespeople like to promote their product as simply being "Super IRAs" with all the advantages of an IRA, except you can invest all the money you can afford. "Super IRAs" they're not. There are disadvantages to variable annuities that erase many of the advantages, enough so to rule out some as not being good investments at all and bringing some down to the point of being so much on the bubble that they're awfully close to call and therein lies some of the controversy.

I must admit that when some variable annuities first came on the scene my first impression was they had the potential of being comparable (in the investment world) to what sliced bread has been to sandwich making. My first thoughts were they only had to bring a wider variety of mutual fund selections to the table to really be great. This began to happen, but, having my own investment programs pretty well committed, I didn't analyze the newer broader offerings to any real degree but generally held the assumption that they would be good investment avenues for a lot of us.

Then one of my favorite magazines, *Forbes*, began to feature articles that questioned the real, true value of variable annuities as investment vehicles. After reading several of these articles, I went back to my analyzation board and took a hard second look.

Pros

With the type of variable annuity I'm talking about, you invest a certain amount of money, $5,000, $50,000, or whatever, with an established insurance company that has tied in with a mutual fund family or several, enabling you to have the advantages of investing almost any sum of money you can afford in a mutual fund. You can even shift from one mutual fund or money fund offered to another and back within an allowable time frame, and all this with the same tax-deferred advantages of an IRA. This, at first glance, seems to be the perfect answer for some Hits-Plus (without margin) investing after your IRA is fully funded. The Henry and Helen Hits-Plus S&P 500 Index portfolio would seem to be an excellent example of where the variable annuity vehicle would be just perfect.

Unlike IRAs you are not compelled to start withdrawing from your variable annuity at age 70 1/2. You can wait until you're 85 years old if you wish. Why would one want to wait that long? If you had built a tremendous IRA and had other well established portfolios and you didn't need the income it would mean you could continue to build more in a tax-sheltered program. Of course it would always pay you to get legal and tax advise before making such decisions as regulations are always subject to change.

There are even some possibilities of using a type of Super Hits-Plus approach within some variable annuities. At the time of this writing I am not aware of any variable annuity that offers a good small company stock index fund as one of their investment choices. I expect that this will change in the not-too-distant future.

In the meantime one might consider utilizing a well managed growth or aggressive growth mutual fund within a good variable annuity that has a track record of closely reflecting the past performance of a small company stock index. If you choose to go with this approach you would move your investment from this fund to the variable annuity's bond fund and money fund when directed by the Hits-Plus strategy and back into the growth fund when so directed by Hits-Plus. I wouldn't recommend this strategy unless you are planning to be in the variable annuity for at least eight to ten years.

Cons

The disadvantages are:

1. The same 10% IRS penalty and ordinary income tax situation is in effect for any withdrawal occurring before the age of 59 1/2.

2. In addition to the above penalty the variable annuity company may charge its own penalty or back-end load for early withdrawal. This usually starts at 7% and goes down to zero over a seven-

year period (it can be better or worse with different companies). This means if a person bought a variable annuity at the age of fifty and absolutely had to have the money four years later he/she would face a 10% penalty from the IRS,perhaps a 4% or 5% penalty from the annuity company, plus ordinary income tax due on a portion of the withdrawal amount.

3. Buying mutual fund oriented variable annuities is not the same as investing directly in the mutual funds. The big bug-a-boo is the extra expenses that come with the variable annuities. These come mainly in the form of mandatory insurance death benefits. This is basically for term-insurance required by law, so the variable annuity maintains the veneer of a regular insurance annuity with a guaranteed death benefit for the owner's heirs. This, plus usually higher than normal management fees, gives the variable annuities a higher annual expense cost ranging from 1% to 2% higher than the same regular mutual funds would incur. However the insurance factor could be a big help if the investor died after the first year or two and the variable annuity had lost money since the inception of the annuity contract. Then the insurance would keep a loss from occurring which would be good news for the heirs.

The 1% to 2% higher annual expense cost may not seem like much, but when you consider that if your mutual fund would normally produce a +15% performance in a given year and that performance would be reduced to +13%, then it takes on a different look. After all, +13% vs. +15% actually represents 13.3% less in money growth for that year. With a one lump $10,000 investment, the results ten years later would be $33,946 vs. $40,456 without figuring taxes. However, the growth in the regular mutual fund investment would be taxed every year, so, actually, you would have less total dollars in the

225

regular mutual fund account than in the variable annuity mutual fund account. But, your annual withdrawals will be taxed higher from the variable annuity account than from the regular mutual fund account. Remember, the variable annuity is just tax deferred not tax exempt. Your own accountant could best calculate how this would affect you.

A Major Breakthrough

This chapter has undergone over four re-writes because of rapid changes taking place with variable annuities and in particular with Vanguard entering the field.

Vanguard has teamed with National Home Life Assurance Company to offer what appears to be an ideal investment vehicle for the Hits-Plus investors who are over 59 1/2 years old or those who are younger and feel they will not need their investment dollars before they reach the age of 59 1/2. Even if they do (for any reason) need to withdraw their funds before they reach 59 1/2, with Vanguard there is no surrender charge even if you withdraw just one year later. Of course, for the under 59 1/2 withdrawal there would be the IRS 10% penalty on income and gains and income tax to pay on gains.

With Vanguard, we have the lowest combination of insurance company expense and mutual fund management expense. The total expense for the Vanguard variable annuity is just .95%, less than one percent and less than most mutual funds alone charge for management.

I guess I'm beginning to sound like a Vanguard salesperson, which I'm not, having no connection with the company whatsoever. But, the features Vanguard offers are very inviting.

There are four portfolios within the Vanguard Variable Annuity:

- Money Fund
- Balanced Fund
- High-Grade Bond Fund
- S&P 500 Index Fund

This means the Hits-Plus investor could invest in the S&P 500 Index and then later, if indicators so direct, switch to a combination of the Money Fund and the High-Grade Bond Fund. All the while under the tax-sheltered umbrella of the annuity. Vanguard does not offer the Small Capitalization Stock Fund that mirrors the Russell 2000 as a variable annuity at the time of this writing. However I have been informed that this is the most requested of additional funds for Vanguard to add to their variable annuity offerings so it just might become available in the future.

At this time the Vanguard variable annuity plan prospectus states: "...you may make two substantive exchanges from each portfolio (at least 30 days apart) during any calendar year." These exchanges may be directed by mail or telephone.

It seems that this would accommodate the Hits-Plus investor under most circumstances. *Frankly, I am excited about the possibilities of the Vanguard Variable Annuities for the long-term investor to build up a tax-deferred retirement fund.*

There is also the hopeful possibility that the competition that Vanguard has brought to the variable annuity marketplace will cause other mutual fund-oriented variable annuity plans to become more competitive in the areas of total expense and surrender charges.

CHAPTER SIXTEEN

To Margin or Not to Margin

"So far as my coin would stretch; and where it would not, I have used my credit."

-- *William Shakespeare*

Now, I don't believe Bill Shakespeare invested in the stock market, but I understand that he did quite well writing plays. Judging from this Shakespeare quote, I would guess he would have used margin if he were investing in the stock market today.

The use of margin really got a bad name with the stock market crash in 1929 and deservedly so. In many cases you could buy stocks by putting up just 10% in cash. It doesn't take an intellectual giant to see that when real gambling speculators invested almost all of their cash and used 90% margin the market only had to dip down slightly for them to be wiped out overnight. This high leverage use of margin in the twenties was one of many factors that contributed to the 1929 crash and ensuing depression.

Your Home May Be on Margin

Today the maximum use of margin is 50% and that seems to be working quite nicely. Actually, almost all of us have used margin without thinking about it in those terms. If you bought your home with a down payment and a mortgage loan this is in essence using margin. If your home goes up in value you have leveraged a higher profit with the loan. If the value of your home goes down you could lose more money when you sell it. You could have more difficulty selling it if you don't have extra funds to retire the loan. And if you have too much difficulty making your mortgage payments you could lose your home.

The same is true of automobile loans except, with the rare exception of certain classic cars, your automobile will always go down in value.

The use of credit is the backbone of business and very necessary for most of our citizens to enjoy a decent standard of living in today's economy. However, we must always be prudent in our use of credit. An overextended use of credit in any shape, form, or fashion could cause us much sorrow.

I acknowledge that I took certain liberties in writing about the use of margin with Hits-Plus. I stayed with today's margin requirements instead of changing to whatever the margin limits were at the time in history that was depicted. Frankly, the reasons were 1) I found acquiring good historical data on margin limits was difficult; 2) I doubt margin requirements in the future will change much from what they are today; and 3) I doubt that on-the-button historical data (in this case) would have changed overall the historical performance very much.

I also used the prevailing average prime rate for the years in question as our margin rate for its historical use with Hits-Plus. With the early use of margin, when your investment capital has not reached substantial levels, you will probably have to pay a little more than the prevailing prime rate for your margin loan. But, once you build up your investment portfolio (especially over $50,000) you will find you can usually negotiate a margin loan rate that will be below the prevailing prime rate.

I will certainly not try to talk anyone into using margin in their investment program, although there's no doubt it has worked well with Hits-Plus and Super Hits-Plus in historical tracking.

Using margin is simply borrowing money from your broker (in my case, Charles Schwab & Co.) to buy additional shares in your chosen mutual funds; you use your portfolio as collateral for the loan. We do this with Hits-Plus when our strategy tells us that the odds are in our favor that the S&P 500 will perform well for us in the upcoming year. I recommend paying off the margin loan at the end of each calendar year unless the first year's use of one-third margin failed to produce an up year and you'll be going with full 50% margin for the next year. In this case, you simply reposition with the broker for the greater use of margin for that next upcoming year. The interest you pay to your broker for margin loans to buy additional shares is tax-deductible.

The Difference Margin Makes

So how much difference would the use of margin make over the years with Hits-Plus? I will not dump another table on you. If you want one you can easily make your own with a little calculator and just leave off the use of margin for those years Hits-Plus utilized it. You will find that from 1929 through 1949 (the 21-year period) the use of margin took $10,000 to $126,742 vs. $10,000 growing to $87,393 with the non-use of margin. That means the margin user achieved an average annual compounded return of +12.85% while the non-margin user had an average annual compounded return of +10. 87%. This two percentage points difference translated into $39,349 or 45% more money at the end of the 21-year time frame.

With the 1950 through 1993 (44-year) experience, the margin user ran $10,000 up to $6,101,434 while the non-margin user took $10,000 to $4,797,165. That's an average annual compounded return of +15.69% for the margin user vs. +15.06% average annual compounded performance for the non-margin user. This, however, translated into $1,304,269 more dollars for the margin user.

? Using Margin With Super Hits-Plus ?

Actually, you may not be able to use margin with the Super Hits-Plus system in the *traditional* manner. At the time of this writing the Vanguard Index Small Cap Mutual Fund (that seeks to mirror the Russell 2000) is not offered by Charles Schwab & Co. or by any other discount broker (that I know of) that can conduct business in all 50 states. Freeman Welwood & Co. (see Appendix B) does offer the Vanguard Index Small Cap Fund with a 1% load and offers margin. Freeman Welwood & Co. is currently listed to do business in the states of Washington, Alaska, Oregon, Idaho, Montana, Hawaii and Northern California. Of course, other discount brokers may add the Vanguard Index Small Cap Fund to their offerings in the future.

If one did want to use margin (with the Super Hits-Plus System) and they did not live in a state where a broker could offer the Vanguard Index Small Cap Fund and margin, what could they do? They could then turn to obtaining a bank loan and pledging their shares in the mutual fund portfolio as collateral. Depending on their borrowing strength, interest charges could be a bit more than the interest charged by a broker.

In the case of the hypothetical portfolio of "Helen" in Chapter 14 she would have had to borrow only $500 to use margin in 1971 with the Super Hits-Plus System. In 1975 she would have needed to borrow $3,215, but she had total portfolio holdings (at that time) valued at $25,237 so obtaining a bank loan should have been no problem. The only other year Helen would have used margin with her Super Hits-Plus program was 1979. This would have called for a loan of $8,674. The total value of her portfolios was $63,788 so a bank should have been happy to make her a loan.

In any case with Super Hits-Plus the margin user would have turned $10,000 into $23,902,444 from 1950 through 1993 while the non-margin user turned $10,000 into $17,307,301 over the same time period. *That's a 19.34% average annual compounded return for the margin user vs. 18.47% for the non-margin user* ... but a big $6,595,143 difference in end-of-period (44 years) results.

Still this does not tell the whole story. The investor must be comfortable with the use of margin and realize that there may be times when there could be considerable psychological stress when faced with the margin decision and uncertain market condition, especially when called on to go with full 50% margin after a 1/3 margin year failed to produce positive results.

The final decision will be up to the individual. You might decide that you'll have 50% of your funds in the Hits-Plus S&P 500 strategy and you will not use margin with it but that you will use margin with the rest of your portfolio. And if 50% of your funds are in a tax sheltered IRA, etc. you would not and could not use margin with that portfolio.

Before you make your final decision about the use of margin you might like to read the next chapter.

CHAPTERSEVENTEEN

The Psychological Makeup of the Investor

"There is only one thing about which I am certain, and that is that there is very little about which one can be certain."
-- W. Somerset Maugham

"He who can have patience can have what he will."
-- Benjamin Franklin

Remember back in Chapter Four where we led off the chapter with the Graham & Dodd quote, "The market is a voting machine, whereon countless individuals register choices which are the product partly of reason and partly of emotions." And remember J. Kenfield Morley wanted to know "...whether you wanted to eat well or sleep well." And we wanted both.

It is certainly true that the market is influenced by the psychological emotions of the investor every bit as much as it is by the logic of the objective analytical investor. The very theme of Hits-Plus maintains that before long, logical reason will win over (at least for a while) as the market searches for its proper value level.

Often the emotional investor will follow a "crowd behavior," sometimes correctly, but all too often he or she will jump on a trend well after the rainbow ride is over and the trend is about to head south. Then there's the "Contrarian." This investor will almost always go against the crowd and supposedly buy value in individual stocks and wait for logic to catch up. There's a mighty good case for the ultimate correctness of the contrarian. The main problem is that sometimes the wait for the contrarian to be proven correct, with selective stocks, can be a little tiresome. However, to some degree, Hits-Plus is a contrarian approach to the market in that we will invest stronger after the market has been down two years, which is usually when the crowd is least optimistic. And we will usually move out of the market after two up years, which is when the crowd is riding an optimistic high. The prime difference is that the Hits-Plus investor is a contrarian with "the market" (the S&P 500 or a small company stock index) instead of with individual selected stocks.

As much as we should be aware of the crowd psychological factor that effects the stock market we should be even more aware of our own psychological make-up as an individual person and as an investor.

Where's the Investor's Psychiatrist?

I don't mean we should have ourselves psychoanalyzed before beginning an investment program. On second thought, they now have sports psychologists, so maybe investor psychologists could be an entirely new career field. I'm only kidding; I think.

I have talked a little about whether the use of margin would come within your personal comfort zone and I have stated that some might find the volatility that can occur with the use of the Super Hits-Plus strategy as being a little too stressful.

Forty-Four Years of Little Stress

Let's take a quick look back at Hits-Plus investing in the S&P 500 Index from 1950 through 1993 from the psychological stand point.

From 1950 through 1955 I don't see a thing that should have bothered any investor; every year was just great, unless you were the type of person who might see someone else do a little better than you over some specific time frame and then get all upset about it. No matter how well you do as an investor there will always be someone who gets lucky with a hot issue and takes a big rocket ride up. It's like reading about the big million dollar winners in Las Vegas. Do you really hope to go out there and duplicate their feat? You usually hear about the high roller winners but not about the dead broke losers.

1956 could have bothered some because Hits-Plus took us out of the market and into U.S. Treasury Bills and Intermediate Term Government Bonds, and we would have been slightly better off had we stayed in. But overall we must choose an investment strategy and stick with it with determined patience and discipline. This is even more evident with Super Hits-Plus as there are a number of years when we were in bonds and T-Bills while the SCSI made fantastic gains. We would all like to be right all of the time, but that just won't happen.

In 1957 we followed the January Barometer and we sold out at the end of January with a -4% loss. The January Barometer proved to be correct so that should have pleased us, but there will be years when the January Barometer will be wrong. Will you get all upset and abandon its use then?

1958 was the first year that called for the Hits-Plus investor to use margin. I hope you have already decided if you have the psychological make-up that allows you to be comfortable with borrowing money to invest in the market or not. I don't promote this issue one way or the other; the individual investor should be at ease with which ever direction he/she takes.

1968 would have bothered some investors as we were

out of the market when it performed with a nice +11.1% gain. Again we must understand that "Hits- Plus" can't guide us correctly every time; it's not a perfect foolproof system. It just so happens that historically it has been right so much more often than it has been wrong. In fact, in this case the very next year, 1969, proved we were correct.

The 1960s as a whole were not premium investment years, but in comparison to the performance of other investment vehicles Hits-Plus and Super Hits-Plus really did quite well.

1987: The Pressure Was There

1987 probably would have bothered any Hits-Plus investor until October 19th. It would have appeared that with our sideline position in T-Bills and Bonds we had missed out on one of the best bull market years ever. Would you have tossed out the Hits-Plus strategy sometime around August 1987 and jumped back into the market? If 1987 had ended as a big up year would you have cursed Hits-Plus and gone to a dart board system of picking stocks? These are questions we must ask ourselves and we should give honest answers to these questions in order to arrive at some understanding of our own psychological make-up as an investor.

` In any event, the time frame from 1950 through 1993 should not have been a difficult or a very stressful time for most investors.

Gut Wrenching, Mind Twisting Twenty-One Years

A look back at 1929 through 1949 is an entirely different matter. We all hope that there will never be a re-run of anything close to the depression years and the World War II years. But, we can't predict the future and we should ask ourselves how do we think we would have reacted during such topsy-turvy investment years?

1929 performed a lot like 1987 as the S&P 500 was up +33% through August and then the crash came in October. What happened after that would test the mettle of anyone. As an investor how would you have stood up during the depression years?

The first use of the Fail-Safe Sell Signal would have been a traumatic experience for most anyone when you have to sell out your investment position at a -31% loss from its highest high. Then to be whipsawed by buying back in only to be sold out again would surely have discouraged the toughest trader. One could draw some solace from the fact that the Hits-Plus investor is doing much better than the others but certainly not all that great. Finally when we were out of the market during the depression years, U.S. Treasury Bills and Intermediate-Term Government Bonds did very little as far as performance.

Now is a good time to talk about patience. A certain amount of patience is necessary for any investor and during the thirties you would have needed a lot of patience to have stayed with any investment program.

It's No Action-Packed Horse Race

If you have never invested in the stock market before and you consider yourself a person who really likes action then you may need to adjust your outlook. The stock market is not a horse race or a blackjack game. Some first time investors buy into the market and then eagerly check their mutual fund listings each day hoping to see dramatic jumps. They think even -15% drops, followed by +17% gains would be better than what appears to be "just sitting there." Where's the action? Can't we blow on the dice and make something happen? Sorry, it doesn't work that way.

When and if you go to the horse races you could see and bet on horses in eight to ten different races in the space of a few hours. But, that is gambling, not investing, and there is a difference.

With stock market investing and the Hits-Plus strategy, a one-year period may be like a single horse race that lasts only minutes. It's like so last year was an up year or down year instead of that last horse race delivered a winner or a loser in a few minutes.

Your Hits-Plus mutual fund portfolio could end the year being up +18% or more with part of that coming from dividends buying additional shares and part coming from per share increase (appreciated growth). The tracking of the year's performance could border on boredom for some, but I can get very excited about my portfolio growing +18% in a year, and I hope you can, too. As a saver and investor you must be patient or develop patience and discipline.

Remember, with the 1929 through 1949 Hits-Plus tracking, that after 1932 (a four-year period) we had -11.1% less money than when we started. Never mind that a buy-and-hold investor would have been down -64.2%. Now that is a time when we must have patience and strong discipline.

Margin Twice in a Row

Then, for the margin user, there comes the year 1941 when we used one-third margin and still the market went down. This meant that the margin investor should go with full 50% margin for 1942. With Pearl Harbor just being bombed and the United States fully involved in World War II, it would have taken some real courage and discipline for the Hits-Plus margin investor to borrow even more money for his upcoming 1942 investment year.

As I hope you can see, this is an exercise to help you decide what exactly is your personal psychological make-up as an investor. *How will you face different possible investment situations and investing decisions?*

I do not mean for this chapter to sound all negative. There were many more good years than bad. Hits-Plus and Super Hits-Plus had a lot more upside power and a lot less downside experiences than any investment strategy that I know of.

Remember in the 44-year period from 1950 through 1993, Hits-Plus only had three down years and all three together loss less than -2%.

You could put all of your savings and investment dollars in fixed income vehicles and sit back. But, I wonder if our old friend Harvey or the $250 a month or the $300 a month annuity retiree experienced any greater psychological health than the Hits-Plus investor. I think not.

Of course, as I said before, I don't know anyone who owns a working crystal ball, so I have to proclaim the usual disclaimer that past performance cannot serve as a guarantee that future results will be similar.

CHAPTER EIGHTEEN

Another Look at Dollar Cost Averaging

"If thou wouldst keep money, save money; If thou wouldst reap money, sow money"
-- Thomas Fuller

Another look at dollar cost averaging? Have we taken the first look?

We have touched on the aspects of dollar cost averaging several times. I also say "another look" because if the reader has read much at all about investing, you already have some familiarity with this investment approach.

Dollar cost averaging is one of the oldest and still one of the best investment programs. In fact, for many of us, at one time or another, it's almost a must because we just don't have a big one lump sum to start with.

With dollar cost averaging you simply budget a certain amount of money monthly, quarterly, or even annually and

Table 18.1

XYZ Mutual Fund Quarterly Investing

Quarter	Amount Invested	Share Price	Shares Purchased	Total Invested	Total Value
1	$500	$8	62.50	$ 500	$ 500
2	$500	$10	50.00	$1,000	$ 1,125
3	$500	$7	71.43	$1,500	$ 1,287
4	$500	$9	55.55	$2,000	$ 2,155
1	$500	$10	50.00	$2,500	$ 2,895
2	$500	$11	45.45	$3,000	$ 3,684
3	$500	$11	45.45	$3,500	$ 4,184
4	$500	$13	38.46	$4,000	$ 5,445
1	$500	$13	38.46	$4,500	$ 5,445
2	$500	$12	41.67	$5,000	$ 5,526
3	$500	$11	45.45	$5,500	$ 5,566
4	$500	$14	35.71	$6,000	$ 7,583
1	$500	$13	38.46	$6,500	$ 8,622
2	$500	$14	35.71	$7,000	$ 8,622
3	$500	$16	31.25	$7,500	$10,353
4	$500	$15	33.33	$10,206	$10,206
4	$500	$17	29.41	$8,000	$12,067

244

then invest that specified amount every month, quarter, or year with no real regard to where the market is at the time of investment (if you're not following Hits-Plus or another market timing program). Over a long period of time you will find you have bought some shares at high prices, but at other times you acquired shares at real bargain prices and the end results will almost always be very good. Our first look at dollar cost averaging will be in the traditional manner without any market timing approach.

Let's take a quick glance at Table 18.1, which utilizes a hypothetical mutual fund with (NAV) share prices changing as you invest ($500 a quarter) on a quarterly dollar cost averaging plan.

After four years of investing in the XYZ Mutual Fund you have acquired 709.83 shares of stock with a total value of $12,067. You purchased shares at various prices from a bargain price of $7 per share to a high of $17. You paid an average price of $11.94 giving you a compounded quarterly return of a little less than +21%. Of course, the share prices could start falling and the total value of your stock portfolio would drop, but you would stick to the dollar cost averaging program and keep acquiring shares at lower prices in hopes that XYZ would ultimately rebound and you would reap the rewards.

Let's take our dollar cost averaging program a little further. Let's imagine that our next twelve quarters of investing will be during years similar to 1973, 1974 and 1975, two terrible years, and then finally a good year (See Table 18.2).

There would have been times when it would have taken courage to keep buying shares in the XYZ Mutual Fund as the price keeps falling. We would have had to rationalize to ourselves "O.K., so the price is dropping, so what. That just means we can acquire more shares at a lower price and the day will come when a bull market will take us back to the top of the mountain."

But, this whole book is about Hits-Plus so how does dollar cost averaging work with the Hits-Plus strategy?

Table 18.2

XYZ Mutual Fund Quarterly Investing Continued

Quarter	Amount Invested	Share Price	Shares Purchased	Total Invested	Total Value
1	$500	$15	33.33	$ 500	$11,147
2	$500	$13	38.46	$1,000	$10,161
3	$500	$12	41.67	$1,500	$ 9,879
4	$500	$11	45.45	$2,000	$ 9,556
1	$500	$11	45.45	$2,500	$10,056
2	$500	$10	50.00	$3,000	$ 9,642
3	$500	$8	62.50	$3,500	$ 8,214
4	$500	$9	55.55	$4,000	$ 9,740
1	$500	$11	45.45	$4,500	$12,405
2	$500	$12	41.67	$5,000	$14,032
3	$500	$13	38.46	$5,500	$15,702
4	$500	$15	33.33	$6,000	$18,667

246

Dollar Cost Averaging with Hits-Plus

Dollar cost averaging works very simply, actually. If our monthly, quarterly, or yearly budgeted investment sum is enough to meet the minimum investment requirements of our chosen Hits-Plus or Super Hits-Plus mutual fund, we just invest exactly the way Hits-Plus directs us to at the time and also move our total portfolio around in the manner the Hits-Plus rules indicate.

In other words, if Hits-Plus has us in an S&P 500 Index Mutual Fund we invest our dollar cost averaging quarterly (or whatever time period) investment sum in that S&P 500 Index Fund. When and if Hits-Plus directs us to shift to a money fund and bond fund we shift our entire portfolio accordingly and then invest our regular dollar cost averaging amount into the new portfolio. The same would be true of Super Hits-Plus

There have been periods of time when a quarterly dollar cost averaging investment program would have been a better approach than with a monthly program, but usually the sooner you put your money to work in the mutual fund that Hits-Plus directs you to the better. However, primarily in the interest of time and space, I will track the 1970 through 1993 period with a quarterly dollar cost averaging approach.

In this quarterly dollar cost averaging I will use $625 per quarter (i.e., $208.33 per month, $2,500 per year). In reality the minimum initial purchase for most mutual funds will be higher than $625. With the Vanguard funds the minimum initial purchase is $3,000 or $500 for IRA accounts. After the initial purchase just $100 is required to make additional purchases. If you don't have the $3,000 for the initial investment simply save it in your bank account until you have it. In this study I have taken the liberty of dollar cost averaging $625 from the beginning.

1970 First Quarter-to-End of January

Quarterly Investment	$625
Share Price	$60.06
Total Shares	10.41
End-of-Quarter Share Price	$55.59
End-of-January Total Value	$579

1969 had been a down year so Hits-Plus called for us to invest in the S&P 500 Index on the first trading day of January and await the results of the January Barometer. January was down -7.4% so we sold out of the S&P 500 and split our money between U.S. Treasury Bills and Intermediate-Term Government Bonds. As you can see, we are following Hits-Plus directives exactly except we invest our money quarterly, as we save it, instead of with the one lump sum.

1970 February and March

Total Funds	$579
U.S. T-Bills	$289.50
Bond Fund	$289.50
End-of-March Value	$597

Our T-Bill and Bond money decreased to $597 by the end of March. On the first trading day in April we invest our second quarter's $625 again in T-Bills and Bonds as Hits-Plus calls for us to do for the remainder of the year.

1970 Second Quarter

Quarterly Investment	$625
Total Investment	$1,222
U.S. T-Bills	$605
Bond Fund	$617
Total Value (End of Quarter)	$1,231

1970 Third Quarter

Quarterly Investment	$625
Total Investment	$1,856
U.S. T-Bills	$929
Bond Fund	$927
Total Value (End of Quarter)	$1,914

1970 Fourth Quarter

Quarterly Investment	$625
Total Investment	$2,539
U.S. T-Bills	$1,256
Bond Fund	$1,283
Total Value (End of Quarter)	$2,634

At the end of the year the total value of our investment was $2,634. At the end of 1970 we have had two down years in a row, according to Hits-Plus, so it calls for us to be fully invested back in the S&P 500 Index and to use one-third margin.

1971 First Quarter

Quarterly Investment	$625
Money from T-Bills & Bond Fund	$2,634
Investment	$3,259
Margin Loan	$1,630
Total Invested Including Margin	$4,889
Share Price	$62.46
Total Shares	78.27
Share Price End of Quarter	$68.52
Total Gross Value End of Quarter	$5,363

As you can see, we still followed the Hits-Plus directives exactly. In reality, we might not be able to use margin with this small total investment sum, and, if we could, the loan rate would be more than prime. But, for our research purposes we will still assume the use of margin. In any event, there would be little difference between the use or non-use of margin in the early years.

1971 Second Quarter

Quarterly Investment	$625
Share Price	$68.52
Additional Shares Purchased	9.12
Total Shares	87.39
Total Gross Value	$5,987
Share Price End of Quarter	$68.64
Total Gross Value End of Quarter	$5,998

1971 Third Quarter

Quarterly Investment	$625
Share Price	$68.64
Additional Shares Purchased	9.11
Total Shares	96.50
Total Gross Value	$6,624
Share Price End of Month	$68.23
Total Gross Value End of Quarter	$6,584

1971 Fourth Quarter

Quarterly Investment	$625
Share Price	$68.23
Additional Shares Purchases	9.16
Total Shares	105.66
Total Gross Value	$7,209
Share Price End of Quarter	$71.41
Total Gross Value End of Quarter	$7,545
Total Value after Loan Paid	$5,822

For 1972 we stayed in the market, invested our $625 the first trading day in January, and awaited the January Barometer. January was up. Throughout 1972 we bought into the S&P 500 Index at the beginning of each quarter. At the end of the year we held 114.67 shares and with the share price being $84.96 the total value was $9,742.

At the end of 1972 we had had two up years in a row so we sold our S&P 500 Index shares and put the money in U.S. Treasury Bills and Intermediate-Term Government bonds and continued to invest the $625 at the beginning of each quarter. As we know now, this was a good move as the market tumbled in 1973. At the end of 1973 our total value in the T-Bills and Bonds was $12,907.

In 1974 we shifted back into the S&P 500 Index to see what January would do. January was down so back in the T-Bills and Bonds we go and avoid another bear market year. 1974 ends with a total value of $16,260, but we do not go immediately back into the S&P 500 Index because if we had been in the market we would have been sold out by the -30% "Fail-Safe Sell Signal;" therefore, we must wait until the +21% Fail-Safe Buy Signal is flashed. We still continue to invest the $625 at the beginning of each quarter to where Hits-Plus says it should go. On the first trading day of February, 1975, the Fail-Safe Buy Signal is flashed and we buy back into the S&P 500 Index complete with the use of one-third margin.

Keep Tracking to Keep on Track

I think now the reader can grasp exactly how dollar cost averaging works with the use of Hits-Plus. It's not difficult at all. You spend a little time tracking the S&P 500 Index on a monthly basis and follow the Hits-Plus rules. You still use the January Barometer when called for. You still use margin when called for (if you choose to use margin). You still track and watch to see if the S&P 500 Index falls -31% from its end-of the-month highest high, thereby flashing the Fail-Safe Sell Signal. And if the Fail-Safe Sell Signal is flashed, you will continue to track the market for a +21% rise from its end-of-the-month lowest low. Here's how things would have continued with the $625 per quarter dollar cost averaging with Hits-Plus:

End of 1975 Total Value:	$23,881
End of 1976 Total Value:	$32,323
End of 1977 Total Value:	$35,940
End of 1978 Total Value:	$38,032
End of 1979 Total Value:	$48,892
End of 1980 Total Value:	$67,877
End of 1981 Total Value:	$78,805
End of 1982 Total Value:	$95,121
End of 1983 Total Value:	$119,250
End of 1984 Total Value:	$136,210
End of 1985 Total Value:	$182,357
End of 1986 Total Value:	$218,697
End of 1987 Total Value:	$230,358
End of 1988 Total Value:	$271,793
End of 1989 Total Value:	$360,321
End of 1990 Total Value:	$394,558
End of 1991 Total Value:	$518,012
End of 1992 Total Value:	$543,323
End of 1993 Total Value:	$600,239

This is earning you an average quarterly compounded return of over +15.5%. Not bad at all. Whereas if you had simply invested your $625 per quarter in the S&P 500 Index with a buy-and-hold (no market timing) strategy, you would have had a total value of $382,788 at the end of 1993. That's over $200,000 less than with the use of Hits-Plus.

Of course, you can use the same dollar cost averaging approach *with the Super Hits-Plus strategy and the same investment of $625 per quarter from 1970 through 1993 would have grown to $1,042,644 (without margin).* That's by investing $2,500 ($625 quarterly) a total of $60,000 spread over a 24-year period and earning an average quarterly compounded return of over 18.25%.

To add a little more to the "Believe it or not" aspect of what you could have achieved from 1970 through 1993 with a $625 per quarter program with Super Hits-Plus, think about this. If you had stopped investing the $625 per quarter (but kept up Super Hits-Plus management) after the first eight years (at the end of 1977) your portfolio would have still grown to a value of $910,041 by the end of 1993. Bear in mind that's with just investing a total of $20,000 spread over an eight-year period. Of course not all time frames would have performed this good, but then some would have done better.

What helped with the dollar cost averaging program was that actually during the early years the market didn't perform so well which allowed the dollar cost average advocate to buy more shares at a lower price that would be worth much more years later.

But although this was a fairly good 24-year investment time period remember it did contain the big 1973-74 bear market and since Super Hits-Plus is not perfect it had us outside of the market (and in T-Bills and Intermediate Government Bonds) during a number of those red-hot Small Company Stock Index years from 1975 through 1983. But after the dust settles Super Hits-Plus is, without a doubt, the performance champion.

Progressive Dollar Cost Averaging

Actually, I believe you should add one other factor to your dollar cost averaging program to make it "Progressive Dollar Cost Averaging." If you have determined the amount of money you can save and invest on a monthly or quarterly basis then you should start with the program and by all means stick to it. But, hopefully over the years you will be receiving raises and promotions that will increase your take home income. When this occurs you should increase your monthly or quarterly savings and investments also. No, I'm not saying for you to put the entire net increase take home into your dollar cost averaging program. With your much deserved salary increase you certainly should spend a little more on life's enjoyments. If your raise brings you $400 more per quarter you should look to putting perhaps $40 to $80 more per quarter in your savings and investment program. This will help a great deal to assure you of reaching a higher total value goal. If you believe you will have to stop your savings and investment program after eight years or so, as Henry and Helen did in Chapter Fourteen, then maybe you should put an even larger portion of your new take-home salary increase in your monthly or quarterly investments.

You Will Get Promotions, Right?

I will assume, for a moment, that the reader is a young person just starting his or her career, has a strong work ethic, and will pursue the necessary training, etc., to keep his or her career on a progressive track. If this is true, then raises and job position promotions will come. In reality, we know that they will not come in a fixed time frame but for the purpose of demonstrating the "Progressive Dollar Cost Averaging" program, we will give the hypothetical investor +6.4% more each year to invest from the beginning of 1971 through 1977 and then he/she will stop investing altogether and just let Hits-Plus take the one lump that is achieved by the end of 1977 on through 1993.

In other words, the investor will start his or her "Progressive Dollar Cost Averaging" program at the beginning of 1970 with $625 a quarter; in 1971 the quarterly investment will go to $665 per quarter, $708 per quarter in 1972, $753 per quarter for 1973, $801 per quarter in 1974, $852 per quarter for 1975, $907 per quarter in 1976, and $965 per quarter for the final investment year in 1977.

With this "Progressive Dollar Cost Averaging" program utilizing Hits-Plus the investor will have a portfolio value of $42,938 at the end of 1977. That's +19.47% more than one would have had with a straight $625 per quarter dollar cost averaging program with Hits-Plus.

What is even more astounding is that although the investor would stop putting more money into his or her investment portfolio after the initial eight years, the $42,938 achievement would go on to grow to $501,303 by the end of 1993. That's only $98,936 less than what the straight dollar cost averaging Hits-Plus investor would have had at the end of 1993, even with a continuation of investing $625 per quarter for the entire 24-year period. Remember, too, that the dollar cost averaging investor who did not invest with Hits-Plus but used a buy-and-hold investment strategy in the S&P 500 Index only had $382,496 after 24 years of investing $625 every quarter, whereas the Progressive Dollar Cost Averaging Hits-Plus investor invested less than half that total amount and invested for just the first eight years.

Progressive dollar cost averaging did even better with Super Hits-Plus. Using the same quarterly program amounts, as just illustrated, and stopping the investing after 1977 (but continuing to switch in and out of the market as directed by Super Hits-Plus) the Super Hits-Plus investor would have a portfolio value of $1,079,481 at the end of 1993.

Incredible as it may seem a total of just $25,096 spread over the first eight years of investing resulted in a portfolio of over a million dollars (taxes not figured).

This really points out the power of Progressive Dollar Cost Averaging that enables you to make excellent progress in the early years putting you well ahead of other strategies. It also re-emphasizes the power of Hits-Plus and Super Hits-Plus.

Dollar cost averaging is one of the oldest and highest regarded investment strategies. I've heard it said that the only thing wrong with dollar cost averaging is that you can't use it with a one lump sum investment.

But, of course, you can and this is an approach that makes a lot of sense to some investors. A close friend of mine who read the first draft of this book reported back to me that he really liked the Hits-Plus System, but he had some reservations. In fact, he was somewhat nervous about any particular investment strategy and with good reason.

My friend's situation is that he's 59 years of age, has a nice one lump sum to invest, but wants to retire in six years. He's not comfortable with how the market looks at this time and Hits-Plus is on a January Barometer year. He's nervous that if his first investment year is a bad down year this will put a lot of stress on him and if he experiences two down years or flat years in a row this really would stress him out.

I suggested that he might consider dollar cost averaging over a two to three-year period. He could invest one-third of his one lump sum now and the next two thirds the following year or over the next two years. This could also be done quarterly to ease into the program a little slower.

The fact is everyone's individual financial and investment position is different and they certainly must take this into consideration. Often a dollar cost averaging approach will be very helpful to an individual's personal situation.

CHAPTER NINETEEN

Obtaining Your Investment Capital

"The average man...is always waiting for something to happen to him instead of setting to work to make things happen."
-- A.A. Milne

"I'm a great believer in luck, and I find the harder I work the more I have of it."
-- Thomas Jefferson

"If you want to become really wealthy...you must have your money work for you. The amount you get paid for your personal effort is relatively small compared with the amount you can earn by having your money make money."
-- John D. Rockefeller

I originally thought of this chapter being keyed toward young people just starting out in a career and I still intend for that to be the main focus. However, it's never too late to start a savings and investing program, and old dogs can indeed be taught new tricks. If you're 45 years old, 55, or even 65 hopefully you still have a number of great years ahead, and if you don't currently have an investment program in place and working, you should certainly get started now.

Actually, I will still address this chapter toward the just starting out, young people, but many of the concepts presented are good principals for anyone to embrace.

Many times, years ago, I would talk to my contemporaries about plans for the future and what we might do to make our plans work out. All too often the truth of the A.A. Milne quote was borne out.

Don't Wait for the Ship or the Luck

"One day my ship will come in," some would say. However, they never said where their ship was sailing from, what cargo it was carrying, or what course it was taking.

"Maybe I'll get lucky like the other rich folks did," others might remark. Get lucky? Sure there are some who have inherited wealth and a minute few who experienced a lot of luck, but they are very small in number. The vast majority of those who have comfortable wealth (and yes, wealth is a relative term) arrived at that status by working hard and working smart.

Hard work is necessary, but that alone will not do it. If hard work was all that was needed then we could all go out and dig ditches or any other number of back breaking jobs and wait for riches to come our way. There is physical hard work and mental hard work, either of which can bring in decent incomes, but to this element we must be smart. I don't mean rocket scientist I.Q. smart. I mean logical, rational thinking with discipline and a plan of action.

A Road Map for Your Financial Trip

I don't believe any of us would attempt to drive an automobile from the East coast to the West coast, or vice-versa, without setting a practical agenda. We would check out our automobile to be sure it was in good condition, and we would get out a good road map and plan the trip. We would estimate the mileage and time to drive from one location to another in a day's travel. We would probably make reservations for our overnight stays. This planning would not be difficult, but it would be necessary. Then once our travel plans were made, our job would be to stick to those plans, as close as possible, to assure a fun-filled, safe, and secure trip. Sure, there could be a flat tire experienced along the way, plus a wrong turn or two, but with a little discipline and by sticking with our plans we'd have a great trip.

The same is true if you want to take an investment trip to achieve a plateau of financial comfort. You must get ready for the trip. You must have a road map and a plan. You must set all of this in action and stick with it. You'll find the trip will be exciting, fun, and very rewarding.

There is no magic wand you can wave or mysterious words you can utter while rolling your eyes a certain way to get you started with investment capital and a continuing program enabling you to reach your financial goals in an "oh so easy manner."

That task is up to you, and it might call for a few small sacrifices to begin with on your part. "Sacrifices, oh no!" you might scream. "You're talking hardships, right?" Not necessarily. Call it a challenge or a slight adjustment in your lifestyle for a while to make your lifestyle much better in the future.

Establishing the Budget

First you must determine how much money you can logically save and invest. To do this you must establish a personal budget, and to do this you need to track your spending. Spend a dollar or two on a cheap ledger and start keeping up with every dollar you spend every month. Your rent or house payment, utilities, groceries, insurance premiums, haircuts, gasoline and maintenance for the automobile (if you own one), car payments, credit card payments, cigarettes (if you smoke), booze (if you drink), eating out, and spending on hobbies. Indeed, track all of your spending and you may find some surprises. You'll also find that after you do this for a while it's very helpful as you can look back at corresponding months in a past year and know when that annual or quarterly insurance premium will be coming up. You can look back and know when high utilities months come up and when other larger quarterly, semi-annual, and annual bills will be due.

Most of all, I think you will be surprised how much unnecessary spending you may be doing in certain areas. I found I was subscribing to more magazines, newspapers, and services than I could possibly use. I still subscribe to a lot of periodicals, but I did not renew those that I never read or needed to read. Put check marks beside those expenditures you can cut out, cut back on, or otherwise control.

Can you save $20 per week? $30 a week? The amount you determine you can save should be within your comfort zone. It should be a sum with some aggressive ambition, but know yourself well enough not to set a savings goal so high that it will become a hurting sacrifice to the point where you will chuck the whole idea and go back to waiting for your ship to come in.

Automobile Poor or Portfolio Rich

In your quest to budget a savings and investment sum, look at the big spending areas, as well as the small expenditures. Where I live there is not a lot of public transportation so automobile ownership is just about a must for the family or individual, but it doesn't have to be a Mercedes, BMW, Cadillac, or even a new car. Over the years I have owned new cars and used cars. I have done very well with good used cars by carefully shopping and spending a little extra for an extended warranty to cover the major components of the car.

I see so many young people, just out of high school or college, head straight for the new car dealer and buy all the automobile they can possibly purchase with a relatively small down payment and lots of credit. It's not unusual now to see new cars sold on a 72-month loan. That's six years and that, in most cases, is completely ridiculous. If they had bought a good two- or three-year-old lower priced economical used car and saved and invested the difference it would have resulted in a big leap forward toward reaching their financial goals.

No Big Spender. No Miser

Stop smoking (if you do) and save your health and your money, up to $1,100 a year or more. Eat out less or at less expensive places. Shop for your clothes more carefully. Look for sales and comparison shop. Maybe you should buy a book like *Penny Pinching: How to Lower Your Everyday Expenses Without Lowering Your Standard of Living* by Lee and Barbara Simmons. I confess I have not read the book but I have read several highly regarded reviews, and it's supposed to be outstanding. I'm not trying to turn you into some never-have-fun miser. Samuel Johnson said, "A man who both spends and saves his money is the happiest man, because he has both enjoyments." You will discover that saving is an enjoyment, bringing a real sense of accomplishment, and I think you will actually enjoy spending better too when you have a sense that your spending is wise and controlled.

Pay Yourself First

There is an old saying that when it comes to saving you should pay yourself first. All this means is that when you set up your personal budget, your budgeted savings amount should be right in there along with the utility bill and rent. Don't be like the people who say, "I'll save what's left over." There's rarely anything left over with that approach. But, when you pay yourself first with the budgeted savings set aside you will usually automatically cut down on behavior spending.

How much should you be able to save and invest? Most of my life, especially in the early career years, I have saved between 10% and 20% of my income, actually nearer 20%. I did this with no real strain, without big incomes in the early years, and all the while my wife, myself, and my children maintained a nice standard of living complete with good automobiles, nice homes, vacations, travel, and college educations. I know of a number of people who beat me in this area so its really not that difficult if you really want to and firmly decide to do it.

So you can save $30 per week. That's good for now. At an average annual +15% compounded return that would give you $23,873 in eight years, $87,000 in fifteen years, $194,641 in twenty years, $421,657 in twenty-five years and over $900,000 in thirty years. But you can probably do better than this. In the preceding chapter we pointed out how you should use progressive dollar cost averaging in your investment program. That is, when you receive a raise, or salary increasing promotion, your savings and investment sum should also go up, not using the entire raise, of course. You deserve to enjoy a little more spending too, but 10% to 20% of that salary increase should go into your savings and investment program. This will better equip you to beat inflation and to reach a very comfortable personal financial level much sooner.

As I mentioned in Chapter Fourteen, I believe it's very important for a married couple to display a keen sense of cooperative teamwork to pursue a good family savings and investment program.

Most couples today, by necessity or choice, are both income earners. Both spouses need a certain amount of independence. I personally believe it's best to pool both salaries and then to budget personal allowances to each for individual pursuits. However, the family budget should be just that, a family budget.

The family budget should be set up to include rent or house payment, utilities, groceries, all insurance premiums, automobile payments and maintenance, etc., and, of course, savings and investment, except savings and investment should be at the top of the list under the "Pay yourself first" approach.

I have seen too many couples display so much independence to the point of "That's my chair and that's his table." "I make the car payment and she makes the house payment." "He's going to spend all he makes, so if I don't do likewise He'll want mine too." Sometimes it goes on and on. "I don't know her business and she doesn't know mine."

Is it any wonder when this type of attitude persists that so little can be accomplished with any kind of family savings and investment program.

If a married couple has any real love and respect for each other, they should be able to work out some mutually satisfactory program and the sooner after they're first married the best.

Ongoing Management a Must

There's little doubt in my mind that if people really make up their minds, utilize discipline, and execute a systematic savings and investment program that they will be successful in reaching their financial goals. But managing their investment portfolios and personal finances is an ongoing lifetime process.

For someone who has nothing saved and invested, a person with a $10,000 portfolio may appear to be wealthy. To the $10,000 person the owner of a $100,000 portfolio seems to be rich. The $100,000 person may look on the net worth of $1,000,000 as being a wealthy plateau. A simple millionaire may think it would take $20 million to $30 million to truly feel wealthy. And on and on it goes.

They all do have one thing in common. If they do not continue to manage their portfolios and personal finances in a logical manner they can all go broke faster than they think. No one can ever reach a net worth position that is totally secure if foolishness prevails.

A few years ago Donald Trump (primarily a real estate mogul) rated a high position in *Forbes* Four Hundred (a list of the top wealthiest individuals); today some financial writers claim he may have a negative net worth. I don't know, but if it is true I would suspect that Mr. Trump's investing so much in "trophies" instead of solid real estate at proper investment multiples and without "pie-in-the-sky" projections would be a main contributing cause.

We know that the Hunt Brothers of Texas lost multiple millions in a wild scheme to corner the silver market.

Some say the Joseph Kennedy fortune has diminished greatly due to non-progressive management and scores of heirs who have demonstrated little interest in business or management.

Almost weekly, you can read about professional sports stars or entertainment stars who earn millions a year declaring bankruptcy. Usually the articles point out poor management and a lifestyle that appeared to represent the idea that they believed they were so rich they couldn't possibly spend themselves broke. They learned otherwise.

The management of your investment and personal finances is an ongoing thing. But, lets get something to manage.

The time to start is now. Get out your road map, track your spending, set up your budget, and head for the rainbow. Have a great trip.

ALMOST
THE FINAL WORD

This is the "almost" final word instead of the "final" word simply because the future will continue to come to us; whereas much of Hits-Plus is based on the premise that history repeats itself, it also recognizes that it does not do this in lock-step with past events.

There will be new elements introduced that will influence the stock market, at least in short term periods. But someone who has an investment strategy that is based on solid long term historical data covering various types of market conditions will certainly be in a much better position to calculate the percentages and probabilities of how the future market will perform.

I will continue to conduct historical stock market research in an effort to fine-tune Hits-Plus and Super Hits-Plus into an even stronger investment strategy.

I will now attempt to answer in advance what I anticipate might be a few criticisms of Hits-Plus and its presentation in this book.

I am sure there will be those who will point out that Hits-Plus is the prime result of historical research and "looking back to see" is not the same as going onward with an investments strategy in "real time." This is true as far as it goes.

Hits-Plus is <u>primarily</u> the result of historical research, but its inception came about over a long period of time—parts of it being tested in "real time" for as much as fifteen years. I have also personally invested with Hits-Plus and Super Hits-Plus programs for some time in "real time." But, I do hasten to add that Hits-Plus was not in effect as a working "real time" model back in the thirties, forties, fifties, or sixties.

Over the past thirty years I must have read and studied hundreds of investment books and investment strategies, some good, some bad, and some mediocre. All were based to a large extent on historical research to support their investment theories. One big difference in these books and the Hits-Plus program is that the historical research in most of the other books covered as little as six to twenty years and many obviously stayed away from the poor performing sixties and would never attempt to historically test their strategies in the thirties and forties.

I think Hits-Plus has gone the whole nine yards with sixty-five years of historical model testing which showed that whereas the strategy is not perfect (there is no perfect strategy), Hits-Plus does emerge as being a solid, outstanding program that in normal times makes the S&P 500 perform like an excellent aggressive growth mutual fund but without the tremendous volatile double digit grizzly bear drops and Super Hits-Plus turns in even greater performance, especially over longer time frames.

Some critics may say I did not figure the cost of federal and state taxes in the end results as much as I should have. My answer is that most investment books do not address the tax question since the tax situation of the thousands of readers of any investment book may differ in a thousand different ways. We all will have to pay our own individual taxes, but the first order of the day is to make a decent return on your investments and then face the tax question.

Other critics may say I have ignored virtually all of the many favorite stock market indicators. They may say I should have given weight to a thirty-nine week moving average indicator, the S&P 500 Price/dividend ratio, the Federal Reserve buy/sell rule, the Sentiment evaluation index, and many other popular indicators.

My answer to this question is that Hits-Plus by its very nature automatically takes into account all such indicators. There are thousands of investors who faithfully follow one or more of these favorite indicators. Some try to give various degrees of weight to all of the more popular indicators. I can't recall a time in investment history when all of the more popular indicators were either totally bullish or totally bearish.

The position of Hits-Plus is that the market is a big voting machine with buyers and sellers casting their votes, often because of directives of their favorite market indicator. This sets up a the market that is constantly searching for its proper real value. So, in effect, these indicators are factored in by the votes of their followers, and Hits-Plus just weighs the historical data and goes with what has always most problematically implied whether the upcoming year will bring a down market or an up market.

Sometimes an argument is raised, usually by someone who is very new to the stock market investment world: "What happens if everyone decides to follow the Hits-Plus program?" The answer to this is simple and the answer is the same in regards to all other investment strategies. There are so many investment ideas, systems, and strategies that no one approach will ever be adopted by enough investors to artificially alter the market or the value of the strategy itself. Hits-Plus, I think, will be followed successfully by a good number of individual investors, but it cannot be followed by the biggest players in the market. The mutual funds, large investment institutions, and managers of large portfolios simply cannot adopt Hits-Plus as a strategy. They cannot move virtually all of their funds out of the market and into T-Bills and Bonds in one gigantic move, and back into the market in another sweeping move. Only individual investors can utilize Hits-Plus, and even if thousands of individuals do this with millions of dollars, it won't make a ripple in the overall complexion of the market, not when one single mutual fund (Fidelity Magellan) controls over $20 billion in investments. And sad but true most individual investors who pick an investment strategy to follow quickly abandon it if it has a poor performing year or two. I stated earlier in this book that "... common sense is actually very uncommon." The same is true when it comes to patience and discipline.

Hits-Plus and Super Hits-Plus are the programs I follow in "real time" and with "real money." None of us can predict the future but we can use reason and logic, and, for this investor, Hits-Plus is the most logical investment strategy on the scene today.

LAST MINUTE UPDATE

"The great rule of moral conduct is, next to God, to respect Time."
-- *Johann Kaspar Lavater*

If you ever write a book you will learn, as I have, that it takes a great deal of time. It takes time to research and write the first draft of the manuscript. It takes time to expose the various drafts to selected readers for constructive criticism. It takes time to critique the feed back from these readers and to utilize some of it in additional re-writing. And it takes time for "blue pencil" editing and all that goes with it.

The original manuscript, of this book, took the performance of Hits-Plus and Super Hits-Plus through 1991. As time passed, this obviously became out-of-date, so the last drafts went through 1993. At this point I hoped publication would take place during 1994. This was not to be as time continued to move.

With all this in mind I have decided to give the readers a last minute update that will take us through July, 1995. I realize that this too will soon be out-of-date, but you have to stop somewhere. Of course, the newsletter, *Hits-Plus Mutual Fund Guide* is published monthly and tracks the performance of Hits-Plus and Super Hits-Plus on a monthly basis.

1994

1993 was an up year with a +10% S&P 500 gain, but 1992 had been a down year so 1994's investment position would be directed by the January Barometer.

January of 1994 was up. However, the January Barometer would prove to be incorrect as *1994 ended up with an anemic +1.2% performance for the Hits-Plus program* (invested in the Vanguard Index 500 Fund. *The Super Hits-Plus investor (investing in the Vanguard Index Small Cap Fund) was down with a -0.51% loss.*

1995

With 1994 being a down year for the S&P 500, once again we are called on to be directed by the January Barometer. Again January is an up month and therefore directing the Hits-Plus and Super Hits-Plus investors to stay invested in 1995 (unless a Fail-Safe Sell Signal is flashed).

So far, *through July, 1995 has been an outstanding year for the Hits-Plus and Super Hits-Plus investors*. Every month has been a plus month. This has occurred only twice since 1926.

Through July 1995 the Hits-Plus investor (in the Vanguard Index 500 Fund) has a total compounded return of +24.1%. The Super Hits-Plus investor (in the Vanguard Index Small Cap Fund) is up +21.2%.

There we have the update through July 1995. Sure it will be out-of-date when you read this, but we have to go to the printers sometime.

INFORMATION JUST ADDED

Don't forget to send for your trial subscription of
Hits-Plus Mutual Fund Guide for up to date information.
See FREE offer on page 285.

Hits-Plus ended **1995** with a total return gain of **+37.5%**. We were in the market in 1996 (because of the Jan. Barometer). **1996** produced a total return of **+22.9%**. **We were out of the market for 1997**.

SUPER HITS-PLUS ended **1995** with a total return gain of **+28.7%**, and **1996** produced a total return of **+18.1%**.

We were out of the market for 1997. And, we are out of the market for 1998. *It appears that the stock market is in a more overvalued position than it's been since 1929.*

Appendix A: Selected Mutual Funds

Capital Preservation Fund
The Benham Group
P.O. Box 7730
San Francisco, CA. 94120-9853
Phone: (800) 472-3389

Dreyfus Index
144 Glenn Curtiss Blvd.
Uniondale, NY 11556-0144
Phone: (800) 242-8671
(718) 895-1396

Newberger/Berman Guardian
342 Madison Ave., Suite 1620
New York, NY 10173
Phone: (800) 877-9700
(212) 850-8300

Portico Equity Index
207 E. Buffalo St., Suite 315
Milwaukee, WI 53202
Phone: (800) 228-1024
(414) 287-3808

SEI Index S&P 500 Index
680 E. Swedesford Rd.
Wayne, PA 19087-1658
Phone: (800) 342-5734
(215) 254-1000

Vanguard Index 500
Vanguard Financial Center PO Box 2600
Valley Forge, PA 19482
Phone: (800) 662-7447
(215) 648-6000

Vanguard Small Capitalization Stock
Vanguard Financial Center PO Box 2600
Valley Forge, PA 19482
Phone: (800) 662-7447
   (215) 648-6000

Bond Funds

California U.S. Govt. Securities
44 Montgomery St.
Suite #2200
San Francisco, CA 94104
Phone: (800) 225-8778

Dreyfus U.S. Govt. Intermediate
144 Glenn Curtiss Blvd.
Uniondale, NY 11556-0144
Phone: (800) 648-9048

Fidelity Intermediate Bond
82 Devonshire St.
Boston, MA 02109
Phone: (800) 544-8888

Value Line U.S. Govt. Securities
711 Third Ave.
New York, NY 10017
Phone: (800) 223-0818

Vanguard Fixed-Income Short-Term Govt. Bond
Vanguard Financial Center
PO Box 2600
Valley Forge, PA 19482
Phone: (800) 662-7447

Appendix B: Selected Discount Brokers

Freeman Welwood & Co., Inc.
2800 Century Square
501 4th Ave.
Seattle, WA 98101
Phone: (800) 729-7585
    (206) 382-5353

Charles Schwab & Co., Inc.
101 Montgomery St.
San Francisco, CA 94104
Phone: (800) 442-5111
    (415) 627-7000

Jack White & Co.
LaJolla Gateway Blvd.
9191 Towne Centre Dr., Suite 220
San Diego, CA 92122
Phone: (800) 233-3411
    (619) 587-2000

Appendix C: Resources

Barron's
200 Liberty St.
New York, NY 10281
Phone: (800) 328-6800, Ext. 292
Current Annual Subscription Rate: $129.00

Forbes
Forbes, Inc., 60 Fifth Ave.
New York, NY 10011
Phone: (800) 888-9896
Current Annual Subscription Rate: $57.00

The Hulbert Financial Digest, Inc.
316 Commerce St.
Alexandria, VA 22314
Phone: (703) 683-5905
Current Annual Subscription Rate: $135.00

Morningstar Mutual Funds Source Book
Morningstar, Inc.,
53 West Jackson Blvd.
Chicago, IL 60604
Phone: (800) 876-5005
Current Annual Subscription Rate: $225

Morningstar Variable Annuity Performance Report
Morningstar, Inc.,
53 West Jackson Blvd.
Chicago, IL 60604
Phone: (800) 876-5005
Current Annual Subscription Rate: $125.00

Morningstar Mutual Funds On Floppy
Morningstar, Inc.,
53 West Jackson Blvd.
Chicago, IL 60604
Phone: (800) 876-5005
Current Annual Subscription Rate: $185.00

Stocks, Bonds, Bills, and Inflation Yearbook
Ibbotson Associates
(annually updates work by Roger G. Ibbotson
    and Rex A. Sinquefield).
Used with permission. All rights reserved.
PO Box # 528456
Chicago, IL 60652-8456
Phone: (800) 758-3557
Current Annual Subscription Rate: $90.00

Stock Trader's Almanac
The Hirsch Organization, Inc.,
PO Box 2069
Rivervale, NJ 07675-9988
Phone: (800) 477-3400
Current Annual Subscription Rate: $31.00

Wall Street Journal
200 Burnett Rd.
Chicopee, MA 01020
Phone: (800) 568-7625
Current Annual Subscription Rate: $164.00

Index

12-b-1 fees, 34
20th Century Growth, 74
401 (k), 56, 194, 222
44 Wall Street Fund, 74-5, 171-2
"73-74 Bear Market", 57, 74, 98, 99, 149-50, 171-2

A

Advisory newsletters, 48
Aesop, 45
Aggressive Growth Funds, 32, 40, 86, 171, 224
America First, 128
American Stock Exchange, 138
Anaconda, 122

B

Balanced Funds, 41
Barron's, 35, 50, 70, 79, 80
Baruch, Bernard, 56
Battle of Britain, 128
Black Thursday, 115
Brouner, Kurt, 31
Brown, W. Paul, 116

C

California U.S. Government Securities, 106
Capital Gains, 59, 68, 188
Capital Preservation Fund, 105-6
CDs (Certificates of Deposit), 60, 166-7, 198
Coasters, The, 51
Compounded Interest/Return and/or gain, 34, 46, 49, 162-3, 167, 169
    explanation of, chap. 13, 198, 231-2, 235, 254, 264, 270
Confucius, 165
Contrarian, 167, 236
CPA (Certified Public Accountant), 221

D

Deflation, 132

DFA (Dimensional Fund Advisors)
    U.S. Small Company 9/10 Mutual Fund, 138-9, 146
Dinda, Bob, 73
Dividends, 34, 40, 47, 59, 69, 79, 89, 105, 194, 240
Dollar Cost Averaging, 38, 189, 193
    explanation of, chap. 18
Donnelly, Barbara, 41
Doolittle, General, 129
Dow Jones, 18, 19, 52, 102
Dreyfus (Index), 19
Dreyfus (U.S. Government Intermediate), 106
DuPont, 122

E

Engle, Louis, 17
Equity/Income Funds, 40
Ecclesiastes 3.2-5, 55

F

Fail-Safe Buy Signal, explanation of, chap. 7
Fail-Safe Sell Signal, explanation of, chap. 7
FDR, 126-7
Felgenhauer, Herman L., 116
Fidelity (Family of), 35
    Fidelity Magellan, 74, 171-2, 268
    Intermediate Bond, 106
Forbes Magazine, 37, 44-9, 223, 263
Ford, Henry, 116
Foreign Exchange, 52
Frank Russell Company, 138
Franklin, Benjamin, 135, 183, 235
Freeman-Welwood & Co., 106, 232
Fuller, Thomas, 243

G

General Motors, 122
Germany, 127, 130,
Graham & Dodd, 51, 235
Great Depression (also depression), 74, 114, 117, 119-20, 123, 132,
    156, 179, 230 238-39

Growth Funds, 40
Guadalcanal, 129
Guardian Mutual Fund, 46

H

Hawley-Smoot, 120
Heard On The Street, 33
Heinlein, Robert A., 43
Henry, Patrick, 43
Hiroshima, 130
Hitler, Adolf, 127-8, 130
Hits-Plus Mutual Fund Guide, 50, 63, 79, 153, 270
Hoover, President, 115
How To Lower Your Everyday Expenses
    Without Lowering Your Standard Of Living,, 261
Hulbert Financial Digest, 48-9
Hulbert Guide to Financial Newsletters, 70
Hulbert, Mark, 48-50, 70
Hunt Brothers, 264
Hirst, Yale, 67-8

I

Ibbotson, 78, 89, 105, 116, 136, 138-9, 153
Income Funds, 40
Index Funds, 19, 40-1
Inflation, 18, 29, 88-90, 97, 132, 179, 188, 198-200, 203,
    216, 262
Intermediate-Term Government Bonds (when used), 41, 78, 82, 83
International Investment Funds, 32, 40
Investing With The Best, 31
IRA (Individual Retirement Account), 56, 66, 68, 153, 194, 203, 206,
    208-15, 218-24, 233, 247

J

Jack White and Co., 106
January Barometer (explanation of), chap. 6
Japan, 127-8, 130
Jefferson, Thomas, 257

K

Kennedy, Joseph, 264

Keoghs, 221-22

L

Lavater, Johann Kaspar, 269
Leningrad, 128
Lepatner, Barry, 44
Lin Broadcasting, 24-5
Livermore, Jesse, 73
Load Funds, 35-7, 39
Loeb, Gerald M., 113
Lynch, Peter, 171

M

Margin, 64-5
   (when to use), 81
   (explanation of), chap. 16
Maugham, W. Sumerset, 235
McDonalds, 24-5
Midway, 129
Milne, A.A., 257-8
Money Funds, 34, 41, 105-6, 166-67, 247
Montgomery Ward, 114
Morgan, J.P., 51-2
Morley, J. Kenfield, 85-6, 235
Morningstar, 37, 41, 48

N

Nagasaki, 130
NASDAQ, 18, 52,138
National Association of Manufacturers, 116
National Home Life Assurance Company, 226
NAV (Net Asset Value), 79-80
Nazis, 128
Neuberger and Berman, 46
New York Stock Exchange, 52, 115, 136, 138
New York's County Trust Co., 116
Nicholas Fund, 74
no-load, 33, 35, 37-9, 66, 106, 218

O

old money concept, 38

P

Palfrey, Frank S.,   116
Parton, Dolly,   155, 163
Pearl Harbor,   128, 160
Porticao Equity Index,   19

R

RCA,   114
RCM Capital Management,   31
Riordan, James J.,   116
Rockefeller, John D.,   257
Rogers, Will,   76
Roosevelt, President (FDR),   124, 126
Rosenburg, Claude,   31-2
Rothchild, Baron,   56
Russell 2000,   18, 138-9, 227, 232
Russia,   128

S

S&P 400 Mid Cap,
S&P 500 Index (explanation of),   18-20, 58
    (1950-1993 performance of),   109
    (1929-1949 performance of),   133
S.E.C. (Securities and Exchange Commission),   48, 124, 134
Samuelson, Paul,   31-2
Sanders, Doug,   197
Schwab, Charles,   66, 106, 218, 231-2
Sector Funds,   32, 40-1
SEI Index,   19, 106
SEP-IRAs,   221-22
Shakespeare, William,   229
Simmons, Lee & Barbara,   261
Small Cap Index Fund,   227
Small Company Stock Index (SCSI),33-4, 136-54, 156-60, 169, 171-2,
    175, 179, 224, 227, 237, 253
Smith, Randall,   33
Smoot-Hawley,   120
Stock Traders Almanac,   67
Stocks, Bonds, Bills, and Inflation Yearbook, (SBBI),   89, 105,
    116, 136, 138-9, 153

Sudetenland, 127
Super Hits-Plus (explanation of), 135-43
Supreme Court, 126

T

T-Bills (U.S. Treasury Bills) when & how to use, 78, 82-4
Teledyne Inc., 24
Time Magazine, 116
Train, John, 85-6
Trump, Donald, 263
Twain, Mark, 67, 217

U

U.S. Steel, 119, 122
U.S.S. Missouri, 130

V

Value Line, 106
Vanguard (family of), 80, 105-7, 138-9
    (Index 500 Fund), 19, 63-4, 79-80, 106, 270
    (Fixed Income Short Term Govt. Bond Fund), 107
    Index Small Capitalization Stock Fund), 139, 153, 232, 270
Variable Annuities, 56, 153, 194, 218, 222-27
Variety ("Wall St. Lays An Egg"), 115

W

Wal-Mart, 24-5, 42
Wall Street Journal, 33, 41, 49-50, 63-4, 79-80, 89, 105
Waterhouse Securities, 106
Whitter, Dean, 73
Wilshire 5000 Index, 18
Wright Aeronautics, 114

Y

Your Money Matters, 41

Another Investment Newsletter You Don't Need (But May Want Anyway)

Yes, I publish a monthly investment newsletter, *Hits Plus Mutual Fund Guide,* and, no, you really don't need it to follow the **Hits-Plus** investment programs. Everything you need to know to invest with the **Hits-Plus** programs is contained in this book.

Of course, you do need certain tools and ongoing information. A subscription to *Barron's* (subscription rate $129 per year) and the *Wall Street Journal* (subscription rate $164 per year) will give you the information to tabulate and track the mutual funds of your choice.

What the monthly *Hits-Plus Mutual Fund Guide* does is track the S&P 500 Total Return, Small Companies Stock Index mutual funds, the January Barometer, Fail-Safe Sell and Buy Signals, and presents the explicit status of all portfolios. The guide also tracks Vanguard and other Variable Annuities.

The *Hits-Plus Mutual Fund Guide* is a simple uncluttered monthly letter, and the annual subscription rate is **only** $69.95. No, you may not really need this newsletter, but you may feel it will save you a lot of time and money and greatly simplify your investing decisions.

Special Offer!

As the owner of this book, you may send this coupon for a **FREE** three-month trial subscription to *Hits-Plus Mutual Fund Guide* ($19.95 value). Photocopies are not accepted.

Return to: Name _____

Hits-Plus Mutual Fund Guide
P.O. Box # 39   Address _____
Tarboro, N.C., 27886
                                    City _____

                                    State _____ Zip _____
